SLEEP AND COGNITION

SLEEP AND COGNITIO

EDITED
BY
**RICHARD R.
BOOTZIN,
JOHN F.
KIHLSTROM**
AND
**DANIEL L.
SCHACTER**

**UNIVERSITY
OF
ARIZONA**

**American Psychological Association
Washington, DC**

Published by
American Psychological Association
750 First Street, NE
Washington, DC 20002

Copies may be ordered from
APA Order Department
P.O. Box 2710
Hyattsville, MD 20784

Designed by Paul M. Levy (Cover design adapted from conference poster designed by
    Elizabeth C. Tang)
Typeset by TAPSCO, Inc., Akron, PA
Printed by Bookcrafters, Chelsea, MI
Technical editing and production coordinated by
    Susan Bedford and Mary Lynn Skutley

First Printing, June 1990
Second Printing, February 1992

Library of Congress Cataloging-in-Publication Data

Sleep and cognition / edited by Richard R. Bootzin, John F. Kihlstrom, and
    Daniel L. Schacter.
        p.   cm.
    Based on the Arizona Conference on Sleep and Cognition, held in Tucson,
Jan. 19–22, 1989.
    Includes index.
    ISBN 1-55798-083-7
    1. Sleep—Congresses. 2. Cognition—Congresses. I. Bootzin, Richard R.,
1940– . II. Kihlstrom, John F. III. Schacter, Daniel L. IV. Arizona
Conference on Sleep and Cognition (1989: Tucson, Ariz.)
    [DNLM: 1. Cognition—physiology—congresses. 2. Sleep—physiology—
congresses. WL 108 S612 1989]
QP425.S664   1990
154.6—dc20
DNLM/DLC   90-672

Printed in the United States of America

To sleep perchance to dream lucidly

I like to process, to think, to scheme,
not to waste my thoughts in dream.
But, if I could somehow become more lucid
during those expressions of my Freudian id,
and remember all, rather than incur a cost
for thoughts I once had, and now find lost.
Then, I might again be willing to step
through the brain's revolving door,
and go back to sleep. And, dream some more.

It's a consequence of the soup we're in

We sleep, we dream,
and scheme for a better life
with a little less stress and a little less strife.
And in this altered state dress our thoughts
with a different blend of aminergic–cholinergic seasoning
—the milieu for a different sort of reasoning
that is hard to recall outside of the dream
no matter how lucid it may be—or seem.

Marta Kutas

CONTENTS

Contributors   ix

Foreword   x

Preface   xii

PART ONE: GENERAL OVERVIEWS

1 The Neurocognition of Sleep Mentation: Rapid   1
   Eye Movements, Visual Imagery, and Dreaming
   John Antrobus

2 Activation, Input Source, and Modulation: A   25
   Neurocognitive Model of the State of the
   Brain–Mind
   J. Allan Hobson

PART TWO: COGNITION DURING SLEEP

3 Event-Related Brain Potential (ERP) Studies of   43
   Cognition During Sleep: Is It More Than a
   Dream?
   Marta Kutas

4 Stimulus Control and Sleep   58
   John Harsh and Pietro Badia

5 Memories in Sleep: Old and New   67
   Pietro Badia

6   Behavioral Responses During Sleep   77
      Frederick J. Evans

7   Learning During Sleep   88
      Eric Eich

8   Lucid Dreaming: Psychophysiological Studies of   109
      Consciousness During REM Sleep
      Stephen LaBerge

9   Cognitive Processing and General Anesthesia   127
      Les Goldmann

PART THREE: COGNITION BEFORE AND AFTER SLEEP

10   Insomnia: The Patient and the Pill   139
      Wallace B. Mendelson

11   The Perception of Sleep Onset in Insomniacs and   148
      Normal Sleepers
      Michael H. Bonnet

12   Are You Awake? Cognitive Performance and   159
      Reverie During the Hypnopompic State
      David F. Dinges

PART FOUR: CLINICAL TOPICS

13   A Network Model of Dreams   179
      Rosalind Cartwright

14   Nightmares (Dream Disturbances) in   190
      Posttraumatic Stress Disorder: Implications for a
      Theory of Dreaming
      Milton Kramer

Index   203

CONTRIBUTORS

John Antrobus, *The City College of the City University of New York*

Pietro Badia, *Bowling Green State University*

Michael H. Bonnet, *Long Beach Veterans Administration Hospital and University of California, Irvine*

Rosalind Cartwright, *Rush–Presbyterian–St. Luke's Medical Center*

David F. Dinges, *University of Pennsylvania*

Eric Eich, *The University of British Columbia*

Frederick J. Evans, *University of Medicine and Dentistry of New Jersey*

Les Goldmann, *Reed College*

John Harsh, *University of Southern Mississippi*

J. Allan Hobson, *Harvard Medical School*

Milton Kramer, *Sleep Disorders Center of Greater Cincinnati*

Marta Kutas, *University of California, San Diego*

Stephen LaBerge, *Stanford University*

Wallace B. Mendelson, *State University of New York at Stony Brook*

FOREWORD

Federal research agencies stopped regularly supporting investigator-initiated "state-of-the-art" research conferences in scientific psychology well over a decade ago. Yet over that same period, scientific psychology has continued to grow—as well as to diversify into many new areas. Thus there have been relatively few opportunities for investigators in new and cutting-edge research areas to convene in special settings to discuss their findings.

The American Psychological Association (APA), as part of its continuing efforts to enhance the dissemination of scientific knowledge in psychology, undertook a number of new initiatives designed to foster scientific research and communication. In particular, the APA Science Directorate, in 1988, initiated the Scientific Conferences Program.

The APA Scientific Conferences Program provides university-based psychological researchers with seed monies essential to organizing specialty conferences on critical issues in basic research, applied research, and methodological issues in psychology. Deciding which conferences to support involves a competitive process. An annual call for proposals is issued by the APA Science Directorate to solicit conference ideas. Proposals from all areas of psychological research are welcome. They are then reviewed by qualified psychologists, who forward substantive suggestions and funding recommendations to the Science Directorate. At each stage, the criteria used to determine which conferences to support include relevance, timeliness, and comprehensiveness of the topics, and qualifications of the presenters. In 1988, seven conferences were funded under the APA Science Directorate program's sponsorship, and six conferences were funded in 1989. We expect to fund six more in 1990, at an annual program expense of $90,000 to $100,000.

The APA Scientific Conferences Program has two major goals. The first is to provide, by means of the conferences, a broad view of specific topics (and, when appropriate, to provide for interdisciplinary participation). The second goal is to assure timely dissemination of the findings presented by publishing a series of carefully crafted scholarly volumes based, in part, on each conference. Thus the information reaches the audiences at each conference as well as the broader psychological and scientific communities. This enables psychology and related fields to benefit from the most current research on a given topic.

This volume presents findings reported at the January 1989 conference, "Sleep and Cognition." Researchers in this area are focusing on a number of fascinating topics. They are applying the methods of contemporary cognitive psychology to traditional areas of interest such as the purpose of dreams and our potential to learn during sleep, as well as exploring newer dimensions like lucid dreaming, cognitive processes under anesthesia, and effects of sleep-inducing medication. Researchers from the typically separate areas of sleep and cognition came together at the conference to exchange ideas and focus on new directions for research.

This volume is representative of what we at the American Psychological Association believe will be a number of exceptional volumes that give readers a broad sampling of the diverse and outstanding research now being done in scientific psychology. We hope you will enjoy and be stimulated by this book and the many others to come.

A list of the conferences funded through this program follows:

Researching Community Psychology: Integrating Theories and Methodologies, September 1988
Psychological Well-Being in Nonhuman Captive Primates, September 1988
Psychological Research on Organ Donation, October 1988
Arizona Conference on Sleep and Cognition, January 1989
Socially Shared Cognition, February 1989
The Role of Experience in Modifying Taste and Its Effects on Feeding, April 1989
Perception of Structure, May 1989
Suggestibility of Children's Recollections, June 1989
Best Methods for the Analysis of Change, October 1989
Conceptualization and Measurement of Organism–Environment Interaction, November 1989
Cognitive Bases of Musical Communication, April 1990
Conference on Hostility, Coping/Support, and Health, November 1990
Psychological Testing of Hispanics, February 1991
Study of Cognition: Conceptual and Methodological Issues, February 1991

Gary R. VandenBos, PhD   Virginia E. Holt
Acting Executive Director   Manager, Scientific Conferences Program
Science Directorate, APA   Science Directorate, APA

PREFACE

Sleep was once a phenomenon of considerable interest to psychologists. One of Freud's most popular books (and arguably one of his best) dealt with dreams. In the classic 1924 study by Jenkins and Dallenbach, sleep provided convincing evidence in favor of the interference theory of forgetting. More than 50 years later, and almost a century after Freud, some of the most frequently asked questions in the introductory psychology course concern what dreams mean and why we seem to forget them. Despite impressive advances in understanding sleep as a biological phenomenon and in understanding the nature of mental processes in the normal waking state, our knowledge of mental life during sleep remains extremely impoverished.

Much of the current scientific interest in sleep can be traced to the discovery in 1953, by Aserinsky and Kleitmen, of the association between rapid eye movements and dreaming. Ironically, however, the discovery of physiologically different sleep stages, and their differential association with dreaming and other mental activities, seems to have transformed sleep from a psychological topic to a biological one. A great deal of work addresses sleep as behavior at a purely biological level, as in studies of the ontogeny and phylogeny of sleep and other biological rhythms. And many major medical centers offer the services of a sleep disorders clinic oriented toward such problems as insomnia (a common symptom in depression and normal aging), narcolepsy, sleep apnea, and parasomnias such as enuresis and somnambulism. But surprisingly little current research focuses on perceptual, memory, and thought processes during this period of activity. There is, of course, a long tradition of work by psychologists on the effects of sleep deprivation on human performance. But research on cognitive processes during sleep itself has received comparatively little attention, both on the conference circuit and in print. Examination of *Sleep Research,* the annual archival publication of the Association of Professional Sleep Societies, reveals relatively little cognitive psychology. Similar trends are apparent in the published proceedings of the biennial European Conferences on Sleep Research and in the volumes of *Advances in Sleep Research.* There is, of course, a large literature (arising primarily from within the psychoanalytic tradition) concerning the interpretation of dreams. Unfortunately, the methodology in these studies is generally clinical and hermeneutic, without the careful controls characteristic of experimental psychology.

Nevertheless, important questions about sleep persist that must be addressed at a purely psychological level: How much information from the environment can be processed by the sleeper? What sorts of mental activities are associated with sleepwalking and sleeptalking? Are dreams meaningful, and if so why aren't they better remembered? What are the possibilities for learning during sleep? Such questions have been asked by psychologists and others, but only rarely have they been addressed with the concepts, principles, and methods of contemporary cognitive psychology. One factor contributing to this situation is the isolation of psychoanalysis, with its interest in dreams, from mainstream scientific psychology. Another is the phenomenology of sleep itself: The sleeper typically appears oblivious to his or her environment, and the occurrence of sleep is generally inferred from this lack of responsiveness and the absence of conscious awareness of events during sleep. The common identification of cognition with consciousness leaves the impression that little or no mental activity occurs during sleep.

Of course, studies in which sleepers are awakened at various points in the night's sleep typically yield reports of thoughts, images, and dreams, but these are rarely remembered spontaneously in the morning. Some individuals engage in episodes of sleepwalking and sleeptalking, which can involve relatively complex speech acts and behavioral sequences—but, again, these are rarely if ever remembered. One explanation for this universally experienced memory deficit is that the cortical centers that mediate complex mental processing are disengaged or deactivated during sleep, with the result that the sleeper does not attend to environmental and mental events occurring during periods of sleep. Because these events are not noticed, they are not processed in a manner that encodes accessible traces of them in memory.

Thus, the most commonly accepted explanation of postsleep amnesia is in terms of consolidation failure. For example, it has been proposed that the low level of cortical arousal characteristic of sleep effectively prevents the sleeper from performing the cognitive operations necessary to encode memory traces of sleep events that are accessible in the subsequent waking state. According to this view, dreams and other sleep events are remembered only when the sleeper awakens during them, permitting retrieval from short-term memory. If the sleeper awakens shortly after a dream has occurred, residual information retrieved from short-term memory may serve as a cue to the retrieval of a highly degraded long-term memory trace. If retrieval is delayed until all traces of the dream have decayed or been displaced from short-term memory, the long-term traces will be virtually inaccessible.

As intuitively appealing as this explanation is, recent empirical work on sleep, as well as theoretical advances in the study of cognition, call it into account. For example, the idea of consolidation failure assumes a rigid distinction between short-term and long-term memory that is not supported by the current literature. Moreover, cognitive theorists have recently begun to distinguish between effortful processes, which require intention and consume attentional resources, and automatic processes, which do not. More important, the domain of automatic processing has expanded to include rather complex mental activities—the kind that ordinarily would be expected to leave residual traces in permanent memory. Finally, studies of both brain-damaged patients and intact subjects support a concept of implicit perception and memory, in which current and past events may influence ongoing experience, thought, and action even though the individual lacks awareness (concurrent or retrospective) of the events themselves.

Recent research on sleep processes bears directly on these theoretical ideas. While sleepers are ordinarily considered unable to engage in complex, intentional cognitive activities during sleep, some evidence tends to contradict this assumption. For example, in the phenomenon of lucid dreaming, selected subjects report that they become aware of the fact that they are dreaming and are able to consciously direct the contents of the dream, while remaining asleep. This claim is difficult to verify objectively, for obvious reasons. But a series of highly provocative and apparently well-controlled studies has shown that subjects can make discriminative responses to verbal suggestions delivered while they are asleep. Although the possibility of sleep learning had been firmly rejected in a widely influential review published in 1955, studies of memory of events occurring during surgical anesthesia strongly suggest that sleep learning may be possible, provided that its success is measured in terms of implicit rather than explicit memory. These preliminary findings, which have emerged from a variety of laboratories employing rather different paradigms, suggest that cognitive activity of considerable complexity may be possible during sleep, provided that it is mediated by automated procedures and assessed by measures that do not require awareness of the events on the part of the subject.

Despite the research possibilities offered by current advances in theory, most texts on sleep, whether intended for undergraduate use or scholarly reference, pay little attention to cognitive processes, aside from our ubiquitous failure to remember our dreams. A major exception to this generalization is *The Mind in Sleep* (Arkin, Antrobus, & Ellman, 1978), which provided a comprehensive account of research on cognitive processes during sleep since the discovery of the EEG correlates of dreaming. The volume focuses on such topics as the difference between stage REM and stage NREM mental activity, factors affecting dream recall, the effects of presleep and intrasleep stimulation, REM deprivation, sleeptalking, and night terrors. Unfortunately, the book is now out of date, especially with respect to current thinking in cognitive psychology; although a new edition has been promised, it is not yet available. Another primary source is a recent monograph, *Dreaming: A Cognitive-Psychological Analysis* (Foulkes, 1985). As comprehensive as the Arkin et al. anthology is, its contributors have almost nothing to say about the problem that concerned Freud most: the meaning of dreams. Foulkes' book approaches this problem from the perspective of cognitive psychology, particularly psycholinguistics and cognitive development. His analysis clearly indicates that sleep researchers and cognitive psychologists have much of interest to say to each other.

In 1986, the Neurosciences Institute of Rockefeller University hosted a small workshop on the remembering and forgetting of dreams, which testifies to an increased interest in sleep among neurobiologists and psychiatrists; but cognitive psychologists were decidedly underrepresented at this meeting. A further impetus to dialog is the recently published report of an ad-hoc committee of the National Academy of Sciences to the Army Research Institute, concerning psychological techniques to enhance human performance (*Enhancing Human Performance: Issues, Theories, and Techniques,* 1988). While generally critical of most of the techniques that have been proposed for this purpose, the Committee strongly urged that further attention be devoted to the phenomenon of learning during sleep. We expect that this suggestion will lead to a greatly improved environment for research on all aspects of cognition in sleep.

The present volume represents the Proceedings of the Arizona Conference on Sleep and Cognition, held in Tucson January 19–22, 1989. A principal concern of the conference was the implications of recent work on implicit memory and other aspects of information-processing outside of awareness for studies of cognitive processes during sleep, and the role of the sleep laboratory as a vehicle for studying various aspects of information processing outside of awareness, in the absence of the active deployment of attention. To this end, selected investigators in the area of sleep who have an interest in cognitive processes were brought together with their counterparts in the area of cognition who have an interest in sleep. The goal of the conference was to create an environment in which representatives of these two quite different areas would meet and exchange ideas in a spirit of open inquiry and constructive criticism and advance the study of cognition during sleep beyond the stage of speculative thought. We hope that one outcome of this meeting, and publication of the Proceedings, will be a new agenda for research on sleep that will carry investigators of both camps well into the 21st century.

Part One of the volume contains two papers in which mental activity during sleep is used as a link between neuroscience and cognitive science. Antrobus provides a sweeping review of the literature on eye movements and imagery in dreaming, with particular reference to cortical activation during sleep. Similarly, Hobson provides an update of the Hobson–McCarley Activation–Synthesis model of dreaming.

Part Two includes a number of papers on various aspects of mental activity during sleep. Kutas offers an authoritative review of the literature on event-related (evoked) potentials during sleep. Harsh and Badia describe a series of experiments on the transfer to sleep of conditioned responses acquired during the normal waking state. Badia continues this discussion, focusing on the acquisition of new conditioned responses during sleep. Evans contributes an overview and update of his extremely provocative studies of response to verbal suggestions during sleep, and the relation of this phenomenon to hypnosis and other dissociative states. Eich provides a new look, originally prepared for the 1988 National Academy of Sciences and Army Research Institute study of techniques for enhancing human performance, at the possibilities for sleep learning. LaBerge summarizes his programmatic research on lucid dreaming, in which the sleeper becomes aware of the fact that he or she is dreaming, and exercises some control over the content of the dream. Finally, Goldmann explores the parallels between information processing during sleep and during adequate surgical anesthesia.

Part Three focuses on cognition in the hypnogogic and hypnopompic states occurring in the transition from waking to sleeping and back again. Mendelson reviews the physiological and cognitive effects of drugs used in treating insomnia. Bonnet examines the factors affecting subjective reports of sleep onset—which, he notes, almost never agree with physiological measures. Dinges summarizes his research on performance impairments in the period after awakening and illustrates his argument with a dramatic example of hypnopompic reverie.

Part Four returns to the question of dreams, this time in a clinical as opposed to an experimental context, with an emphasis on the effects of stress on dreams. Cartwright describes a new study of the dreams of people going through divorce and explores the implications of her findings in relation to the question of the meaning of dreams. Kramer summarizes his ongoing work on nightmares in Vietnam veterans suffering posttraumatic stress disorder.

The Arizona Conference on Sleep and Cognition was supported in part by the Science Directorate of the American Psychological Association. We are grateful to Alan G. Kraut, Virginia E. Holt, and Barbara Calkins of the Science Directorate for their efforts. Matching funds were provided by various units of the University of Arizona (Department of Psychology, Lee Sechrest, Head; Committee on Cognitive Science, Merrill Garret, Director; College of Nursing, L. Claire Parsons, Dean; and the Sleep Disorders Center of the Arizona Health Sciences Center, Stuart Quan, Director) and by the UpJohn Company (James W. Battles, Medical Sciences Liaison). Final preparation of the Proceedings was supported in part by Grant #MH-35856 from the National Institute of Mental Health.

We are grateful to a number of individuals for their efforts in behalf of the conference. Our colleagues Larry E. Beutler, L. Claire Parsons, and Stuart F. Quan served as chairs for the conference sessions. Also at the University of Arizona, Carol Cantor, Lucy Canter Kihlstrom, and Martha L. Glisky provided organizational assistance—as did Karen Shoun of the Doubletree Hotel. Elizabeth C. Tang of Communications: Visual designed the stunning conference poster. Barbara Calkins represented the APA Science Directorate at the Conference; Lynne Lamberg, a science writer with a special interest in sleep, grilled us during breaks and after-hours and forced us to express our ideas in comprehensible English. Professors Robert A. Bjork (UCLA), David Koulack

(Manitoba), and Jonathan Winson (Rockefeller) made vigorous and incisive contributions to the conference sessions. Finally, we thank those investigators who enriched the conference by contributing summaries of their research to the poster sessions: Andrew Brylowski (University of Texas Southwestern Medical Center), Mindy Engle-Friedman (Baruch College, CUNY), Irene P. Hoyt (University of Wisconsin), Robert Nadon (University of Pennsylvania), Kan Paller (Yale School of Medicine), and Jim Wood (University of Arizona).

Richard R. Bootzin
John F. Kihlstrom
Daniel L. Schacter

PART ONE

GENERAL OVERVIEWS

CHAPTER 1

THE NEUROCOGNITION
OF SLEEP MENTATION:
RAPID EYE MOVEMENTS, VISUAL IMAGERY, AND DREAMING

JOHN ANTROBUS

The relation of eye movement to the cognitive process of dreaming during sleep has been a source of speculation since Ladd (1892) suggested that such movement might represent the sleeper's observation of his or her dreams. After the discovery by Aserinsky and Kleitman (1953) of the association between Stage 1 REM (rapid eye movement) sleep and dreaming, REMs, which occupy only a fraction of Stage 1 REM sleep, have been identified as one component of a cluster of phasic activities that are associated with a pontine-geniculate-occipital (PGO) sequence of neural activity. Despite the dramatic frequency and amplitude of PGO activity, the fact that it is not associated with any known function in the waking state has confounded efforts to identify its function in REM sleep.

Pontine-geniculate-occipital activity has been implicated in the production of at least four characteristics of sleep thought and imagery: bizarreness, direction of visual orientation, clarity or vividness of visual imagery, and amount of information processed from nonsensory sources. The apparent pontine origin of the PGO sequence implies that the cerebral cortex and, therefore, higher cognitive processes have no role in initiating eye movement (EM) activity in REM sleep (Hobson & McCarley, 1977). This chapter evaluates the neurocognitive and neurophysiological support for models that have proposed a relation between EMs and the cognitive characteristics of the imagery and thought of REM sleep.

The first 25 years of contemporary sleep mentation research have focused on whether dreaming is isomorphic with Stage 1 REM or whether it is better aligned with a correlated biological characteristic such as the REMs themselves or with concurrent phasic events like the PGO spikes that are readily observed in cats but not in intact human subjects.

Although many studies have reported modest relations between physiological markers and characteristics of Stage 1 REM sleep mentation, the relations have either not been replicated or have proven to be relatively small in magnitude. In short, relative to non-REM (NREM) sleep, REM sleep consistently yields dreamlike mentation reports and descriptions of fanciful, vivid, hallucinatory, and sometimes bizarre imagery and thought, regardless of the presence of physiological markers at different intervals within the REM period. Nevertheless, the behavioral drama of the burst of REMs, particularly in the early part of REM periods, continues to dominate neurophysiological theories of dream production and perpetually continues to puzzle students in this field.

The relatively small payoff of recent psychophysiological studies of dreaming, coupled with the high cost of such research, has discouraged many investigators from continuing the search. However, recent advances in the neurosciences, particularly in neurocognition, have clearly demonstrated that the brain-mind is much more complex than any other subject in the history of science and that most of our working assumptions about the relations between brain concepts and mind concepts have been too simplistic. Thus, one of the goals of this paper is to restate some of the early models of REM sleep and dreaming in an updated context and, thereby, to reorient the direction of future research.

It is now established that REM bursts or clusters within Stage 1 REM sleep are associated with PGO-like activity (McCarley, Winkelman, & Duffy, 1983). It is therefore appropriate to consider all these phasic event bursts or clusters—REMs, phasic submental EMG suppression, periorbital integrated potentials (PIPs), and middle ear muscle activity (MEMAs)—as a family of neural events closely associated in time or neural space.

Because of the greater ease of measurement of REMs and their putative association with visual imagery, most phasic mentation studies have been carried out with REMs. The early phasic–tonic studies pioneered by Foulkes and colleagues (Foulkes & Pope, 1973) tended to regard phasic events as an intensive form of Stage 1 REM sleep. The search for a link to sleep mentation was broadly directed toward dream recall and the vividness of the events experienced. (For an excellent review of this literature, see Pivik, 1978).)

Four positions describing the functional relation between phasic activity and the characteristics of dreaming, or sleep mentation, have been proposed. The first, suggested by Ladd (1892), is the compelling hypothesis that REMs represent the action of the sleeper looking at the events in his or her dream. Associated with this position, but not dependent on it, is the magnitude hypothesis, namely, that periods of "dense" REM activity are associated with an increment in the vividness or clarity of the dreamer's visual imagery.

The Activation–Synthesis model proposed by Hobson and McCarley (1977), which was founded on an articulated neurophysiological model of sleep stage alternation, posits that EM information is initiated by the pons rather than by the cerebral cortex. Receiving EM information from sources not under its control obliges the cognitive apparatus that produces dream imagery to, in effect, "make the best of a bad job" (p. 11), thereby creating mentation that is often bizarre in nature.

The fourth position is a modification of the first and second positions and is based on the across states connectionist model of imagery and thought (ASCIT) proposed by Antrobus (1986, 1990). It argues that, within the Stage 1 REM period, the interval of high frequency REM and PGO activity is associated with a temporary increment in cortical activation. This increased activation supports a general increment in the production of imagery and thought, which in turn leads to an increase in the information in the sleep mentation report.

The EM visual orientation model and the Activation–Synthesis model will be examined first because they contribute to the understanding of whether the cortex is responsible for the initiation and orientation of EM within REM sleep.

LOOKING RESPONSE–EYE MOVEMENT–PGO–VISUAL IMAGERY MODEL

Well after the Aserinsky and Kleitman (1953) discovery of REM sleep, researchers recovered the work of Ladd, who in 1892 first suggested that movement of the eyes beneath the lids of sleeping subjects might indicate that the sleeper is watching his or her dreams. But what exactly is the sleeper watching? Rechtschaffen and Foulkes (1965) evaluated a model in which the internal neural origin of the visual dream image is constructed from random receptor activity in the retina. They taped open the eyes of the sleeper and, in REM sleep, presented a number of illuminated visual forms. However, upon the immediate awakening of the sleeper, they found no evidence to support a model that required retinal information to be transmitted to cortical processing centers.

Meanwhile, Roffwarg, Dement, Muzio, and Fisher (1962) tested a model in which Stage 1 REM EMs are the motor component of looking responses even though the visual cortex receives no visual information from the retina. Problems with the original data analysis and several subsequent failures to replicate the results left this model in a precarious state for over 20 years. Recent research by Herman et al. (1981); Herman, Barker, and Roffwarg (1983); and Herman (1984), however, has supported the position that at least some REMs are associated with directional looking responses within REM sleep. In these studies, judges rated the concordance of EMs as measured by the electrooculogram (EOG) and as inferred from reported visual imagery and body movement. In both the 1962 and 1981 studies, the strength of the association between EOG and imagery reports increased with the judges' (but not with the subjects') confidence in their predictions. This confidence effect indicates that at least some EMs are associated with looking responses during dreaming, but the relation may be obscured during states of reduced cortical activation within REM sleep so that the awakened dreamer is unable to recall the relevant looking cues, or perhaps the frontal eye fields do not influence EM direction until they are sufficiently activated by medial reticular formation (MRF) excitation beyond some minimal level. Note that it is assumed that the visual dream imagery is produced regardless of whether the frontal eye fields are sufficiently active to modify EM direction.

The Herman et al. (1981) study provides the strongest evidence that there is a relation between EM pattern and the visual imagery of REM sleep. However, the evidence is consistent with both the looking hypothesis, which implies that the cortex is the origin of EM control in REM sleep, and the activation–synthesis model (Hobson & McCarley, 1977), which proposes that REMs are controlled by activity that originates in the pons in the form of PGO spike trains. According to the activation–synthesis model, the PGO activity is carried to the occipital and frontal cortices, where the cortex synthesizes the information about REM pattern to create a visual scenario that is consistent with it.

Evidence that the pontine origin of PGO activity is out of cortical reach has come from demonstrations of EMs in REM sleep in decorticate preparations (Jeannerod, 1966; Jeannerod & Mouret, 1962; Mergner & Pompeiano, 1981). Herman (in press) countered this interpretation of the decorticate data by showing that the EM frequency is reduced by 80%, the bursting characteristic is eliminated, and the EM patterns are stereotyped and repetitive. This observation is perhaps the strongest evidence for the cortical control of REMs and against the activation–synthesis position that subcortical units determine the spatial and temporal patterns of REMs.

A second test of the looking response models of REM sleep EMs asks whether the velocities of the EMs are similar to those of looking responses in the waking state. The test is complicated by several factors: (a) the resting muscle tonus is different in the two states, (b) the eyes are covered by the lids during sleep, (c) waking saccadic movement is generally initiated by an extrafoveal external visual stimulus, and (d) waking PGO activity tends to be masked by the larger electromyogram activity in unrestrained animals. In two comparisons of waking and REM EMs, Herman and colleagues (Herman et al., 1981; Herman et al., 1983) found that REM EMs are quite similar to waking saccades with the eyes closed. The left–right patterns of EMs matched the predictions of judges from the verbal reports of the subjects best when judges took account of the imagined head movements of the dreamer. The temporal distribution of EMs in REM sleep is, therefore, more similar to the waking EM distribution when the head is unrestrained than when the head is held in a fixed position. Herman and colleagues concluded, therefore, that the oculomotor system in REM sleep coordinates both eye and head movement.

Aserinsky, Lynch, Mack, Tzankoff, and Hurn (1985), however, argued that, in REM sleep, the eye not only moves more slowly but also evidences a "disengagement of the usual velocity–amplitude relationship seen in waking movements" (p. 9). In the waking state, the angular velocity of the eye is proportional to the angular excursion of the movement. Aserinsky et al. (1985) concluded that there is no evidence to support this relation within REM sleep. However, they may have overstated their case. Their study compared REM EMs with 5.5 min and 11 min of arc excursion with EMs of similar excursion under several waking conditions. All waking conditions, with eyes open or closed, showed a significantly higher velocity during 11-min than during 5.5-min excursions, and the increment was significantly greater than the increment during REM sleep. Nevertheless, the increment was significant in REM sleep at the .005 level. It seems, therefore, that REM sleep may produce an attenuation rather than a disengagement of the velocity–amplitude relation.

ACTIVATION–SYNTHESIS MODEL

The Activation–Synthesis model (Hobson & McCarley, 1977) consists of a neurophysiological activation model (McCarley & Hobson, 1975), which was recently revised (Hobson, Lydic, & Baghdoyan, 1986), followed by a cognitive synthesis process by which the cortex combines the neural information from various activated subcortical locations to form dreamlike mentation. Their "working sketch" (Hobson & McCarley, 1977, p. 1340) of the model assumes that the "forebrain is tonically activated, probably via the midbrain RF that is also responsible for its activation during waking. Thus the forebrain is made ready to process information."

They proposed that the stimuli from which dreams are constructed originate not in the "cognitive areas of the cortex" (Hobson & McCarley, 1977, p. 1347) but in a noncognitive or reflex process in the pontine brain stem, namely PGO activity. Referring to the close association in time of PGO spikes and REMs during Stage 1 REM sleep, they suggested that this process indirectly provides spatial information that can be used in the construction of dream imagery. Because the direction and temporal pattern of waking EMs and vestibular activity provides some form of spatial information, they suggested that the EMs and vestibular activity of REM sleep, even though they are randomly driven by PGO spikes, might initiate similar forms of information processing that might subsequently be synthesized into segments of a dream. This position differs from that of the ASCIT model (Antrobus, 1990) in which these brain stem generators provide only nonspecific activation to widespread areas of neural networks in the association cortex and, thereby, determine the information processing rate rather than more specific spatial information.

According to Hobson and McCarley (1977, p. 1347), the process of transforming this information into a dream is "likened to a computer searching its addresses for key words"; "best fits to the relatively inchoate and incomplete data provided by the primary stimuli are called from memory, the access to which is facilitated during dreaming sleep" by the tonically activated forebrain: "In other words, the forebrain may be making the best of a bad job from the relatively noisy signals sent up to it from the brain stem." The two metaphors, of synthesis and of making the best of a bad job, might be restated today in the more precise parallel distributed processes (PDP) vector models in which neural nets engage in a process of "graceful degradation," in which the output of a particular neural net constitutes the best fit to the current input to that net (McClelland, Rumelhart, & Hinton, 1986, p. 29).

Bizarreness: The Phasic Component of the Activation–Synthesis Model

Hobson and McCarley (1977) suggested that the " 'bizarre' formal features of the dream" may be attributed to "properties of the brain stem neuronal generator mechanism" (p. 1347). They assumed that "the random but specific nature of the generator signals could provide abnormally sequenced and shaped, but spatiotemporally specific, frames for dream imagery; and the clustering of runs of generator signals might constitute time-marks for dream subplots and scene changes. Further, the activation by generator neurons of diffuse postsynaptic forebrain elements in multiple parallel channels might account for the disparate sensory, motor, and emotional elements that contribute to the 'bizarreness' of dreams" (p. 1347).

Hobson and McCarley (1977) as well as Porte and Hobson (1986) further suggested that the large number of the neuronal sources of information activated during REM sleep contributes to the bizarreness of REM mentation. By way of emphasizing an alternative to the psychoanalytic notion that dreams are motivated by the need to disguise unconscious conflictual information, Hobson and McCarley (1977) concluded that the bizarreness of dreams may be attributed to the difficulty of making sense of such random input from subcortical, and therefore noncognitive, generators.

The assumption that phasic brainstem events cause segmentation of the dreamer's experience implies that the phasic events are associated with discontinuity in ongoing cognitive processes, regardless of whether discontinuities are bizarre. Because phasic events are more frequent in REM sleep than in Stage 2 sleep or in waking, the activation–synthesis model posits that discontinuities should be most frequent in REM sleep. As reported by Reinsel, Antrobus, and Wollman (in press), however, changes in topic in mentation reports are the least common in the waking state.

The finding that many characteristics of the REM/NREM report difference disappear after total recall count (TRC; Antrobus, 1983) is partialled out suggests that the greater bizarreness of REM reports may, in part, be contingent on their greater length. TRC is the sum of all words in the mentation report that describe the thought and imagery prior to the awakening or interruption. It excludes commentary, associations, and redundant references. That is, compared with waking thought, all sleep mentation may be somewhat bizarre and, therefore, the more mentation recalled, the more bizarre the report will be. Using the Antrobus (1983; $N = 73$) data set, Porte and Hobson (1986) found that REM reports were, indeed, more bizarre than NREM reports. In an unpublished analysis in our lab, we replicated this finding but found that the bizarreness difference disappeared after TRC was partialled out. An interim conclusion is that if any component of bizarreness does survive the partialling out of TRC, it will be only a minute part of the REM/NREM difference. Knowledge of TRC can correctly sort 92.5% of REM/NREM pairs; knowledge of bizarreness scores may add another 0.5–1.0% at most.

BIZARRENESS: PHASIC VERSUS TONIC REM AWAKENINGS

The Activation–Synthesis and ASCIT models both predict that mentation reports will be more bizarre following phasic (REM, PIP, or MEMA) awakenings than tonic awakenings. The ASCIT model assumes that PGO activity is associated with a widespread increase in cortical activation, sufficient to activate the frontal eye fields that control REMs, so that both more thought and more imagery are produced and reported. To the extent that sleep in general is associated with more bizarre mentation, an increment in TRC should bring with it an increment in bizarre mentation and, conversely, partialling out TRC should eliminate the bizarreness increment. By contrast, according to the activation–synthesis model, phasic events should increase bizarreness but not TRC with sleep stage held constant.

Rechtschaffen, Watson, Wincor, Molinari, and Barta (1972) reported that PIP awakenings produced more bizarre mentation than tonic control awakenings, but they later criticized their failure to obtain the reports under conditions in which the interrogator was blind to the polygraph condition. In a subsequent study, Watson, Bliwise, Friedman, Wax, and Rechtschaffen (1978) used blind procedures to demonstrate the PIP–bizarreness relation but found it in only 1 of 4 subjects. Subsequently, Ogilvie, Hunt, Sawicki, and Samanhalskyi (1982) found a significant association between MEMAs and bizarreness in 9 subjects, averaged across REM and NREM reports. They reported a borderline interaction ($p < .10$) between REM/NREM and phasic–tonic awakening for the dependent variable recall such that, relative to tonic awakenings, phasic events (or MEMAs) were associated with more recall in REM relative to NREM. A slight increment in bizarreness in phasic, relative to tonic, REM reports was not formally tested. Recently, Reinsel, Antrobus, and Wollman (in press) found no difference in the bizarreness of phasic and tonic REM sleep reports of 19 subjects where phasic events were defined by REM bursts, but there was a tendency ($p = .08$) for TRC to be greater following the phasic or REM awakenings. (For a recent review of this literature, see Watson & Deptula, in press.)

Aside from the possible contribution of interference and interruption to bizarreness, the effects of under- or overactivation versus differential patterns of activation among different cognitive modules remain a major question. The notion of an underactivated system that has access to fragmentary information implies a system prone to errors and, therefore, to bizarre output. However, we associate high activation with alert waking performance that is close to error free, whereas high cognitive activation in the absence of an anchoring effect of sensory input, as is the case in REM sleep, creates a very different pattern of cognitive output.

If increased cortical activation is associated with a reduction in bizarre sleep mentation, then the late morning dreams that occur when one sleeps later on weekend mornings should be the least bizarre. Yet, the opposite is true. Kondo (1988) recently compared the mentation reports of subjects who were put to bed 3 hours later than usual (thus, all reports were made 3 hours later) with those obtained on a control night. He argued that the late morning reports would benefit from the rising phase of activation of the diurnal rhythm in addition to the phase of the sleep REM/NREM cycle. All the predictions were supported. The brightness and clarity of the visual imagery, the bizarreness of the report, and the number of words used to describe the mentation, TRC (logTRC), all increased in the late REM and NREM reports in the late-morning delayed-sleep condition. The REM/NREM difference remained unchanged. Because the increment in cortical activation due to the diurnal rhythm is putatively more widespread than the cortical activation associated with REM sleep, the additive effects of the two sources constitutes strong evidence that bizarreness is the consequence of an activated cognitive system, supported by an activated cortical structure, in the presence of high sensory thresholds.

In conclusion, the cognitive data supports a general activation rather than a disruptive activation origin for bizarre mentation. Nevertheless, although the PGO– or phasic–bizarreness relation lacks substantial support at the present, it may be premature to conclude that no relation exists. Future studies must explicitly define and measure bizarreness and recall and must describe effects both with and without partialling out TRC or a similar index of total information reported.

RELATION OF REM SLEEP TO VISUAL IMAGERY: NEUROPHYSIOLOGICAL EVIDENCE

This section examines the evidence for the role of the cerebral cortex, and the cognitive processes it supports, in the control of EMs within REM sleep. Although it may be assumed that many of the structures essential to visual perception contribute to the generation of spontaneous visual imagery, there is no strong evidence about which parts of the brain contribute to the production of spontaneous visual imagery in either waking or sleep. It should be cautioned that cortical models for the generation of visual imagery in response to instruction or command (Kosslyn, 1988), where the concept or meaning precedes the image, may be inappropriate for the production of REM sleep imagery, where the temporal precedence of meaning and image is unknown.

Early sleep imagery studies started by examining the role of the retina in REM sleep. Pompeiano's (1970) finding that there is no neural transmission from the retina to the visual cortex in REM sleep suggests that the visual images of REM sleep have an extraretinal origin and many even have multiple sources. As previously mentioned, Rechtschaffen and Foulkes (1965) found no evidence that the retina is sensitive to illuminated objects presented during REM sleep to subjects whose eyelids had previously been taped open.

Once the cognitive system becomes unresponsive to external stimuli it becomes, by definition, a closed system. At that point, the search for the origin of the information that flows through the system must be expanded to include all the feedforward and feedback pathways that become active when the system is not externally driven as well as an account of how these pathways are state (waking, REM, NREM) dependent. This opens up a variety of new possibilities concerning the relation between REMs and visual imagery. Spontaneous independent activity might occur in spatial, visual movement and higher processing modules but might be transmitted to neighboring modules only when the system is sufficiently activated by the MRF. At that point, a winner-takes-all effect may allow one module to dominate another. For example, a visual module may produce an event that higher cognitive modules are obliged to accommodate to, or the higher cognitive module may inhibit incompatible productions in the lower visual modules. None of this visual dreaming production need involve the oculomotor system unless the frontal eye fields and the brain stem oculomotor systems are sufficiently well-activated.

Because this kind of information is not accessible to introspection in waking or in sleep, one must examine the patterns of neural activity in the structures putatively responsible for the relevant component cognitive processes in order to reduce such speculations to a reasonable model. However, detailed evidence on the neural circuits that control EMs can only come from animal studies, and this necessarily precludes examination of the relation of neural activity to visual imagery in different components of this complex system.

The general strategy pursued here is to identify the pathways that enable EM control in waking perception and to then determine how closely this action pattern operates in REM sleep. In waking perception, the decision to move the eyes is distributed over many cortical and subcortical centers and is based on a wide variety of information classes such as visual, auditory, and eye and head position and velocity as well as on higher cognitive judgments and values. Within the cortex, much of the perceptual and cognitive information is funneled through the frontal eye fields that putatively decide where in space to move the eyes and decide to communicate this, typically, to the superior colliculus, which further refines the decision and passes the command to the oculomotor system that programs the EMs. However, the fine tuning of the motor execution is carried out in a sideways loop into the seventh vermal lobule of the cerebellum (Noda, Murakami, Yamada, & Aso, 1988), which takes account of eye position and velocity relative to head and body position.

Before we examine some of the components that contribute to EMs in waking and sleep, it is important to note that the activation of all components is dependent on MRF activation. This activation, largely pontine in origin, not only activates the cortical areas that produce both visual imagery and EM decisions but also drives the final leg of the oculomotor system, namely, the oculomotor neurons. At the most general level then, the co-occurrence of visual imagery and EMs in REM sleep is dependent on MRF activation. Within REM periods, the occurrence of REM may also be due to a higher level of MRF activation than that which exists during periods of ocular quiescence, but evidence supporting this hypothesis is only indirect. Of particular interest is whether activity in certain components of the oculomotor system during REM sleep can be taken as evidence of information processing analogous to that carried out by the structures during waking perception. We will first look at the relations between the visual cortex, EMs, and MRF activation in waking perception and REM sleep.

Breitmeyer's (1986) analysis of visual masking and saccadic EMs offers a useful hunch about the function of both MRF and PGO activation of the lateral geniculate nucleus (LGN). During waking saccades, the fovea is continuously smeared with a succession of visual patterns. The images appear smeared because the retina input summates before it reaches the cortex. This is not a serious problem at the onset of the saccade because the visual system is only interested in the target stimulus at the termination of the saccade. But a problem does arise if the next-to-final retinal image summates with the target image to smear or mask the target image.

Breitmeyer (1986) cited the work of Cohen, Feldman, and Diamond (1969); Ogawa (1963); Singer (1977a, 1977b); Singer and Bedworth (1973); Singer, Tretter, and Cynader (1975); and Tsumoto and Suzuki (1976) to argue that the MRF, possibly under the guidance of the frontal eye fields, provides phasic activation to the LGN and the LGN-cortical pathway to assist selective processing of the foveal image at the termination of the saccade. Breitmeyer noted that "this reset would occur at the beginning of each new fixation interval by counteracting any persisting effects of saccade suppression exerted on the response of these sustained neurons as a result of the activation of transient channels during the saccade" (1986, p. 77). Perhaps the waking LGN activity level was well below that of REM sleep (McCarley et al., 1983) because of the marked reduction of visual pattern in the waking research environment of their cats. Extended to REM sleep, the Breitmeyer model suggests that looking responses initiated in the cortex, possibly in the frontal eye fields, control with a 60–100-ms latency a LGN–visual cortex activation that, in the absence of retinal input to the LGN, activates or perhaps primes the visual cortex in a manner that supports the construction of visual imagery. This speculation, of course, assumes that the cortex plays some role in initiating saccades in REM sleep. This assumption will be examined after a look at the relation between PGO activity and the occipital cortex projection area for the LGN.

McCarley et al. (1983) plotted cortical evoked potentials that were timed from the onset of REM sleep EMs in human subjects. They observed a parietal-occipital evoked response that began 27.6 ms prior to REM onset and peaked 5.6 ms after REM onset (range = 0–12 ms), followed by a low amplitude negative wave. The location of the spike relative to EM onset in REM sleep was later than the 10–40 ms peak prior to the saccade onset that was reported by Kurtzberg and Vaughan (1982) for waking human subjects. Sample sizes larger than the 5 and 6 subjects that were respectively used in the two studies are necessary to determine if there is a significant difference in the timing and location of the REM and waking EM-triggered cortical-evoked potentials.

Although McCarley et al. (1983) found that EMs were contralateral to the occipital-parietal response, Monaco, Baghdoyan, Nelson, and Hobson (1984), using implanted electrodes, found the EMs to be ipsilateral to the occipital response. This apparent discrepancy may have occurred because scalp electrodes linked to a common reference to measure evoked potentials do not necessarily provide a measure of cortical activity immediately below the electrode (Fein, Raz, Brown, & Merrin, 1988) and because electrodes may respond to electromagnetic projection from neural dipole that are sometimes remote from the electrode (Goff, Williamson, Van Gilder, Allison, & Fisher, 1980; Kaufman, Okada, Tripp, & Weinberg, 1982), perhaps even in the contralateral hemisphere. The assumption of contralateral dipole projection would render the EM-posterior cortex findings of the two studies congruent. Cortical-evoked potentials have never been computed in sleep summed from the termination point of saccades, the onset of fixation. Using an estimated average of 25 ms for saccade duration, however, would place the peak of the cortical response approximately 19 ms prior to fixation. This lead time seems compatible with Breitmeyer's (1986) model of a cortically controlled, MRF-energized preparatory activation of the visual cortex just prior to foveation. Further research with waking saccades is necessary to determine whether the occipital-evoked potentials identify visual cortex enhancement processes tied to the onset of ocular fixation, or rather, to a presaccade decision process.

Of course, there is no foveation following saccades in REM sleep. In light of the salience of visual imagery in that state, however, one might speculate that this phasic activation of the visual cortex supports the visual analysis of whatever information is resident on the visual networks at the time of activation. For example, top-down processes in the association cortex might bias neural nets in earlier modules of the visual system to produce visual images that "fit" ongoing thought (see Antrobus, 1990). However, this conception also presupposes some cortical influence on the timing of PGO activity, a position that has been discounted by the identification of PGO burst cells in the pons.

The argument for pontine control of REMs is based on evidence that EMs in REM sleep appear to originate in the premotor neurons of the pontine reticular formation (Buttner, Buttner-Ennever, & Henn, 1977; Henn, Buttner-Ennever, & Hepp, 1982; Henn, Hepp, & Buttner-Ennever, 1982). Among these neurons are pontine giant cells that project to the oculomotor and vestibular neurons (Pompeiano, 1980). They exhibit similar patterns of discharge in both waking and REM sleep. McCarley, Nelson, and Hobson (1978) identified burst cells, primarily in the brachium conjunctivum, which is one of the neural branches that joins the pons to the cerebellum. Inasmuch as the burst cells are necessary to PGO activity, they appear to be the origin of the PGO wave generator system. They fire at high rates during horizontal EMs and precede ipsilateral lateral geniculate activity (Monaco et al., 1984; Nelson, McCarley, & Hobson, 1983).

Because the majority of the REM burst cells are in the brachium conjunctivum and because the brachium conjunctivum carries the output of the cerebellum to the brainstem, we must consider the possibility that this bursting activity in REM sleep is triggered by cerebellar processes. This hypothesis is also supported by the finding that discharge in the tegmental reticular nucleus of Bechterew, which has cerebellar connections, is coherent with both PGO waves and REMs and is also coupled with EM during waking (McCarley, Nelson, Hobson, & Strassman, 1981).

The role of the cerebellum in coordinating EM and head movement with spatial search is well-known, and the cerebellum is generally thought to fine tune the general EM control commands initiated in the frontal eye fields of the cerebral cortex (Bruce & Goldberg, 1985). Further support for this conjecture is provided by Hobson and McCarley's (1972) demonstration that the Purkinje cells of the cerebellum are more active in REM than in either NREM sleep or waking and that, within REM sleep, they are more active during REMs than ocular quiescence. Activation of the cerebellum in conjunction with REMs is not evidence, of course, that the cerebellum is processing cortical input, but it does demonstrate the operation of one further link between cortex and the oculomotor system during REM sleep EMs.

Although the major pathway from frontal eye fields to the brain stem includes the superior colliculus, little is known about the relation between collicular and cerebellar unit activity. The McCarley et al. (1981) study shows that it does not have direct input to the PGO units.

If the precise route from cerebral cortex to the burst cells of McCarley et al. (1978) in REM sleep is to be identified with precision, it will require extensive prior tagging in the waking state of individual neurons in the frontal eye fields–cerebellum–burst cell sequence. Individual adjacent units, such as hold units and fire units (particularly in the frontal eye fields), often serve quite different functions in waking perception (Bruce & Goldberg, 1985), so that measures of lead time and coherence between different nuclei or fields are of little value if the comparisons are based on random samples of units in each group.

The absence of high frequency and high amplitude burst cells in the cerebral cortex is not, in itself, evidence that the pontine burst cells are free of cortical control. As described later, the oculomotor neurons have unique energy requirements, and only an inefficient brain design would place these cells in the cerebral cortex surrounded by dense associative neuronal pathways and distant from the oculomotor neurons. A better design would place the complex decision making in the cortex and would place the neurons with high volley rates, which it modulates, close to the oculomotor neurons, namely, in the brain stem. The location of the burst cells and the input to the oculomotor neurons in the MRF seem to fit this organization.

BURSTING CELLS AND STATES OF SLEEP AND WAKING

What are the implications of the shifts in firing patterns of individual units across states of sleep and waking? This question constitutes a major puzzle concerning the function of PGO and burst cell activity in REM sleep, particularly their relation to the visual imagery of dreaming sleep. The oculomotor neurons always fire in bursts, proportional in duration to the projected size of the saccade. But many neurons show a bursting pattern only when they are not processing or transmitting information, and this is particularly true of sleep, especially NREM sleep and the transitions from either waking or NREM to REM sleep (Greene, Haas, & McCarley, 1986). Many of the rhythmic neural patterns such as electroencephalogram (EEG) alpha and spindles occur when the eyes close or in sleep states. These bursting patterns are generally terminated by activation from the MRF (McCarley, Benoit, & Barrionuevo, 1983). The bursting and rhythmic patterns within individual units can be determined from the electrochemical properties of the units, but their functions are not understood and may differ from structure to structure (Llinas, 1989).

It is the pattern of firing across a large set of neurons that putatively carries the information processed by a nucleus or field. However, almost nothing is known about how the shifts in spike patterns within a given unit affect the pattern of a network of units within a given structure. Perhaps one exception to this pessimistic picture is the bursting patterns that lead to recruitment of neighboring cells and lead to widespread rhythmic activity. In this case, surely, the neurons carry no cognitive information other than the message that the structure is in an off state.

The information carried by the pattern of PGO spikes is more difficult to decode. The pontine leg shows a bursting pattern (Greene et al., 1986; Nelson et al., 1983), but its input to the lateral geniculate does not (Fourment & Hirsch, 1980), even though other geniculate units do show bursting patterns during REM sleep. Monaco et al. (1984) found that the primary spike in occipital PGO waves is correlated with EM direction and amplitude in REM sleep but not in waking.

In conclusion, it is clear that the information available about the EM production system in REM sleep is, by itself, insufficient to support any strong model regarding EM activity and the cognitive process of visual imagery production. The evidence does not clearly support the cortical origin of EM control proposed by Herman et al. (1981), but neither does it support the Hobson and McCarley (1977) position that the REMs are totally free of cognitive control. Finally, the uninterpretability of cortical PGO bursting and high frequency spiking does not support the activation–synthesis hypothesis that the spikes interrupt ongoing cognitive processes to produce bizarre mentation. Even the EM information identified in the occipital cortex by Monaco et al. (1984) must remain suspect inasmuch as it is not seen in the waking state.

This latter point suggests one recommendation for all future research on this issue, namely, what are the appropriate waking controls for the study of EMs in REM sleep? If dreaming, as imaged perception, provides the context for an EM, then the waking control condition must approximate the imagined perceptual event. Because experimenters have no access to each subject's dreams, they must at the very least employ a variety of illumination levels and visual events as well as head position and movement conditions. Obviously, if a neuron's response is invariant over a range of these conditions, the multiple controls could be eliminated. But McIlwain (1988) has demonstrated at least one case where it is not. The trajectory of an electrically evoked saccade is dependent on the initial position of the eye.

The waking controls of most animal sleep studies have been poorly defined, generally studying animals under low arousal and low illumination with little or no visual pattern or movement, and often placing the animal under restraint (with the exception of Sakai & Jouvet, 1980), so that no head movements are possible. Thus, the conditions that the visual system is designed to respond to rarely occur in the waking control conditions. Obviously, there is no single waking control condition that is suitable for the study of REM sleep saccades.

VESTIBULAR, CEREBELLAR, AND OCULOMOTOR SYSTEM

Vestibular activity has often been suggested as a contributor to the characteristics of dream imagery. The horizontal posture of sleep has been suggested as a factor in the production of dreams of flying and falling. The intimate relation between head movement and eye movement in the waking state is sufficient reason to consider the possible contribution of vestibular activity to EMs in REM sleep. If a relation does exist during sleep, it is additional reason to compare unrestrained with restrained animals in waking control conditions in studies of the neural control of EMs.

During PGO activity in sleep, the pontine giant cells activate the vestibular neurons (Peterson, Franck, Pitts, & Daunton, 1976; Pompeiano, 1970, 1980). Pompeiano (1970) observed that high rates of medial and descending vestibular nuclei firing (80–160 spikes/s) were observed simultaneously with EMs in REM sleep but not in waking or synchronous sleep. Nelson et al. (1983) observed in restrained cats that, in waking, the PGO cells fire in single spikes rather than bursts, as in REM sleep. The similarity of the burst cell to the EM firing pattern is a criterion for ascertaining the similarity in the function of the waking and REM sleep EM control system and the function of PGO spikes. But are these comparisons valid if they fail to account for concurrent vestibular activity?

In the waking state, the medial and superior vestibular nuclei act on the third and sixth nerve to coordinate EMs with head movements during saccadic and tracking EMs, but during sleep there is neither retinal information to control eye trajectories nor head movements with which the EMs must be coordinated. The vestibular neurons extend to the paramedial reticular formation, and in the waking state, both vestibular and reticular neurons contribute to the excitation of the burst cells that control horizontal eye movements in the waking state. However, although the medial vestibular neurons modify EMs, it is the descending vestibular neurons that coordinate eye and head movement information with the cerebellum and higher cortical centers via the medial longitudinal fasciculus to the thalamus and, possibly, from there to the occipital cortex.

Ito (1974) described the vestibular–cerebellar–ocular network by which head movement and vestibular information modifies the cerebellar burst cell firing rates in the waking state. This network suggests part of the circuit by which the vestibular nuclei, which are quite active in REM sleep, can modify EMs via the cerebellar burst cells. Extensive afferents to the cerebellum from the association cortex (Kornhuber, 1974) indicate pathways by which cognitive processes could modify waking saccades and may similarly modify sleep EMs when the cortex is sufficiently activated, as in REM sleep, by the MRF.

The active involvement of the vestibular neurons raises the possibility that saccade control centers are programming REM EMs as though there were simultaneous head movements, as supported by the looking response findings of Herman et al. (1981). This complication emphasizes the difficulty of finding the appropriate waking head movement and visual stimulus conditions against which to compare REM EMs. None of the animal PGO EM sleep studies provide sufficiently explicit descriptions of their waking procedures or systematically vary their waking EM conditions so that an adequate assessment of the REM waking EM similarities and differences can be made.

Although the role of the vestibular nuclei in the modification of sleep mentation has been discussed only in the context of EMs, these nuclei may provide a trigger for dreams of falling or floating. Vestibular activity, when accompanied by a sporadic drop in the Stage 1 REM inhibition of alpha motor neurons, may account for the dreamer's experience of waking following a large body jerk that is accompanied by a dreamed episode of being off balance. The studies of the relation between REM sleep EMs and sleep mentation reports cited earlier by Roffwarg, Herman, and colleagues indirectly support this model. A significantly greater correlation between EM direction and the reported directional shift of the dreamer's gaze is observed when taking account of head movements than when ignoring them. Experimental evidence for this notion could be obtained in human sleep by means of pneumocaloric stimulation of the vestibular system.

PGO–BIZARRENESS MODEL REVISITED

As noted earlier, the Activation–Synthesis account of bizarreness rests on the assumption that PGO activity originates in the pons and is independent of cortical control and, therefore, is free of any input from antecedent cognitive processes. The cortex is informed of EMs by an independent route (Hobson & McCarley, 1977) and does the best it can in synthesizing the information it receives. If, as proposed here, the cortex uses cognitive information from several sources to initiate, control, or modify saccadic EMs via a cerebellar route rather than receives EM information post hoc, then the bizarreness explanation of the activation–synthesis model is not warranted.

Crick and Mitchison Theory of REM Sleep and Neural Nets

Crick and Mitchison (1983, 1986) have recently proposed that the production of REM dreams represents a cognitive process in which neural networks that have been "overloaded" (Crick & Mitchison, 1986, p. 234) as a consequence of waking perceptual and cognitive activity can once again become receptive to new information when they reawaken. The proposal is suggested by the finding that math models of "gridlocked" neural nets can be unlocked by random input to the net. If PGO spikes in REM sleep constitute such a random generator, then it is reasonable to posit such a function for PGO spikes. If, as proposed here, however, PGO spikes are a lawful or nonrandom output of a component of the visuomotor system, then a major assumption of the Crick and Mitchison (1983, 1986) model is untenable.

The evidence reviewed here for the role of the cerebellum in the programming of EMs in REM suggests that the possible role of the cortex in creating the visual imagery that is coordinated with EMs during REM sleep be reexamined. Might not the associative cortex attempt to interpret pattern information initiated in the occipital cortex, which in turn may result in an oculomotor decision to foveat the visual image, an apparent perception, in the foveal projection area of the occipital cortex? And furthermore, might it not be possible, since the retina receives no input in REM sleep and the EM cannot therefore foveate the imaged stimulus, that the movement command is given repeatedly, thereby producing a visual "stutter" that we see as a REM burst?

Visual Imagery and REMs

A number of studies have looked for an association between REMs and other qualities of visual imagery such as vividness, clarity, color saturation, and number of visual features. In "what was in some measure a post hoc analysis" (see, Foulkes and Pope, 1973, p. 115) of reports from phasic and tonic Stage 1 REM and Stage 2, Molinari and Foulkes (1969) found that REM-phasic versus tonic awakenings were associated with more reports of "primary visual experience" (p. 351); tonic REM and Stage 2 reports were associated with "secondary cognitive elaboration" (p. 351), such as reports of thinking, being awake, recognizing, or interpreting. Unfortunately, the two scales were confounded. The Primary Visual Imagery scale was scored residually only if the mentation report did not contain secondary cognitive elaboration. Further, some categories of secondary cognitive elaboration were added "*post hoc* if they proved to discriminate REM (burst) from (quiescent)" (p. 351), that is, phasic from tonic intervals. This procedure of scale construction confounds any conclusion about the relation of visual imagery to phasic Stage 1 REM versus other states of sleep. In 1973, Foulkes and Pope attempted a replication of the study using the same scales, but the phasic-tonic difference in primary visual experience held only for the spontaneous portion of the sleep reports. The authors emphasized that visual imagery, with or without secondary cognitive elaboration, is reported from all phasic and tonic REM sleep awakenings. Reinsel et al. (in press) just found that phasic, relative to tonic, REM reports are not associated with an increase in verbally reported visual imagery as measured by the log of the number of visual nouns, modifiers, and spatial prepositions taken as a rough index of the number of visual features in the report. In a critical review of phasic–tonic relations, Pivik (1978) concluded that, except for the Foulkes and Pope (1973) study, "we appear to be dealing with a rather weak effect" (p. 269).

A major handicap in the search for the neural substrates of visual imagery is that our inferences about visual characteristics have up to now been based exclusively on verbal reports. Rechtschaffen's (1983) recent success with the use of photographs to identify visual characteristics such as color saturation and visual clarity without regard to specific form or meaning offers an experimental tool that encourages us to reassess our models of visual image production. Rechtschaffen constructed a large number of photographic variations of a single scene. He presented a book containing the photographic variations to subjects as they awoke from different classes of sleep and asked them to select the single photograph that was most like their preceding sleep mentation. The model selection was the natural full color, full clarity photograph that had been used to construct the wide range of clarity, brightness, color saturation, and figure–ground variations in clarity and other distortions. One of the most noteworthy achievements of this instrument is its ability to distinguish a characteristic of phasic versus tonic REM mentation that has not been picked up by verbal report measures, specifically visual clarity, scaled in magnitude of focus versus blur in the photograph. Phasic REM visual imagery was judged higher in overall visual clarity than imagery during tonic REM sleep ($p < .02$, $N = 25$). Color saturation, brightness, and the remaining measures showed no change. Because Rechtschaffen did not obtain verbal mentation reports, the relation of the visual responses to verbal indices of visual mentation characteristics is unknown. If, indeed, the photoimagery instrument is sensitive to characteristics of visual imagery in sleep that verbal reports are not sensitive to, then the two types of instruments together may be able to provide a more valid test of the neuropsychological models of sleep mentation that have made predictions about variations in visual imagery. For example, an increase in visual characteristics of mentation during phasic REM is a critical prediction for the EM models of dreaming. The absence of support from verbal reports (Reinsel et al., in press) may be rectified by the photoimagery measure.

Recently, Antrobus, Hartwig, Rosa, Reinsel, and Fein (1987) scaled variations on a single color photograph for brightness and clarity of focus using a magnitude estimation technique where 100 represented the focus and brightness of normal waking vision. Photos were arranged in a 4×4, Brightness $\times$ Focus matrix. Upon awakening, subjects selected the photo that best represented the visual quality of each of the brightest and clearest (maximum = 5) objects or persons in their sleep mentation. Across all conditions, the brightness of visual imagery approximated that of visual perception more than did the clarity of focus, and both indices were highest during waking, slightly lower for REM, and lowest for NREM imagery responses. Brightness means were 88, 77, and 51, and clarity means were 79, 69, and 44 for waking, REM, and NREM states, respectively. The result suggests that there may be different neural control mechanisms for the two properties and that it may be worthwhile, in future research, to distinguish among various properties of visual imagery.

Despite Rechtschaffen's support for the phasic REM–visual imagery model, the precise relation between the clarity of visual imagery, on the one hand, and the REM sleep PGO and subcortical and cortical pattern of activation, on the other, is unclear. Although the PGO-associated occipital response (Nelson et al., 1983) may include no external visual pattern information, it may produce a general depolarization of pattern receptor cell units in areas 16, 17, and 18 so that higher order hypercomplex cells of the peristriate cortex can be activated to produce visual patterns that are consonant with the cognitive sequences generated in the associative cortex. Thus, mentation may be produced throughout REM sleep but may generate more visual detail during PGO-vestibular-related activation of the occipital cortex.

Although the role of the vestibular nuclei in the modification of sleep mentation has been discussed only in the context of EMs, these nuclei may provide a trigger for dreams of falling or floating. Vestibular activity, when accompanied by a sporadic drop in the Stage 1 REM inhibition of alpha motor neurons, may account for the dreamer's experience of waking following a large body jerk that is accompanied by a dreamed episode of being off balance. The studies of the relation between REM sleep EMs and sleep mentation reports by Roffwarg, Herman, and colleagues cited earlier indirectly support this model. A significantly greater correlation between EM direction and the reported directional shift of the dreamer's gaze is observed when head movements are considered rather than ignored. Experimental evidence for this notion could be obtained in human sleep by means of pneumocaloric stimulation of the vestibular system.

CONCLUSION

This chapter has reviewed evidence in support of the position that the PGO–EM link is part of a feedforward system for the control of waking saccades. Although waking saccades may be elicited by either visual or auditory input, the executive decision to emit a saccade during waking and REM sleep appears to be made in the cortex. Although this system is down throughout most of sleep, the activation of the cortex, vestibular, and oculomotor system by the MRF during portions of stage 1 REM is sufficient for the system to output PGO and REM periodically. The cognitive role in this cerebral cortex–cerebellum–PGO–EM sequence is demonstrated by the association of EMs in REM sleep with the clarity and direction of visual imagery and with the total amount of information reported. Eye movements and other phasic activity in REM sleep are therefore interpreted as evidence of a temporary increment in the activation of the cortex, including the visual association structures that generate the imaginal characteristics of dreaming.

The lawfulness of this control system is evidence against the interpretation of PGO activity as a random process. Therefore, it is evidence against both Hobson and McCarley's (1977) proposal that PGO is a random process that may, among other things, account for the bizarreness of sleep mentation and Crick and Mitchison's (1986) proposal that PGO activity is a random process that frees gridlocked neural nets during REM sleep.

References

Antrobus, J. S. (1983). REM and NREM sleep reports: Comparison of word frequencies by cognitive classes. *Psychophysiology, 20,* 562–568.

Antrobus, J. (1986). Cortical and cognitive activation, perceptual thresholds, and sleep mentation. *Journal of Mind and Behavior, 7,* 193–210.

Antrobus, J. (1990). *Cognitive and cortical activation and sleep mentation.* Manuscript submitted for publication.

Antrobus, J., Hartwig, P., Rosa, D., Reinsel, R., & Fein, G. (1987). Brightness and clarity of REM and NREM imagery: Photo response scale. *Sleep Research, 16,* 240.

Aserinsky, E., & Kleitman, N. (1953). Regularly occurring periods of ocular motility and concomitant phenomena during sleep. *Science, 118,* 361–375.

Aserinsky, E., Lynch, J. A., Mack, M. E., Tzankoff, S. P., & Hurn, E. (1985). Comparison of eye motion in wakefulness and REM sleep. *Psychophysiology, 22,* 1–10.

Breitmeyer, B. C. (1986). Eye movements and visual pattern perception. In E. C. Schwab & H. C. Nusbaum (Eds.), *Pattern recognition by humans and machines* (pp. 65–87). New York: Academic Press.

Bruce, C. J., & Goldberg, M. E. (1985). Primate frontal eye fields: I. Neurons discharging before saccades. *Journal of Neurophysiology, 53,* 603–635.

Buttner, U., Buttner-Ennever, J. A., & Henn, V. (1977). Vertical eye movement related unit activity in the rostral mesencephalic reticular formation of the alert monkey. *Brain Research, 130,* 239–252.

Cohen, B., Feldman, H., & Diamond, S. P. (1969). Effects of eye movement, brain stem stimulation, and alertness on transmission through lateral geniculate body of monkey. *Journal of Neurophysiology, 32,* 583–594.

Crick, F., & Mitchison, G. (1983). The function of dream sleep. *Nature, 304,* 111–114.

Crick, F., & Mitchison, G. (1986). REM sleep and neural nets. *Journal of Mind and Behavior, 7,* 229–250.

Fein, G., Raz, J., Brown, F. F., & Merrin, E. L. (1988). Common reference coherence data is confounded by power and phase effect. *Electroencephalograph and Clinical Neurophysiology, 69,* 581–584.

Foulkes, D., & Pope, R. (1973). Primary visual experience and secondary cognitive elaboration in stage REM: A modest confirmation and extension. *Perceptual and Motor Skills, 37,* 107–118.

Fourment, A., & Hirsch, J. C. (1980). Synaptic potentials in cat's lateral geniculate neurons during natural sleep with special reference to paradoxical sleep. *Neuroscience Letters, 16,* 149–154.

Goff, W. R., Williamson, P. D., Van Gilder, J. C., Allison, T., & Fisher, T. C. (1980). Neural origins of long latency evoked potentials recorded from the depth and cortical surface of the brain in man. In J. E. Desmedt (Ed.), *Progress in clinical neurophysiology* (Vol. 7, pp. 126–145). Basel, Switzerland: Karger.

Greene, R. W., Haas, H. L., & McCarley, R. W. (1986). A low threshold calcium spike mediates firing pattern alternations in pontine reticular neurons. *Science, 234,* 738–740.

Henn, V., Buttner-Ennever, J. A., & Hepp, K. (1982). The primate oculomotor system: I. Motoneurons. A synthesis of anatomical, physiological, and clinical data. *Human Neurobiology, 1,* 77–85.

Henn, V., Hepp, K., & Buttner-Ennever, J. A. (1982). The primate oculomotor system: II. Premotor systems: A synthesis of anatomical, physiological, and clinical data. *Human Neurobiology, 1,* 87–95.

Herman, J. H. (1984). Experimental investigations of the psychophysiology of REM sleep including the question of lateralization. *Research Communications in Psychiatry and Behavior, 9,* 53–75.

Herman, J. (1989). Transmutative and reproductive properties of dreams: Evidence for cortical modulation of brain stem generators. In J. A. Antrobus and M. Bertini (Eds.), *The neuropsychology of dreaming sleep.* Hillsdale, NJ: Erlbaum.

Herman, J. H., Barker, D. R., & Roffwarg, H. P. (1983). Similarity of eye movement characteristics in REM sleep and the awake state. *Psychophysiology, 20,* 537–543.

Herman, J. H., Roffwarg, H. P., Taylor, M. E., Boys, R. M., Steigman, K. B., & Barker, D. R. (1981). Saccadic velocity in REM sleep dreaming, normal visual activity, and total darkness. *Psychophysiology, 18,* 188.

Hobson, J. A., Lydic, R., & Baghdoyan, H. A. (1986). Evolving concepts of sleep cycle generation: From brain centers to neuronal populations. *Behavioral and Brain Sciences, 9,* 371–448.

Hobson, J. A., & McCarley, R. W. (1972). Spontaneous discharge rates of cat cerebellar Purkinje cells in sleep and waking. *Electroencephalograph and Clinical Neurophysiology, 33,* 457–469.

Hobson, J. A., & McCarley, R. W. (1977). The brain as a dream state generator: An activation–synthesis hypothesis of the dream process. *American Journal of Psychiatry, 134,* 1335–1348.

Ito, M. (1974). The control mechanisms of the cerebral motor systems. In F. O. Schmitt & F. G. Worden (Eds.), *The neurosciences: Third study program* (pp. 293–303). Cambridge, MA: MIT Press.

Jeannerod, M. (1966). The phasic phenomena of paradoxical sleep. *Revue Lyonnaise du Medicine, 15,* 27–44.

Jeannerod, M., & Mouret, J. (1962). Etude des mouvements oculaires observes chez l'homme au cours de la veille et du sommeil [The study of eye movements in man observed during the course of waking and sleep]. *Society de Biologie de Lyon, 25,* 1407–1410.

Kaufman, L., Okada, Y., Tripp, J., & Weinberg, H. (1982). Evoked neuromagnetic fields. *Annals of the New York Academy of Sciences, 388,* 197–213.

Kondo, T. (1988). *Late REM activation and sleep mentation.* Unpublished master's thesis, The City College of New York.

Kornhuber, H. H. (1974). Cerebral cortex, cerebellum, and basal ganglia: An introduction to their motor function. In F. O. Schmitt & F. G. Worden (Eds.), *The neurosciences: Third study program* (pp. 267–280). Cambridge, MA: MIT Press.

Kosslyn, S. M. (1988). Aspects of a cognitive neuroscience of mental imagery. *Science, 240,* 1621–1626.

Kurtzberg, D., & Vaughan, H. G. (1982). Topographic analysis of human cortical potentials preceding self-initiated and visually triggered saccades. *Brain Research, 243,* 1–9.

Ladd, G. (1892). Contributions to the psychology of visual dreams. *Mind, 1,* 299–304.

Llinas, R. R. (1989). The intrinsic electrophysiological properties of mammalian neurons: Insights into central nervous system function. *Science, 242,* 1654–1664.

McCarley, R. W., Benoit, O., & Barrionuevo, G. (1983). Lateral geniculate nucleus unitary discharge in sleep and waking: State- and rate-specific aspects. *Journal of Neurophysiology, 50,* 798–818.

McCarley, R. W., & Hobson, A. (1975). Neuronal excitability modulation over the sleep cycle: A structural and mathematical model. *Science, 189,* 58–60.

McCarley, R. W., Nelson, J. P., & Hobson, J. A. (1978). Ponto-geniculo-occipital (PGO) burst neurons: Correlative evidence for neuronal generators of PGO waves. *Science, 201,* 269–272.

McCarley, R. W., Nelson, J. P., Hobson, J. A., & Strassman, A. (1981). A cross-correlogram study of PGO-related neuronal activity in tegmental reticular nucleus, central tegmental field, and superior colliculus. *Sleep Research, 10,* 38.

McCarley, R. W., Winkelman, J. W., & Duffy, F. H. (1983). Human cerebral potentials associated with REM sleep rapid eye movements: Link to PGO waves and waking potentials. *Brain Research, 274,* 359–364.

McClelland, J. L., Rumelhart, D. E., & Hinton, G. E. (1986). The appeal of parallel distributed processing. In J. L. McClelland & D. E. Rumelhart (Eds.), *Parallel distributed processing: Explorations in the microstructure of cognition* (Vol. 1, pp. 3–44). Cambridge, MA: MIT Press.

McIlwain, J. T. (1988). Effects of eye position on electrically evoked saccadis: A theoretical note. *Visual Neuroscience, 1,* 239–244.

Mergner, T., & Pompeiano, O. (1981). Basic mechanisms for saccadic eye movements as revealed by sleep experiments. In A. Fuchs & W. Becker (Eds.) *Progress in oculomotor research* (pp. 107–114). New York: Elsevier/North Holland.

Molinari, S., & Foulkes, D. (1969). Tonic and phasic events during sleep: Psychological correlates and implications. *Perceptual and Motor Skills, 29,* 343–368.

Monaco, A. P., Baghdoyan, H. A., Nelson, J. P., & Hobson, J. A. (1984). Cortical wave amplitude and eye movement direction are correlated in REM sleep but not in waking. *Archives Italiennes de Biologie, 122,* 213–223.

Nelson, J. P., McCarley, R. W., & Hobson, J. A. (1983). REM sleep burst neurons, PGO waves, and eye movement information. *Journal of Neurophysiology, 50,* 784–797.

Noda, M., Murakami, J., Yamada, Y., & Aso, T. (1988). Saccadic eye movements evoked by microstimulation of the fastigial nucleus of macaque monkeys. *Journal of Neurophysiology, 60,* 1036–1052.

Ogawa, T. (1963). Midbrain reticular influences upon single neurons in lateral geniculate nucleus. *Science, 198,* 855–857.

Ogilvie, R., Hunt, H., Sawicki, C., & Samanhalskyi, J. (1982). Psychological correlates of spontaneous middle ear muscle activity during sleep. *Sleep, 5,* 11–27.

Peterson, B. W., Franck, J. I., Pitts, N. G., & Daunton, N. G. (1976). Changes in responses of pontomedullary reticular neurons during repetitive, cutaneous, vestibular, cortical and tectal stimulation. *Journal of Neurophysiology, 39,* 564–581.

Pivik, R. T. (1978). Tonic states and phasic events in relation to sleep mentation. In A. M. Arkin, J. Antrobus, & S. Ellman (Eds.), *The mind in sleep* (pp. 245–276). Hillsdale, NJ: Erlbaum.

Pompeiano, O. (1970). Mechanisms of sensorimotor integration during sleep. In E. Stellar & J. M. Sprague (Eds.), *Progress in physiological psychology* (Vol. 3). New York: Academic Press.

Pompeiano, O. (1980). Cholinergic activation of reticular and vestibular mechanisms controlling posture and eye movements. In J. A. Hobson & M. A. B. Brazier (Eds.), *The reticular formation revisited* (pp. 473–512). New York: Raven Press.

Porte, H. S., & Hobson, J. A. (1986). Bizarreness in REM and NREM reports. *Sleep Research, 15,* 81.

Rechtschaffen, A. (1983). Visual dimensions and correlates of dream images. *Sleep Research, 12,* 189.

Rechtschaffen, A., & Foulkes, D. (1965). Effect of visual stimuli on dream content. *Perceptual and Motor Skills, 20,* 1149–1160.

Rechtschaffen, A., Watson, R., Wincor, M. Z., Molinari, S., & Barta, S. C. (1972). The relationship of phasic and tonic periorbital EMG activity to NREM mentation. *Sleep Research, 1,* 114.

Reinsel, R., Antrobus, J., & Wollman, M. (in press). *Bizarreness in waking and sleep mentation: Waking, REM-NREM, and phasic-tonic differences in bizarreness.* In J. A. Antrobus and M. Bertini (Eds.), *The neuropsychology of dreaming sleep.* Hillside, NJ: Erlbaum.

Roffwarg, H. P., Dement, W., Muzio, J., & Fisher, C. (1962). Dream imagery: Relationship to rapid eye movements of sleep. *Archives of General Psychiatry, 7,* 235–258.

Sakai, K., & Jouvet, M. (1980). Brain stem PGO on cells projecting directly to the cat dorsal lateral geniculate nucleus. *Brain Research, 194,* 500–505.

Singer, W. (1977a). Brain stem stimulation and the hypothesis of presynaptic inhibition in cat lateral geniculate neurons. *Brain Research, 61,* 55–68.

Singer, W. (1977b). The effect of mesencephalic reticular stimulation on intracellular potentials of cat lateral geniculate neurons. *Brain Research, 61,* 35–54.

Singer, W., & Bedworth, N. (1973). Inhibitory interaction between X and Y units in cat lateral geniculate nucleus. *Brain Research, 49,* 491–507.

Singer, W., Tretter, F., & Cynader, W. (1975). Organization of cat striate cortex: A correlation of receptive-field properties with afferent and efferent connections. *Journal of Neurophysiology, 38,* 1080–1098.

Tsumoto, T., & Suzuki, D. A. (1976). Effects of frontal eye field stimulation upon activities of the lateral geniculate body of the cat. *Experimental Brain Research, 25,* 291–306.

Watson, R. K., Bliwise, D. L., Friedman, L., Wax, D., & Rechtschaffen, A. (1978). Phasic EMG in human sleep: II. Periorbital potentials and REM mentation. *Sleep Research, 7,* 57.

Watson, R., & Deptula, D. (in press). Phasic integrated potentials and ego boundary deficits. In J. Antrobus & M. Bertini (Eds.), *The neuropsychology of dreaming sleep.* Hillsdale, NJ: Erlbaum.

CHAPTER 2

ACTIVATION, INPUT SOURCE, AND MODULATION:
A NEUROCOGNITIVE MODEL OF THE STATE OF THE BRAIN–MIND

J. ALLAN HOBSON

Three factors that are of relevance to the level, source, and mode of information processing by the brain–mind state can be quantitatively estimated from neurophysiological data. They are (a) activation (Factor A), which estimates the electrical energy level of the information processing system from the rate of discharge of midbrain reticular formation neurons; (b) input source (Factor I), which estimates the provenance of data to be processed by the system from the ratio of external to internal stimulus strength values; and (c) mode of processing (Factor M), which estimates the way that data will be treated by the system by calculating the ratio of cholinergic to aminergic neuronal discharge.

The model is called AIM as both a shorthand eponym combining the first letters of each of the three factors and as a method of conveying the aspirations of a still evolving concept. Since each of the three factors of AIM can be defined in cognitive terms and can be measured as a neurobiological variable, the model is both conceptually promising and empirically anchored. The ultimate goal is to unify the brain and mind in a new way. This unity is implied by the hybrid term *brain-mind,* implying a functional identity of the two domains.

When we mathematically combine Factors A, I, and M in various ways, both explanatory and predictive principles emerge that render the model heuristically valuable whatever its ultimate verity may be when it is corrected or elaborated in the light of new data. The key to the success of the concept— and its major limitation—is its focus on the global states of waking, sleeping, and dreaming and its focus on the very superficial formal aspects of cognition during those states while ignoring, for the time being, many fascinating cognitive details that also characterize and differentiate those states.

FORMAL ASPECTS OF BRAIN–MIND STATES

The reasons for choosing the state level as a frame of reference for model construction are compelling. From the cognitive point of view, mental activity has long been known to be differentiated strikingly at this global level of analysis. For example, such major cognitive faculties as perception, volition, and memory change almost qualitatively as we pass from waking through non-REM (NREM) or slow wave sleep to REM sleep and dreaming. For example, consider the difference between waking vision and dream vision: In waking, visual perception is shaped by external data that have both stable and faithful representations in our mind's eye; in dreaming, imagery that is no less clear and no less vivid arises spontaneously and changes unpredictably, often without reference to even historical reality.

The robust nature of these mental state changes and the relative invariance of their correlation with neurobiological factors suggests that they are deeply rooted in, if not causally dependent on, the physical state of the brain. It is the strength of this connection that supports the idea of a unified brain–mind system. Within the past 35 years, new and powerful neurobiological techniques, especially in electrophysiology and neuropharmacology, have yielded abundant, replicable, and richly diversified sets of quantitative data regarding the states of the brain associated with these robust cognitive state variables (Hobson, 1988a, b, 1989; Hobson & Steriade, 1986). Thus, in connection with the visual perception example cited previously, we now know from studies of waking cats and monkeys how retinal signals encoding photic intensity are processed in the lateral geniculate body and are relayed to the visual cortex for further elaboration as animals perform visually guided tests. During REM sleep, many of the same central neural structures are both endogenously activated and autostimulated when humans dream visually detailed scenes. It is this psychophysical parallelism, so clearly differentiated from state to state, that lies at the heart of AIM. Knowing what we already know, we ought to be able to begin to sketch a unified model.

PROBLEMATIC PREMISES OF THE MODEL

Subjectivity

Reports by human subjects of their internal mental states, despite wide variability and notorious unreliability in special cases, have both consensual and face validity that cannot be denied. The global level of the model accommodates this problem nicely by concentrating on the most unequivocal and universal aspects of mental states, their formal properties. Thus, if 80 of 100 subjects report visually vivid, constantly animated, emotionally charged, narratively coherent but bizarrely organized mental experience on experimental awakening from REM sleep, I tend to believe that most of the 80 subjects, and perhaps even all 100 subjects, actually had such an experience.

Isomorphism

The correlation of these formal mental state variables with brain states as they can now be measured in humans justifies the assumption of an isomorphic relation between the consensually validated subjective experiences and the objectively recordable states of the brain. This correlation may be even stronger than is now supposed given the uncertainties of accurate reports of subjective data out of sleep and the relative superficiality of the currently recordable electroencephalogram (EEG) parameters of brain activity. *Isomorphic* is defined as a similarity of form in the two domains of brain and cognition (McCarley & Hobson, 1977). Thus, for example, if memory is poor for dreams, we can assume that the biological substrate of memory is impaired. If, conversely, dream vision is sharp and intense, we can assume that the visual brain is strongly activated in a way that simulates wake-state activation and stimulation.

Animal Models

To overcome the problem posed by the inaccessibility of the human brain to deep neurobiological analysis, we have recourse to animal models whose brains can be studied at the level of regions, nuclei, neuronal populations, individual neurons, membranes, and even molecular neurotransmitters (Hobson, Lydic, & Baghdoyan, 1986). As payment for the rich data that are thus obtainable, we accept the uncertain assumption that all mammalian brains, or at least those of the human, monkey, and cat, share common mechanisms of state control so that we can build our model up from subhuman data sources. This strategy makes no assumptions about whether the animals studied experience consciousness as we humans know it. I will now briefly discuss the evidence that encourages such assumptions and provides the substantive ground for the AIM model.

PSYCHOPHYSIOLOGY OF BRAIN–MIND STATES

The brain-mind is periodically activated and deactivated as humans move from waking through NREM to REM sleep (see Figure 1). We further know that the electrical aspects of such activation are shared by man and cat (see Figure 2). Assumptions underlying the quantification of activation (Factor A in the model) are thus quite strongly justified. Indeed, the activation concept is widely accepted and applied by cognitive psychologists, usually in models that are considerably more specific and more limited than is AIM (Anderson, 1985; Chapter 1, by J. Antrobus in this volume). Thus, the truly innovative aspects of the new model are related to Factor I (input source) and Factor M (mode of processing), which have not yet been considered by model-building cognitive psychologists. (The reader seeking a more detailed discussion of Factor A should consult Hobson, in press.)

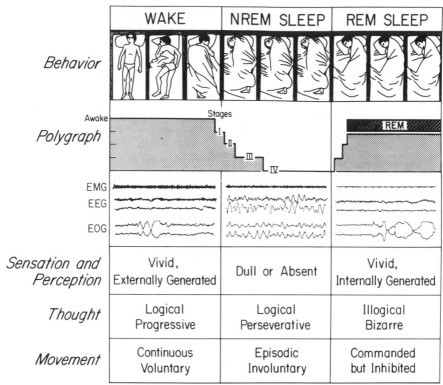

Figure 1 Three brain-mind states in humans. (States of waking, non-REM [NREM] sleep, and REM sleep have behavioral, polygraphic, and psychological manifestations. In the behavior channel, posture shifts (detectable by time-lapse photography or video) can occur during waking and in concert with phase changes of the sleep cycle. The sequence of these stages is represented in polygraph channel displaying EMG, EEG, and EOG tracings. Three lower channels describe other subjective and objective state variables.)

The source of data, or input source, changes progressively from a strongly external stimulus drive (SE) in waking to a strongly internal stimulus drive (SI) in REM sleep. Parallel to the decrease in activation that characterizes the wake–NREM transition is thus a decline in the access of external data to the system. That this decrease in external data is not a linear function of the decrease in activation is shown by the exponential increase in threshold to external stimulation at sleep onset. This exponential change in input source probably depends on the sudden occurrence of thalamocortical oscillation (seen in the EEG as spindling) that interferes with the effective transfer and central processing of sensory data. Since the strength of the external data stimulus is the reciprocal of the threshold, a value for SE can be derived by computing the inverse of threshold. We can therefore assert, as shown by Bonnet's studies (Chapter 11, by M. H. Bonnet in this volume), that values for the external data function could be directly derived from human data.

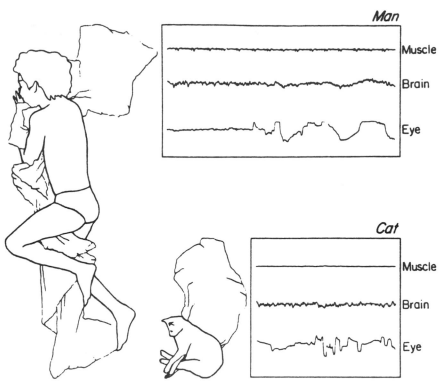

Figure 2   A comparison of REM sleep electrographic features in man and cat, based on a time-lapse photographic study by Theodore Spagna.

As the NREM sleep state evolves toward REM sleep in the cat (see Figure 3), we notice an increase in SI with the evolution of the pontine-geniculate-occipital (PGO) waves (Callaway, Lydic, Baghdoyan, & Hobson, 1987). The increase in SI parallels the resurgence of activation, but the cross-correlation is no more linear than the relation of activation to SE at sleep onset; rather, it is similarly and strikingly exponential. It is also significant that the thalamo-cortical oscillation of NREM sleep subsides inversely with the increment in PGO wave frequency. At a later and critical point in the transition from NREM to REM, the PGO waves are no longer the isolated, large-amplitude single spikes and wave complexes but become clustered into groups of 6–10 smaller waves (see Figure 4). That the PGO waves are genuinely sensory stimuli of entirely internal provenance is made clear by the discovery that during REM sleep eye movement direction is encoded in the left-to-right amplitude difference of the waves in the two lateral geniculate bodies and occipital cortices (Callaway et al., 1987; Monaco, Baghdoyan, Nelson, & Hobson, 1984). This discovery further justifies the assumption that these internally generated sensory stimuli actually arise on the motor side in keeping with two important concepts: First, that motor commands arising in the upper brain are abundant in REM sleep but are quenched by inhibition of the anterior horn cells in the

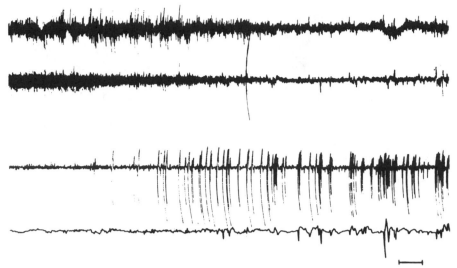

Figure 3   Transition from non-REM (NREM) to REM sleep in the cat.

spinal cord and, second, that REM sleep is characterized by a marked increase in the excitability of internal communication systems of the brain.

We are thus justified in postulating that in REM sleep there is not only the diminished access to external data by the brain-mind that is typical of all sleep but also an increase in the strength of internally generated data. It seems likely, moreover, that these PGO waves are a reflection of the disinhibition of the efferent copy or corollary discharge systems of the brain by which sensori-motor integration has been conceptualized since the time of the German neurophysiologist, Hermann von Helmholtz (for a discussion, see Hobson, 1988a). Although PGO waves are not easily recorded from human subjects, recent evidence supports the assumption that they do exist in our species and that they also signal the direction of eye movement from brainstem motor centers to the cerebral cortex (McCarley & Ito, 1983; McCarley, Winkelman, & Duffy, 1983).

In the shift from waking through NREM sleep to REM, the brain-mind has thus been deactivated (Factor A) with a concurrent decrease in the access of external data to the system and then reactivated with a concurrent increase in internal stimulus strength. We can therefore say with confidence that the cognitive differences between waking and REM sleep could not possibly depend only (if at all) on a changed level of activation. Rather, it is clear that both the waking and REM sleep states differ from NREM sleep and that they differ in equal degrees on this dimension. This difference parallels the cognitive downshift in NREM sleep that was pointed out by Antrobus (Chapter 1, by J. Antrobus in this volume). Input source, however, has shifted radically from external (in waking) to internal (in REM sleep), whereas NREM sleep

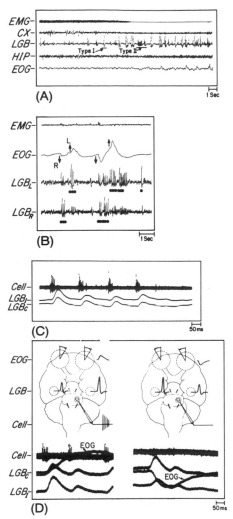

Figure 4   Pontine-geniculate-occipital (PGO) waves and relation to REM sleep and eye movement direction. (A) NREM–REM transition showing PGO waves. (B) Side-to-side alternation of primary waves. (C) Burst cell and PGO waves. (D) Efferent copy model. Subscripts: C = contralateral, I = ipsilateral.

shows constantly changing intermediate values of input source. Thus, different data are being processed by the equally activated brain in the two states. Now the question becomes, Is the data being processed in the same or in different ways?

Factor M, estimating the mode of processing, is designed to capture and to estimate the strength of such shifts in information processing from waking to dreaming, such as the shifts from linear to parallel, from logical to analogic, and from analytic to synthetic. The most likely candidate for a neurobiological mediator of these mode shifts is the modulatory neuronal systems of the brain whose generic name is suggestive of such a function (Laborit 1986).

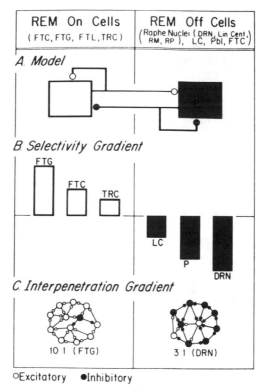

OExcitatory ●Inhibitory

Figure 5   Schematic illustration of the hypothesized relation between physiological selectivity and anatomical interpenetration of REM-on (left column) and REM-off (right column) cells whose reciprocal interconnections are modeled in Factor A.

We know that many modulatory neuronal populations of the brainstem show progressive changes in tonic discharge rate, and in the release of their respective neurotransmitters, over the sleep cycle in the cat. According to this concept, the extracellular concentration of neuromodulators over time is a function of the tonic discharge rate of the neurons that manufacture and release them. As yet, we have no evidence that such changes occur in humans, which makes Factor M the weakest link in the model. This is unfortunate because it is in many ways the most conceptually interesting aspect of the model. We must therefore regard its introduction as speculative and must await direct proof that the human brain is biochemically altered in the same way and to the same degree as that of the cat (see Figures 5 and 6).

With this caveat in mind, we may tentatively state that the value of Factor M decreases from a high ratio of aminergic to cholinergic neurotransmitter concentration in the brain during waking to a low ratio in REM sleep. In other words, the brain-mind becomes progressively less aminergic and more cholinergic as we pass from waking to dreaming (see Figure 7).

In this view, information processing transactions take place in a radically different biochemical climate according to whether the brain-mind is awake

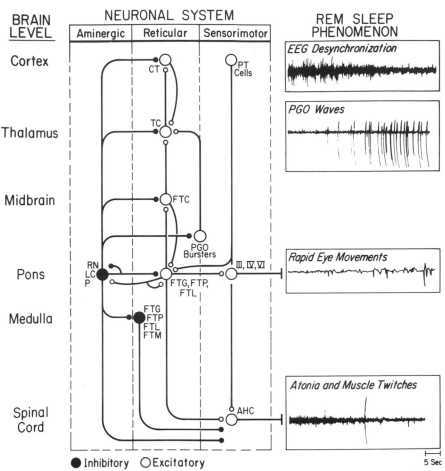

BRAIN LEVEL	NEURONAL SYSTEM			REM SLEEP PHENOMENON
	Aminergic	Reticular	Sensorimotor	

Figure 6   Schematic representation of the REM sleep generation process.

or is in REM sleep. This concept is an intracerebral and informational update of Hess's (1954) distinction between the ergotrophic (or catabolic) functions of the sympathetic nervous system and the trophotropic (or anabolic) functions of the cholinergic nervous system. The shift from an emphasis on energy (in Hess's concept) to an emphasis on information processing (as in the AIM model) is prompted by the recognition that such neurotransmitters as acetylcholine, norepinephrine, and serotonin exert their modulatory actions via second messengers, with effects on the activity of the intracellular metabolism of the genome as well as on the conductance of neuronal membranes (Black et al., 1987; Hobson, 1988b). It is now widely accepted that changes in membrane conductance that constitute signals from cell to cell must lead to alterations in the protein structure of ion channels, receptors, or enzymes if neurons are to retain a trace (or memory) of their excitation. For example, whether a postsynaptic cell remembers the information conveyed by its cho-

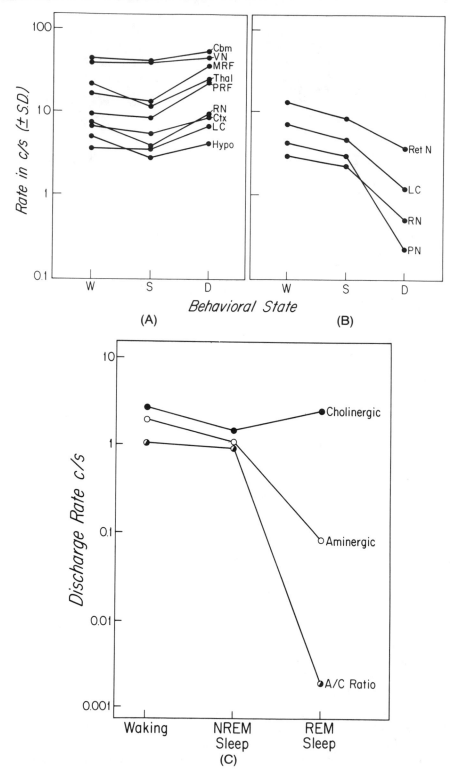

Figure 7 Behavioral state and neuronal discharge rate. (A) D-on cells. (B) D-off cells. (C) State-dependent changes in aminergic to cholinergic ratio.

linergically mediated input may depend on whether it is coactivated by an aminergic neuron releasing dopamine, serotonin, or norepinephrine (Flicker, McCarley, & Hobson, 1981).

In any case, we know that the noradrenergic and serotonergic neuronal populations of the brainstem shift from high levels of discharge in waking to intermediate levels in NREM sleep and to very low levels in REM sleep. This means that the brain is aminergically deafferented or "demodulated" in REM sleep compared with waking. (See Mamelak & Hobson, 1989, for a discussion of this concept and its implications for cognition.)

NEUROBIOLOGICAL QUANTIFICATION OF AIM

The activation values of several neuronal populations are shown in the left panel of Figure 8. Although the absolute values vary widely from neuron to neuron, it is generally true that in NREM sleep the average level is about half that in waking and REM sleep. We may thus use the ratio 2:1:2 as the relative value of activation across the three states.

The estimate of input source is more complex because SE and SI vary conversely, with the former value falling rapidly at NREM sleep onset and the latter rising rapidly at REM sleep onset. Using Bonnet's data (Chapter 11, by M. H. Bonnet in this volume), we note that since the auditory threshold changes from 10 dB in waking to 40 dB in NREM sleep, SE suddenly falls by a factor of about 4:1 at sleep onset. We do not know what happens in REM sleep, but the data of Harsh and Badia (Chapter 4, by J. Harsh and P. Badia in this volume) indicate that the sensory threshold actually falls a bit as REM develops, perhaps by a factor of 2:1. Thus, we may estimate SE in REM as 2. If PGO spike frequency is used as the estimate of internal stimulus strength, SI has the relative values of 1:2:100 (based on absolute values of 0.1 c/s for waking, 0.2 c/s for NREM, and 10.0 c/s for REM). If input source is the ratio of SE/SI, solving for input source gives the following values: wake = 4.00, NREM = 0.50, and REM = 0.02.

Factor M is a ratio function that measures the relative strengths of the aminergic and cholinergic systems. From the neuronal data in the right panel of Figure 8, we obtain values for aminergic modulation (MA) of 2.00 in waking, 1.00 in NREM sleep, and 0.01 in REM sleep. The values for cholinergic modulation (MC) are not precisely estimable at this time but may be conservatively quantified as being proportional to Factor A: Thus, MC has values of 2 for waking, 1 for NREM, and 2 for REM. The equation $M = MA/MC$ yields M values of 1.00 for waking, 1.00 for NREM, and .005 for REM.

COMBINING THE VALUES OF AIM

In a previous paper, the merits of various arithmetic and graphic representations of AIM were explored (Hobson, in press). The numerical value of A × I × M was first plotted as a function of sleep cycle phase, which revealed interesting properties at sleep onset (Chapter 11, M. H. Bonnet in this volume) and during REM sleep (Chapter 4, by J. Harsh and P. Badia in this volume). Then

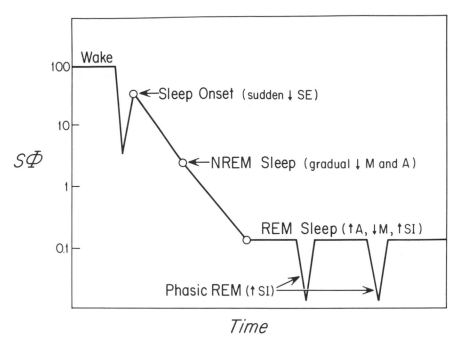

Figure 8   At sleep onset, a sudden and precipitous drop in the value of S could be caused by the sudden drop in the value of SE (with eye closure) after a slow decline in activation.

a three-dimensional state–space representation was explored (see Figure 9). When each variable is one of three dimensions of the state space, the instantaneous positions of points with coordinates A, I, and M represent the moment-to-moment value of the brain–mind state. The clusters or "clouds" of instantaneous values of AIM for waking are seen to fall in the back, upper right corner, in the center of the space for NREM, and in the front, lower right corner for REM. Of course, these positions are arbitrary, but their interrelations are revealing.

One virtue of the state–space conceptualization of AIM is that it can also accommodate a much wider continuity of values and a more richly varied continuity of states than can be integrated by any other existing schema. To demonstrate this property, we can begin to contemplate and comprehend such otherwise puzzling dissociative phenomena as lucid dreaming (Chapter 8, by S. LaBerge in this volume) and reverie (Chapter 12, by D. F. Dinges in this volume).

AIM IN LUCID DREAMING
In lucid dreaming, the paradox to be explained is the recovery of self-reflective awareness by subjects who report becoming conscious of dreaming and who can then signal out of REM sleep, when the somatic musculature is paralyzed, by executing complex voluntary eye movement sequences. The other physio-

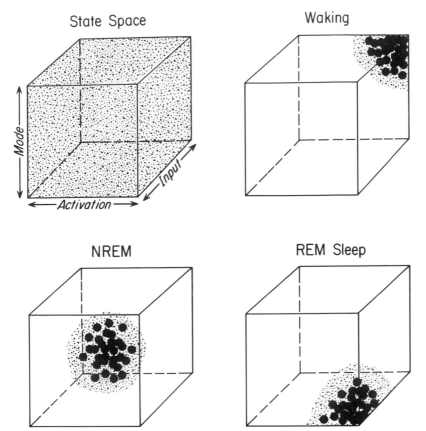

Figure 9   Three dimensional state space defined by the values for brain activation (A), input source and strength (I), and mode of processing (M).

logical signs of REM sleep are still present. It has been difficult for many sleep scientists to understand what physiological mechanisms could allow such wake state motor behavior as voluntary movement to occur during REM sleep because, by definition, motor output is blocked in REM. The AIM model allows us to consider another possibility: that lucid dreaming is a unique and specific state of the brain-mind. Because it has some features of waking and some features of REM, it is a hybrid state. Where would lucid dreaming fall in the state space?

It seems unlikely that a change in activation could account for the results because the level of cognitive activation is, if anything, higher than in REM sleep or in waking. Rather, one suspects a change in input source, with a temporary suppression of internally generated signals, allowing cortical commands to dominate the oculomotor apparatus in a wake-state fashion. Put another way, the usually weak top-down forces gain control of the usually strong bottom-up forces that are battling for control of the brain-mind in REM sleep. We might imagine Factor I as increasing toward waking values (i.e., toward the back of the state space, though still keeping to the right side because activation remains high). Since the REM-PGO generator network in the brain stem is activated via aminergic disinhibition, one way that such an effect could be enhanced is by turning on the locus coeruleus and raising the value of MA, which would put a brake on the cholinergic REM sleep generator. This would have the effect of moving AIM upward in the state space. The net effect of raising Factors I and M toward waking levels, while conserving a high level of Factor A, would be to locate lucid dreaming on the right-hand wall of the state space in the midpath of the rapid reset trajectory of the system when REM suddenly gives way to waking at the end of each REM cycle.

This view predicts (a) that lucid dreamers will frequently awaken from REM sleep once dream consciousness is achieved and (b) that lucidity will be easiest to induce at times in the night when the system is likely to be changing from REM to waking. This might be true during the brief period of descending to Stage 1 episodes at sleep onset but will be even more likely at the end of REM periods late in the night. This hypothesis could be tested in longitudinal home-based studies of experienced lucid dreamers.

REVERIE

Dramatic state dissociations occur on arousal from NREM sleep, especially in sleep-deprived subjects (Chapter 12, by D. F. Dinges in this volume). Although they are electrically awake (that is, showing signs of high levels of activation) and capable of input-output processing of the wake state type (that is, also having high levels of input source), such individuals appear to be unable to keep a cognitive test task in mind, and hence they perform poorly. They may even confabulate and produce garbled language only loosely rooted in the task structure imposed by the experimenter. Thus, we are again dealing with a paradox: Features of wake are hybridized with features of NREM sleep.

Variations of this functionally significant anomaly occur naturally in children with night terrors and in adults (such as physicians and other night-shift workers) who find themselves unable to perform complex cognitive tasks when suddenly aroused from NREM sleep by duty calls. Broughton (1968) has dubbed these phenomena disorders of arousal. Dinges (Chapter 12, by D. F. Dinges in this volume) has postulated that "sleep inertia" may mediate this phenomenon because, despite their best intentions, the subjects feel irresistibly pulled back down into sleep.

What could this inertial element of the brain-mind be, according to AIM? Factors A and I are probably not the culprits because the EEG is fully activated and wakelike input-output processing is possible. It seems rather that it is attention, the ability to hold a concept or task in mind and focus on it, that is defective. This would result if Factor M remained effectively low, so that the cortex, while electrically activated and capable of input-output transactions, remained biochemically demodulated. How could such an event occur?

Suppose that, early in the night, the serotonergic and noradrenergic systems of the brain have been operating at half-speed for 1 to 3 hours. And suppose further that the concentration of these two neurotransmitters in the cortex has fallen to 50% of waking levels. An arousal signal might immediately turn on the noradrenergic and serotonergic neurons electrically, but the concentrations of serotonin and norepinephrine in the extracellular fluid of the forebrain would climb back to their wake state levels only gradually. Ten to fifteen minutes of sustained firing might be needed to raise the concentration of these modulatory compounds to levels consonant with sustained attention and with memory.

In this view, sleep inertia is a hydraulic process, like the time taken for a large reservoir to refill when a small valve is opened, no matter how high the pressure in the supply chamber. One of the virtues of AIM is thus its distinction between electrical phenomena or "sparks" (mediating rapid changes in Factors A and I) and biochemical phenomena or "soup" (mediating slower changes in Factor M). Future development of this aspect of the model must take these even slower circadian and hormonal soup-like processes into account. In reverie, the net effect on AIM of raising Factors A and I while keeping Factor M low would be to move AIM to the back, lower right-hand corner of the state space. A testable prediction of this formulation is that treatment of subjects with biogenic amine-reuptake blockers will protect against reverie by maintaining higher levels of Factor M throughout sleep.

CONCLUSION

On the assumption that the states of waking and sleep effect cognition via neurobiological mechanisms, a three-factor model is proposed. Reflecting the electrical energy level of the brain is Factor A (for activation), which has a well-established cognitive analogue in network modeling parlance. The provenance of the information to be processed is assessed by Factor I (for input source), which measures the relative access and strength of external versus internal stimuli or data. Factor I also relates to motor activity via the corollary discharge or efferent copy concept. The most speculative and original component of the model is Factor M (for modulation), the estimated ratio of aminergic to cholinergic neurotransmitter concentration, which measures the mode of information processing manifested by the brain-mind. By mediating attention, learning, and memory processes, Factor M alters the capacity of the activated brain-mind to focus and perform intentional analytic computations of its data.

References

Anderson, J. (1985). *Cognitive psychology and its implications* (2nd ed.). New York: Freeman.

Black, I. B., Adler, J. E., Dreyfus, C. F., Friedman, W. F., LaGamma, E. F., & Roach, A. H. (1987). Biochemistry of information storage in the nervous system. *Science, 236,* 1263–1268.

Broughton, R. (1968). Sleep disorders: Disorders of arousal. *Science, 159,* 1070–1078.

Callaway, C. W., Lydic, R., Baghdoyan, H. A., & Hobson, J. A. (1987). Ponto-geniculo-occipital waves: Spontaneous visual system activation occurring in REM sleep. *Cellular and Molecular Neurobiology, 7,* 105–149.

Flicker, C., McCarley, R. W., & Hobson, J. A. (1981). Aminergic neurons: State control and plasticity in three model systems. *Cellular and Molecular Neurobiology, 1,* 123–166.

Hess, W. R. (1954). The diencephalic sleep centre. In E. D. Adrian, F. Bremer, & H. H. Jasper (Eds.), *Brain mechanisms and consciousness* (pp. 117–136). Oxford, England: Blackwell.

Hobson, J. A. (1988a). *The dreaming brain.* New York: Basic Books.

Hobson, J. A. (1988b). Homeostasis and heteroplasticity: Functional significance of behavioral state sequences. In R. Lydic (Ed.), *Clinical physiology of sleep* (pp. 199–220). Bethesda, MD: American Physiological Society.

Hobson, J. A. (1989). *Sleep.* San Francisco: Scientific American Library.

Hobson, J. A. (in press). A new model of brain–mind state: Activation level, input source and mode of processing (AIM). In J. Antrobus & M. Bertini (Eds.), *The mind-brain in dreaming sleep: Activation and asymmetry.* Hillsdale, NJ: Erlbaum.

Hobson, J. A., Lydic, R., & Baghdoyan, H. A. (1986). Evolving concepts of sleep cycle generation: From brain centers to neuronal populations. *Behavioral and Brain Sciences, 9,* 371–448.

Hobson, J. A., & Steriade, M. (1986). Neuronal basis of behavioral state control. In V. Mountcastle & F. E. Bloom (Eds.), *Handbook of physiology: The nervous system* (Vol. 4, pp. 701–823). Bethesda, MD: American Physiological Society.

Laborit, H. (1986). *L'Inhibition de l'action* [The inhibition of action] (2nd ed). Montreal, Canada: Masson.

Mamelak, A. N., & Hobson, J. A. (1989). Dream bizarreness as the cognitive correlate of altered neuronal behavior in REM sleep. *Journal of Cognitive Neuroscience, 1,* 201–222.

McCarley, R. W., & Hobson, J. A. (1977). The neurobiological origins of psychoanalytic theory. *American Journal of Psychiatry, 134,* 1211–1221.

McCarley, R. W., & Ito, K. (1983). Intracellular evidence linking pontine reticular formation neurons to PGO wave generation. *Brain Research, 280,* 343–348.

McCarley, R. W., Winkelman, J. W., & Duffy, F. H. (1983). Human cerebral potentials associated with REM sleep rapid eye movement: Links to PGO waves and waking potentials. *Brain Research, 274,* 359–364.

Monaco, A. P., Baghdoyan, H. A., Nelson, J. P., & Hobson, J. A. (1984). Cortical PGO wave amplitude and eye movement direction are correlated in REM sleep but not in waking. *Archives of Italian Biology, 122,* 213–223.

PART TWO

COGNITION DURING SLEEP

CHAPTER 3

EVENT-RELATED BRAIN POTENTIAL (ERP) STUDIES OF COGNITION DURING SLEEP:
IS IT MORE THAN A DREAM?

MARTA KUTAS

Punctate stimuli presented to an awake human leave an electrical trail as they travel from sensory transducers through the central nervous system (CNS). This electrical signature, typically represented as a waveform of voltage in time, is known as the *evoked response or potential* (EP). Current-day dogma has it that the EP reflects the potential field created from the summation of the excitatory and inhibitory postsynaptic potentials synchronously activated by an incoming stimulus. With the discovery of new brain wave components, it has become clear that some waves are more intimately related to internal events (such as preparing to move) than to external stimuli. Hence, the term *evoked* was subsumed by the general term *event-related* (EP being expanded to ERP). The transient ERP comprises a series of negative and positive peaks identified by their time synchrony to an eliciting stimulus. Each peak (also referred to as a component) is identified by its polarity and latency relative to stimulus onset (although on occasion a psychological label finds itself unabashedly attached to an ERP component). An ERP component is further characterized by the relative distribution of its amplitude across the scalp and by its waveshape (i.e., morphology).

Over the past 20 years, much research has been aimed at discovering the specific functions that relate changes in these EP characteristics to variations in stimulus parameters such as intensity, rate of presentation, frequency, and modality (see Regan, 1972, 1989). More important for our present purpose, much energy has also been spent compiling a vocabulary of components that describe many of the critical information-processing transactions in the brain that underlie cognition. A fuzzy but sizeable vocabulary exists. Thus, for example, some component changes have been related to selective attention (e.g., N1, Nd) and others have been related to anticipation and preparation (contingent negative variation [CNV] and readiness potential [RP]). Still others have been linked to sensory mismatches (N2-P3a), orienting (N_2), preperceptual mismatches (mismatch negativity [MMN]), surprise (P3b), novelty (P3a), and semantic processing (N400) (Gaillard & Ritter, 1983; Hillyard & Picton, 1987; Johnson, 1988; Johnson, Rohrbaugh, & Parasuraman, 1987; Kutas & Van Petten, 1988).

One undeniable benefit of some ERP components as measures of human brain activity is that they can be recorded regardless of a person's level of arousal or mental state. Of course, this is not to say that a person's state may not alter the amplitude or latency of the electrical response recorded but rather that a subject need not be awake or fully conscious of the eliciting stimulus to generate a measurable response. Insofar as we know what process is indexed by a part of an ERP waveform, the differential behavior of the peaks and troughs of the ERP can be used to make inferences about the psychology and physiology of the brain, be it awake or asleep. However, insofar as the processes underlying the ERP are less clear, it may be necessary to vary arousal states to learn more about the mappings between ERP components and cognitive operations.

EVENT-RELATED POTENTIALS IN SLEEP

Given that electroencephalographic (EEG) criteria have proven indispensable for differentiating among the various sleep stages (e.g. Rechtschaffen & Kales, 1968), it is surprising how infrequently ERP measures have been chosen as a means of evaluating the psychological and computational capabilities of the brain during the different sleep stages. In part, this may reflect our intuitions and the prevailing belief that not much processing (especially of external stimuli) goes on during sleep. Then again, the lack of cognitive ERP studies during sleep may be a reaction to the difficulty of pinning a cognitive operation uniquely to a specific positive or negative wave, even under conditions in which subjects are unquestionably awake and behaving. If one is fairly certain that there is little in the way of cognition during sleep and one is equally uncertain about interpreting a measure of cognitive activity (within existing frameworks), then one would be a bit foolhardy to jump right into the research fray. Few have.

Indeed, most research utilizing ERP recordings during sleep has focused on clinical rather than cognitive uses of the technique. By this view, the ERP

I extend sincere thanks to C. Van Petten for her helpful comments on this manuscript. Research efforts were supported by a Research Scientist Development Award from the National Institute of Mental Health (MH00322) and by a grant from the National Institute of Child Health and Human Development (HD22614).

is a clinical tool that provides an index of the integrity of the sensory pathways in the central nervous system. For diagnostic purposes, the most informative EP components are those that are consistently elicited by specific stimulus parameters in the face of fluctuations in arousal or attention. Studies over the past 20 years have indicated that the auditory brain evoked potential (ABEP), also known as the auditory brain stem response (ABR) or the brainstem evoked response (BER), provides just such a response. The ABR consists of a series of small vertex-positive waves occurring within the first 10 ms after an abrupt stimulus (Campbell, Picton, Wolfe, Baribeau-Braun, & Braun, 1981; Chiappa, Gladstone, & Young 1979; Stockard, Stockard, & Sharbrough, 1978). Peak 5 of the response is usually recognizable to within 20 dB of the behavioral auditory threshold (Galambos & Hecox, 1978; Picton, Woods, Baribeau-Braun, & Healy, 1977; Picton, Stapells, & Campbell, 1981). While there is considerable intersubject variability in component amplitudes, the latencies of the BER peaks are remarkably stable across replications, provided that the subject's age, gender, and body temperature as well as the physical properties of the eliciting stimulus and recording parameters are held constant (e.g., Moore, 1983). Such reliability, in fact, has sanctioned the development of a normative data base against which deviant responses can be judged. Abnormalities in the timing of various components relative to norms signal a possible cause for concern in either audiological or neurological domains. With a few exceptions that have been difficult to replicate (Lukas, 1980, 1981), it has been demonstrated that the first five waves of the BER are insensitive to attentional manipulations in an awake adult (Picton & Hillyard, 1974; Woldorff, Hansen, & Hillyard, 1987; Woods & Hillyard, 1978). Thus, ABR measurement has become a routine means of objective audiometry, especially for subjects who are unwilling or unable to undergo traditional methods of examination (e.g., neonates, young children, demented individuals).

The insensitivity of the BER to arousal levels and attentiveness in awake subjects suggests that the BER should be the same regardless of whether the subject is awake or asleep. The literature on this question is, however, contradictory. For instance, Amadeo and Shagass (1973) reported latency shifts as large as 0.25 ms in different stages of sleep. In contrast, Hellekson, Allen, Greeley, Emery, and Reeves (1979) found no differences in the latency of any ERP components between waking and light naps. Osterhammel, Shallop, and Terkildsen (1985) noted only minor changes in the latency of Peak 5 for only some subjects and only for low intensity stimuli. Campbell and Bartoli (1986) suggested that such inconsistencies in the literature may be due to a number of factors including (a) failure to control the stimulus input (that is, using loudspeakers rather than headphones), (b) failure to control for covariation in core temperature during the night (Jones, Stockard, & Weidner, 1980; Marshall & Donchin, 1981; Stockard, Sharbrough, & Tinker, 1978), and (c) small sample size.

Campbell and Bartoli (1986) evaluated the BER at different intensities and rates of stimulus presentation during wakefulness, Stages 2 and 4, and

REM sleep while maintaining precise control over the stimulus input (with an ear-mold hearing aid device) and monitoring temperature in 9 female subjects (18–25 years old). They reported that regardless of (a) the stage of sleep, (b) the time of night, (c) the rate of stimulus presentation, and (d) the intensity of the stimulus, sleep did not appear to have a significant effect on any of the components of the click-evoked ABR. They concluded "that auditory information is transmitted without alteration from the periphery through the brainstem relay centres during sleep" (p. 146). Before we accept this conclusion, we must remember that the BER is a sensitive index of the timing operations of the auditory system but is silent about the processing of the contents of the auditory signal.

Components of the auditory evoked response occurring between 10 and 100 ms have also been called into service for clinical hearing assessments. These components, referred to as *middle latency responses* (MLR), come in the form of transient or steady-state responses. Transient responses are evoked whenever stimuli are presented at slow rates (10/s or less), whereas steady-state responses arise when stimuli are presented at such a high repetition rate that the responses to successive stimuli overlap (e.g., Stapells, Linden, Suffield, Hamel, & Picton, 1984). The auditory MLR has received considerable attention in audiometry because of the possibility that it might allow determination of frequency-specific auditory thresholds. And indeed, threshold estimates from MLRs correlate well with behavioral thresholds, with the estimates from the steady-state response being less variable than those derived from transient responses (Galambos, Makeig, & Talmachoff, 1981; Goldstein & Rodman, 1967; Klein, 1983; Mendel et al., 1975; Shallop & Osterhammel, 1983; Stapells, 1984). Moreover, the effects of stimulus rate on the amplitude of the steady-state MLR are quite similar during wakefulness and sleep. For example, although the amplitude of the response is smaller during sleep, the maximum amplitude is still recorded at stimulus rates between 30–50 tones/s. The amplitude of the response increases as the intensity of the stimulus increases. A similar stimulus-intensity/response-amplitude function occurs at all stages of sleep, although the slope of the suprathreshold intensity–amplitude relation is lower during sleep than waking. Likewise, a similar intensity phase (i.e., latency) relation occurs in all stages of sleep and wakefulness, with the phase of the response decreasing as the suprathreshold intensity of the stimulus increases. Thus, while the steady-state MLR is sensitive to changes between sleep and wakefulness, it is little affected by transitions across the different sleep stages (e.g., Linden, Campbell, Hamel, & Picton, 1985). As such, it holds promise as a viable technique for generating electrophysiological audiograms at different frequencies during sleep.

COGNITIVE EVENT-RELATED POTENTIALS

There are few reports comparing components of the auditory ERPs later than 100 ms to standardized stimuli in the different states of wakefulness and sleep. Although during sleep there seems to be an overall reduction in the amplitude of electrical responses to sensory stimulation, this is not true of every component. Thus, it is important to consider different time regions of the ERP separately. For example, the amplitude of the N1 (around 100 ms) component is usually reduced during sleep (Anch, 1977; Bell & Campbell, 1988), whereas the amplitude of the following P2 component has been found to be highly variable (Buchsbaum, Gillin, & Pfefferbaum, 1975). The most profound change in the longer latency ERP components is the addition of a large negative N2 wave with a peak latency of 300–500 ms occasionally followed by a P3 component around 800 ms (e.g., Kevanishvili & von Specht, 1979; Ornitz, Ritvo, Carr, Panman, & Walter, 1967; Picton, Hillyard, Krausz, & Galambos, 1974; Ujszaszi & Halasz, 1986; Weitzman & Kremen, 1965; Williams, Tepas, & Morlock, 1962).[1] Components of the auditory ERP later than 100 ms have been found to be too variable to be useful in the clinic.

These data clearly demonstrate that sensory stimuli are afforded some processing during sleep, often with stimulus–response functions, that resemble those of wakefulness. These observations, together with the data demonstrating that people are capable of making both simple and discriminative manual responses during sleep (Granda & Hammack, 1961; Williams, Morlock, & Morlock, 1966), suggest the possibility of applying cognitive ERP paradigms. Very few investigations of this type have been reported. Those that have have focused on ERPs associated with anticipation or with physical mismatches embedded in a stimulus sequence.

During wakefulness, to be forewarned to is to be forearmed. That is, being warned of an impending stimulus makes it possible to react more quickly and more accurately. In most theories, the facilitatory influence of the preparatory set on motor reactions and perceptual judgment is attributed to different subprocesses of attention. Does this adage hold for sleep as well? Is it possible to talk about different types of attention during sleep? In the waking adult, differential preparation is reflected in specific patterns of CNS activity that develop across preparatory intervals. For example, in both human and nonhuman animals it has been found that, during intervals of preparation and anticipation, there develops an expectancy wave; this potential is referred to as the contingent negative variation (CNV), *contingent* because it is assumed to index the contingency between the warning and imperative stimulus and *variation* because that is the way the British say potential.

Walter, Cooper, Aldridge, McCallum, & Winter (1964) first observed the CNV in a reaction time task with a fixed foreperiod between the warning stimulus and the imperative stimulus. Accordingly, they proposed that this cortical electronegativity reflected the priming of the frontal lobes for action. Current-day views of the CNV based on human and animal experiments also have proposed major involvement of the frontal lobes as well as the ascending reticular activating system (ARAS) in CNV generation and modulation (Skin-

---

[1] This N2 and P3 should not be mistaken for the N2 and P3 components that are referred to in the ERP studies of human information processing in awake adults.

ner & Yingling, 1977). Moreover, Marczynski (1978) argued that it is the cholinergic component of the ARAS that is involved in the genesis of surface negative potentials of this type.

Studies demonstrating that CNVs can be elicited without a motor response requirement have shifted the emphasis from response priming to mobilization of effort for anticipated activity, wherein the amplitude of the CNV indexes the total allowance of effort devoted to preparatory activity (for reviews see Hillyard, 1973; Tecce, 1972). Most investigations thus have emphasized the relation between the CNV and *intensive* (e.g., alertness, arousal, concentration, effort, expectancy) rather than *selective* aspects of attention. And to some extent this seems reasonable. Generally, attentiveness to the eliciting stimuli yields larger CNVs than distraction, more difficult tasks yield larger CNVs than easy tasks, and anticipation of noxious or informative stimuli yields larger CNVs than benign or uninformative stimuli (for a review, see Donchin, Ritter, & McCallum, 1978). However, the relation is by no means a simple one: Too difficult a task, too stressful a task, or too many simultaneous task requirements often yield a CNV of a diminished amplitude. Despite this complex function between CNV amplitude, attentional resources, and arousal (e.g., Tecce & Hamilton, 1973), it is possible to determine the relation under specified circumstances during waking and to contrast it with that obtained under the same conditions during sleep.

One such study was conducted by Salamy, Lester, and Jones (1975). In this experiment, 3 subjects were asked to respond (i.e., press a microswitch taped to their right hand) to white noise forewarned by a tone occurring 1 s ahead on 3 consecutive nights. Recordings were obtained prior to sleep, during REM sleep, and immediately after morning awakening. The results suggested that, although the subjects responded correctly 65% of the time in REM sleep, a CNV either did not develop or was dramatically attenuated during REM sleep. However, there are aspects of the data that warrant caution. For instance, it would be informative in interpreting the ERPs to compare the waveforms associated with a response against those elicited on no-response trials. Given the limited number of trials per average ($n = 16$), however, it is unlikely that the data could have been sorted on the basis of behavior (e.g., by reaction time). The noise level of the data presented, especially in the REM condition, indicates that caution is well-advised. Moreover, as the authors noted but dismissed, the reaction times during REM were significantly slower (five- to sixfold) than when the subjects were awake. While the relation between CNV amplitude and reaction time is typically not linear, very prolonged reaction times tend to be associated with very small CNVs. Finally, the recordings were restricted to two electrode locations, vertex (Cz) and the left occiput, each referred to the left mastoid. Given that the latter part of a CNV elicited by a simple, right-handed response typically has a slight contralateral predominance over the motor strip, recordings from the central scalp locations and over the left hemisphere might provide a more precise test of the hypothesis. In any case, a replication of this type of study as well as recordings of CNV in a discriminative reaction time task would be worthwhile before we close the book on slow negative potentials and REM sleep.

The relation between CNV amplitude and non-REM (NREM) sleep has been studied by Bruneau, Martineau, Ragazzoni, and Roux (1980). Like the study of Salamy et al. (1975), the recordings were limited to the vertex and occiput (in this case the right occiput) referenced to the left earlobe. Recordings were taken when subjects were awake and while they were asleep. During sleep, three fifths of the recordings were obtained during Stages 1–2, approximately two fifths were obtained during Stages 2–3, and several more were obtained during Stages 3–4. The two conditions in which CNVs were anticipated involved a weak sound (i.e., click) followed 880 ms later by an ankle jerk or Hoffman reflex (a monosynaptic spinal segmental reflex triggered by electrical stimulation of the 1A fibers of the muscle spindles in the calf [soleus muscle]). The ankle jerk was elicited in one case by the fall of a hammer beside the Achilles tendon and in the other by electrical stimulation of the sciatic nerve. Given the lack of an explicit task, this is not the most auspicious paradigm for eliciting CNVs. Moreover, the trials in which the click was paired with an ankle jerk were interspersed with blocks in which the click and the ankle jerk were each presented alone in the series, without pairing. Again, this type of equivocation in the warning stimulus to imperative stimulus contingency has been shown to reduce CNV amplitudes somewhat, albeit most severely when the single and paired trials are interspersed within a single experimental run. Although the data from sleep and waking were collected in counterbalanced order across the subjects, there is no indication that order of presentation made a difference on the size of the effects. On the whole, it seemed as if a CNV developed between the warning stimulus and the imperative stimulus during waking, whereas during NREM sleep the results were more variable with a clear large *positivity* developing prior to the imperative stimulus in some cases. The authors suggested that all of the ERPs recorded during sleep were probably K complexes (biphasic, negative–positive) and that the slow potential changes obtained by the sound and ankle jerk pairing were abolished. Again, I believe that more testing with a design better suited for CNV-elicitation and a more detailed mapping of the potentials across the scalp are warranted before we generalize this conclusion. Given the controversy surrounding the existence of a CNV as a unitary phenomenon as opposed to a combination of an orienting response to the warning stimulus (O wave) and a preparation for movement in response to the imperative stimulus (E wave), it might also be informative to manipulate the foreperiod interval during sleep studies. This latter approach has been used to separate the two components in waking subjects (e.g., Rohrbaugh & Gaillard, 1983).

Thus, is being forewarned helpful in sleep as well? The answer, based on ERPs, is that we do not know. First, one would want to know whether a warned signal is responded to more quickly than an unwarned signal and whether the effect of warning varies with sleep stage. The results of such a behavioral study would aid in the interpretation of slow potential studies and would be less costly to pursue. If the CNV requires active engagement of attentional mechanisms and this is not possible during sleep, then no CNVs will be expected. However, we must question whether the concept of attention can be invoked in the same breath as sleep. If the CNV is truly an indicator of CNS excitability, one might expect differences in CNV generation and maintenance between REM and NREM sleep. While it would not be surprising to find that CNVs are smaller during sleep than during waking, it is theoretically crucial to determine whether there are any significant differences in CNV amplitude, morphology, and scalp distribution during the different stages of sleep. The critical role of muscarinic cholinergic mechanisms both in REM sleep (e.g., Hobson, 1988) and in the generation of slow negative potentials such as the CNV (Marczynski, 1978; Pirch, Corbus, Rigdon, & Lyness, 1986) suggest that, if CNVs are to be recorded during sleep, they should vary across the stages, especially between REM and NREM. In addition, if the proposed involvements of REM sleep and CNV amplitude in some aspect of memory have some validity, one might expect differential effects of sleep stages on CNV generation and amplitude. Certainly, any study of these issues should attempt to gather the relevant ERP data from the same subjects during the different sleep stages under the same experimental conditions (difficult as this may be).

To date, intuition and evidence lead me to argue that the so-called cognitive ERP components require at least a modicum of attention for their elicitation. The most likely candidate as an exception to this rule is the MMN.[2] The MMN was first identified and was subsequently studied by Naatanen and associates (Naatanen, 1986; Naatanen & Gaillard, 1983; Naatanen, Gaillard, & Mantysalo, 1978; Naatanen, Sams, & Alho, 1986). The MMN is a negative component beginning around 100 ms after a stimulus change in a repetitive homogeneous stimulus stream, even when the change is not consciously perceived. That is, if subjects are asked to attend to one ear in a dichotic listening task and to ignore stimuli in the other ear, tones in the unattended ear that deviate from the ongoing sequence of tones elicit an MMN. The larger or more obtrusive the deviation and the less frequently it occurs, the larger the MMN. Naatanen has proposed that the MMN reflects the activity of an automatic, preperceptual neuronal mismatch process; namely, the neurophysiological basis of echoic memory in audition. The MMN has been found to be modality specific and is presumed to be independent of and insensitive to attentional manipulations.

The latter presumption was tested in a situation considered to provide "the most extreme case of attention to environmental stimuli, namely sleep" (Paavilainen et al., 1987, p. 247). Seven subjects who were instructed to wake up early in the morning took part in an experiment that same evening, during which they listened to tones as they read a book; gradually, they fell asleep.

---

[2] However, I could easily argue that it does not properly belong in the arsenal of cognitive components.

Tone bursts (50 ms of a sine wave at 75 dB SPL) were presented at a constant interstimulus interval of 510 ms. Ninety percent of the tones were 1000 Hz, whereas 10% were 1050 Hz. While awake, subjects read a book and ignored the tones; afterward they slept while sequences of 800 tones were presented. The ERPs to the frequent (i.e., standard) tones were characterized by a P1 and an N1 component. As had been previously reported, the N1 component was reduced significantly as the subjects grew drowsy, and it disappeared as they entered Stage 1 sleep. In contrast, the P1 component grew larger in amplitude with progressing stages of NREM sleep. The reading condition was as expected: The less frequent (i.e., deviant) stimulus was characterized by a large MMN peaking between 150 and 200 ms, followed by a P3a-like deflection between 250 and 300 ms. As drowsiness set in, 4 of the subjects continued to produce significant MMNs and a nonsignificant hint of the P3a. By Stage 1 sleep and thereafter, none of the ERPs to deviant tones contained an MMN. Three of the subjects continued to show a small, late positivity in response to the deviant stimulus during Stage 1 sleep. By Stage 2 sleep there were no differences in the ERPs elicited by standard and deviant tones. Although some data were recorded during Stages 3 and 4, the ERPs to deviant tones were described as distorted by "the low frequency and high amplitude brain waves characteristic to these sleep stages" (Paavilainen et al., 1987, p. 249). In addition, no ERPs were recorded during REM because the subjects' sleep architecture was abnormal. These peculiarities included longer-than-normal Stage 2, spontaneous awakening after one or two sleep cycles, and insufficient numbers of reliable periods of REM. This last observation aside, the results of this experiment clearly show that the MMN is not elicited by deviant stimuli during sleep.

It is important to comment that Paavilainen et al. (1987) were the first to propose that additional experiments with the mismatch negativity during sleep be carried out and to suggest that such follow-up experiments should use larger stimulus deviations. They based this recommendation on the fact that larger deviations are associated with larger MMNs and on the observation by Csepe, Karmos, and Molnar (1987) of an MMN (30–70 ms) during slow wave sleep in cats. Csepe et al. presented 3- and 4-kHz tones as deviant and standard tones, respectively, at a number of different target-to-standard probability ratios (five levels between 5% and 50%) and found MMNs of an increased latency at some recording sites but only at the lowest deviant probabilities. While it is sometimes difficult to compare ERP components across species, the cat recordings met enough of the necessary criteria to be considered similar to the MMN recorded in man. As such, they also suggested that Paavilainen et al.'s (1987) study with humans be modified and tried again. In addition to using a greater deviation as they proposed, I also recommend using (a) variable intervals between stimuli (e.g., between 300 and 500 ms), (b) recording epochs of at least 800 ms poststimulus, and (c) acclimating the subjects to sleeping in the laboratory so that their sleep patterns are normal.

FUTURE DIRECTIONS AND POSSIBILITIES

As is evident from this review of the scant literature on cognitive electrophysiological investigations of sleep, the door is wide open for studies of this type. What follows are some of my thoughts on possible directions to pursue.

Although the CNV requires that subjects somehow appreciate the contingency between two stimuli, there are other slow, long-lasting negative potentials of the same family that are easier to record. For example, recordings made prior to limb movements indicate the presence of a slow-rising negativity that begins in some cases as early as 1.5 s before movement onset (measured relative to the response in the moving muscles with electromyography [EMG]). This negativity, variously called the readiness potential, *bereitschaftspotential,* and N1 of the motor potential, is largest over the motor strip and, at least in its latter half, has a strong contralateral predominance (e.g., Kornhuber & Deecke, 1965). In a series of experiments, Libet (1985) made inferences about the timing of conscious awareness based on the onset time of the readiness potential relative to each subject's verbal report of the intention to move. Within an experimental psychology tradition, Coles and colleagues (e.g., Coles & Gratton, 1986; Gratton, Coles, Sirevaag, Eriksen, & Donchin, 1988; see also de Jong, Wierda, Mulder, & Mulder, 1988) have used the asymmetric portion of the readiness potential as a measure of differential preparation and have used it to make inferences about information flow through the black box we call a brain (Coles, Gratton, Bashore, Eriksen, & Donchin, 1985). Do we need to be paying attention to make use of partial information? What are the odds of recording RPs to spontaneous movement during sleep—during any stage? If a lucid dreamer can make voluntary movements based on presleep instructions, will these movements be preceded by a readiness potential? And if RPs are recorded during sleep, must we modify our conceptions of preparation and voluntariness?

The past 10 years of ERP research have witnessed a strong push in the areas of language processing and memory, sometimes in combination (Kutas, 1988; Kutas & Van Petten, 1988; Neville, Kutas, Chesney, & Schmidt, 1986). For example, ERPs to words and pictures show clear repetition effects (Nagy & Rugg, 1989; Rugg, 1985, 1987; Rugg, Furda, & Lorist, 1988; Rugg & Nagy, 1987). To what extent is attention necessary to yield this repetition effect? How will the brain respond to an auditory passage that it has been exposed to earlier in the day? How will it respond the next morning to a passage that it has heard during sleep, either slow wave or REM? Will anomalous sentences seem less strange to subjects if they have been experienced previously during sleep? Both behavioral and ERP measures may provide answers to such questions, albeit not necessarily the same ones. The ERP measure has on occasion proven to be more sensitive to implicit memories than to reaction time measures (e.g., Besson, Fischler, Boaz, & Raney, 1989). If forced to bet, I would put my money on the ability of implicit memories or procedural learning (linguistic and nonlinguistic) to penetrate the sleeping brain to a greater degree than those of an explicit or declarative nature. If semantic processing truly reflects lexical processing without awareness, as claimed by some researchers (for a review, see Holender, 1986), then two associatively or semantically related words might prime each other during sleep as well. Examining ERP signs of semantic association during sleep might shed light on these issues (e.g., Kutas & Hillyard, 1989).[3] Certainly, my views on language processing, ERPs, and sleep would be affected by empirical evidence on these matters. In fact, it is precisely because my intuitions run counter to any notion wherein people can simultaneously cogitate about external events and enjoy sleep that I have proposed ways to prove myself wrong.

References

Amadeo, M., & Shagass, C. (1973). Brief latency click-evoked potentials during waking and sleep in man. *Psychophysiology, 10,* 244–250.

Anch, M. (1977). The auditory evoked brain response during adult human sleep. *Waking and Sleeping, 1,* 189–194.

Bell, I., & Campbell, K. (1988). In T. W. Picton (Ed.), Human event-related potentials. *EEG handbook* (Vol. 3, p. 364). Amsterdam: Elsevier.

Besson, M., Fischler, I., Boaz, T. L., & Raney, G. (1989). *Effects of automatic semantic priming on explicit and implicit memory tests.* Manuscript submitted for publication.

Bruneau, N., Martineau, J., Ragazzoni, A., & Roux, S. (1980). Event-related slow potentials evoked during ankle jerk conditioning in wakefulness and NREM sleep. *Electroencephalography and Clinical Neurophysiology, 49,* 93–101.

Buchsbaum, M., Gillin, J. C., & Pfefferbaum, A. (1975). Effect of sleep stage and stimulus intensity on auditory average evoked responses. *Psychophysiology, 12,* 707–712.

Campbell, K. B., & Bartoli, E. A. (1986). Human auditory evoked potentials during natural sleep: The early components. *Electroencephalography and Clinical Neurophysiology, 65,* 142–149.

Campbell, K. B., Picton, T. W., Wolfe, R. G., Baribeau-Braun, J., & Braun, C. (1981). Clinical evoked potential studies: II. Auditory brainstem responses. *Sensus, 1,* 9–19.

Chiappa, K. H., Gladstone, K. J., & Young, R. R. (1979). Brainstem auditory evoked responses: Studies of waveform variation in 50 normal human subjects. *Archives of Neurology, 36,* 81–87.

Coles, M., & Gratton, G. (1986). Cognitive psychophysiology and the study of states and processes. In E. R. J. Hockey, A. W. K. Gaillard, & M. G. H. Coles (Eds.), *Energetics and human information processing.* Dordrecht, The Netherlands: Martinus Nijhof.

Coles, M. G. H., Gratton, G., Bashore, T. R., Eriksen, C. W., & Donchin, E. (1985). A psychophysiological investigation of the continuous flow model of human information processing. *Journal of Experimental Psychology: Human Perception and Performance, 11,* 529–553.

---

[3] In a fantasy world of science, I would also be interested in knowing whether segments of the EEG activity of any given individual recorded during the day would correlate highly with a segment of equal length recorded later that evening during REM sleep. That is, is there any evidence for the notion that certain processing sequences are replayed for the purpose of consolidation during sleep?

Csepe, V., Karmos, G., & Molnar, M. (1987). Evoked potentials correlates of stimulus deviance during wakefulness and sleep in cat-animal model of mismatch negativity. *Electroencephalography and Clinical Neurophysiology, 66,* 571–578.

de Jong, R., Wierda, M., Mulder, G., & Mulder, L. J. M. (1988). Use of partial stimulus information in response processing. *Journal of Experimental Psychology: Human Perception and Performance, 14,* 682–692.

Donchin, E., Ritter, W., & McCallum, W. C. (1978). Cognitive psychophysiology: The endogenous components of the ERP. In E. Callaway, P. Tueting, & S. H. Koslow (Eds.), *Event-related brain potentials in man* (pp. 349–441). New York: Academic Press.

Gaillard, A. W. K., & Ritter, W. (Eds.). (1983). *Tutorials in event related potential research: Endogenous components.* Amsterdam: Elsevier/North-Holland.

Galambos, R., & Hecox, K. E. (1978). Clinical applications of the auditory brainstem response. *The Otolaryngologic Clinics of North America, 11,* 709–722.

Galambos, R. S., Makeig, S., & Talmachoff, P. J. (1981). A 40-Hz auditory potential recorded from the human scalp. *Proceedings of the National Academy of Sciences, 78,* 2643–2647.

Goldstein, R., & Rodman, L. (1967). Early components of averaged evoked responses to rapidly repeated auditory stimuli. *Journal of Speech and Hearing Research, 10,* 607–705.

Granda, A. M., & Hammack, J. T. (1961). Operant behavior during sleep. *Science, 133,* 1485–1486.

Gratton, G., Coles, M. G. H., Sirevaag, E., Eriksen, C. W., & Donchin, E. (1988). Pre- and poststimulus activation of response channels: A psychophysiological analysis. *Journal of Experimental Psychology: Human Perception and Performance, 14,* 331–344.

Hellekson, C., Allen, A., Greeley, H., Emery, S., & Reeves, A. (1979). Comparison of inter-wave latencies of brain stem auditory evoked responses in narcoleptics, primary insomniacs and normal controls. *Electroencephalography and Clinical Neurophysiology, 47,* 742–744.

Hillyard, S. A. (1973). The CNV and human behavior. *Electroencephalography and Clinical Neurophysiology,* Suppl. 33. Amsterdam: Elsevier.

Hillyard, S. A., & Picton, T. W. (1987). Electrophysiology of cognition. In F. Plum (Ed.), *Handbook of physiology, Section 1: The nervous system: Vol 5. Higher functions of the nervous system, Part 2* (pp. 519–584). American Physiological Society, pp. 519–584.

Hobson, J. A. (1988). *The dreaming brain.* New York: Basic Books.

Holender, D. (1986). Semantic activation without conscious identification. *Behavioral and Brain Sciences, 9,* 1–66.

Johnson, R., Jr. (1988). The amplitude of the P300 component of the event-related potential: Review and synthesis. In P. K. Ackles, J. R. Jennings, & M. G. H. Coles (Eds.), *Advances in Psychophysiology* (Vol. 3, pp. 69–138). Greenwich, CT: JAI Press.

Johnson, R., Jr., Rohrbaugh, J. W., & Parasuraman, R. (Eds.). (1987). Current trends in event-related potential research, *Electroencephalography and Clinical Neurophysiology,* Suppl. 40. Amsterdam: Elsevier.

Jones, T. A., Stockard, J. J., & Weidner, W. J. (1980). The effects of temperature and acute alcohol intoxication on the brain stem auditory evoked potential in the cat. *Electroencephalography and Clinical Neurophysiology, 49,* 23–30.

Kevanishvili, Z., & von Specht, H. (1979). Human slow auditory evoked potentials during natural and drug-induced sleep. *Electroencephalography and Clinical Neurophysiology, 47,* 280–288.

Klein, A. J. (1983). Properties of the brain-stem slow wave component: 1. Latency, amplitude, and threshold sensitivity. *Archives of Otolaryngology, 109,* 6–12.

Kornhuber, H. H., & Deecke, L. (1965). Hirnpotentialanderungen bei Wilkurbewegungen und passiven Bewegungen des Menschen: Bereitschaftspotential und re-afferente Potentiale [Changes in brain potential during voluntary and passive movements in man: The readiness potential and reafferent potential]. *Pfluegers Archiv für Gesammelte Physiologie, 284,* 1–17.

Kutas, M. (1988). Review of event-related potential studies of memory. In M. S. Gazzaniga (Ed.), *Perspectives in memory research* (pp. 181–218). Cambridge, MA: MIT Press.

Kutas, M., & Hillyard, S. A. (1989). An electrophysiological probe of semantic association. *Journal of Cognitive Neuroscience, 1,* 38–49.

Kutas, M., & Van Petten, C. (1988). Event-related brain potential studies of language. In P. K. Ackles, J. R. Jennings, & M. G. H. Coles (Eds.), *Advances in psychophysiology* (Vol. 3, pp. 139–187). Greenwich, CT: JAI Press.

Libet, B. (1985). Unconscious cerebral initiative and the role of conscious will in voluntary action. *Behavioral and Brain Sciences, 8,* 529–566.

Linden, R. D., Campbell, K. B., Hamel, G., & Picton, T. W. (1985). Human auditory steady state evoked potentials during sleep. *Ear and Hearing, 6,* 167–174.

Lukas, J. H. (1980). Human attention: The olivo-cochlear bundle may function as a peripheral filter. *Psychophysiology, 17,* 444–452.

Lukas, J. H. (1981). The role of efferent inhibition in human auditory attention: An examination of the auditory brainstem potential. *International Journal of Neuroscience, 12,* 137–145.

Marczynski, T. J. (1978). Neurochemical mechanisms in the genesis of slow potentials: A review and some clinical implications. In D. Otto (Ed.), *Multidisciplinary perspectives in event-related brain potential research* (pp. 25–36). Washington, DC: U.S. Government Printing Office.

Marshall, N. K., & Donchin, E. (1981). Circadian variation in the latency of brainstem responses: Its relation to body temperature. *Science, 212,* 356–358.

Mendel, M. I., Hosick, C. E., Windman, T. R., Davis, H., Hirsh, S. K., & Dinges, D. F. (1975). Audiometric comparison of the middle and late components of the adult auditory evoked potentials awake and asleep. *Electroencephalography and Clinical Neurophysiology, 38,* 27–33.

Moore, E. J. (Ed.). (1983). *Bases of auditory brain-stem evoked responses.* New York: Grune & Stratton.

Naatanen, R. (1986). Neurophysiological basis of the echoic memory as suggested by event-related potentials and magnetoencephalogram. In F. Klix & H. Hagendorf (Eds.), *Human memory and cognitive capabilities* (pp. 615–628). Amsterdam: Elsevier/North-Holland.

Naatanen, R., & Gaillard, A. W. K. (1983). The orienting reflex and the N2 deflection of the ERP. In A. W. K. Gaillard & W. Ritter (Eds.), *Tutorials in event-related potential research: Endogenous components* (pp. 119–329). Amsterdam: Elsevier/North-Holland.

Naatanen, R., Gaillard, A. W. K., & Mantysalo, S. (1978). The early selective attention effects on evoked potential reinterpreted. *Acta Psychologica, 42,* 313–329.

Naatanen, R., Sams, M., & Alho, K. (1986). The mismatch negativity: The ERP sign of a cerebral mismatch process. In W. C. McCallum, R. Zappoli, & F. Denoth (Eds.), *Cerebral psychophysiology, electroencephalography and clinical neurophysiology* (Suppl. 38, pp. 172–178). Amsterdam: Elsevier.

Nagy, M. E., & Rugg, M. D. (1989). Modulation of event-related potentials by word repetition: The effects of inter-item lag. *Psychophysiology, 26,* 431–436.

Neville, H. J., Kutas, M., Chesney, G., & Schmidt, A. (1986). Event-related brain potentials during the initial encoding and subsequent recognition memory of congruous and incongruous words. *Journal of Memory and Language, 25,* 75–92.

Ornitz, E. M., Ritvo, E. R., Carr, E. M., Panman, L. M., & Walter, R. D. (1967). The variability of the auditory averaged evoked response during sleep and dreaming in children and adults. *Electroencephalography and Clinical Neurophysiology, 22,* 514–524.

Osterhammel, P. A., Shallop, J. K., & Terkildsen, K. (1985). The effect of sleep on the auditory brainstem response (ABR) and the middle latency response (MLR). *Scandinavian Audiology, 14,* 47–50.

Paavilainen, P., Cammann, R., Alho, K., Reinikainen, K., Sams, M., & Naatanen, R. (1987). Event-related potentials to pitch change in an auditory stimulus sequence during sleep. In R. Johnson, Jr., J. W. Rohrbaugh, & R. Parasuraman (Eds.), *Current trends in event-related potential research* (EEG Suppl. 40). Amsterdam: Elsevier/North Holland.

Picton, T. W., & Hillyard, S. A. (1974). Human auditory evoked potentials: II. Effects of attention. *Electroencephalography and Clinical Neurophysiology, 36,* 191–200.

Picton, T. W., Hillyard, S. A., Krausz, H. I., & Galambos, R. (1974). Human auditory evoked potentials: I. Evaluation of components. *Electroencephalography and Clinical Neurophysiology, 36,* 179–190.

Picton, T. W., Stapells, D. R., & Campbell, K. B. (1981). Auditory evoked potentials from the human cochlea and brainstem. *Journal of Otolaryngology, 10,* 1–41.

Picton, T. W., Woods, D. L., Baribeau-Braun, J., & Healey, T. M. J. (1977). Evoked potential audiometry. *Journal of Otolaryngology, 6,* 90–119.

Pirch, J. H., Corbus, M. J., Rigdon, G. C., & Lyness, W. H. (1986). Generation of cortical event-related slow potentials in the rat involves nucleus basalis cholinergic innervation. *Electroencephalography and Clinical Neurophysiology, 63,* 464–475.

Rechtschaffen, A., & Kales, A. (1968). *A manual of standardized terminology, techniques, and scoring system for sleep stages of human subjects.* Washington, DC: U.S. Government Printing Office.

Regan, D. (1972). *Evoked potentials in psychology, sensory physiology and clinical medicine.* London: Chapman & Hall.

Regan, D. (1989). *Human brain electrophysiology: Evoked potentials and evoked magnetic fields in science and medicine.* Amsterdam: Elsevier/North Holland.

Rohrbaugh, J. W., & Gaillard, A. W. K. (1983). Sensory and motor aspects of the contingent negative variation. In A. W. K. Gaillard & W. Ritter (Eds.), *Tutorials in event related potential research: Endogenous components* (pp. 269–310). Amsterdam: Elsevier/North-Holland.

Rugg, M. D. (1985). The effects of semantic priming and word repetition on event-related potentials. *Psychophysiology, 22,* 642–647.

Rugg, M. D. (1987). Dissociation of semantic priming, word and non-word repetition by event-related potentials. *Quarterly Journal of Experimental Psychology, 39A,* 123–148.

Rugg, M. D., Furda, J., & Lorist, M. (1988). The effects of task on the modulation of event-related potentials by word repetition. *Psychophysiology, 25,* 55–63.

Rugg, M. D., & Nagy, M. E. (1987). Lexical contribution to non-word repetition effects: Evidence from event-related potentials. *Memory and Cognition, 15,* 473–481.

Salamy, J., Lester, J., & Jones, K. (1975). REM sleep and contingent negative variation development. *Electroencephalography and Clinical Neurophysiology, 39,* 201–204.

Shallop, J. K., & Osterhammel, P. A. (1983). A comparative study of measurements of SN-10 and the 40/sec middle latency responses in newborns. *Scandinavian Audiology, 12,* 91–95.

Skinner, J. E., & Yingling, C. D. (1977). Central gating mechanisms that regulate event-related potentials and behavior. In J. Desmedt (Ed.), *Progress in clinical neurophysiology: Attention, voluntary contraction, and event-related cerebral potentials* (Vol. 1, pp. 30–69). Basel, Switzerland: Karger.

Stapells, D. R. (1984). *Studies in evoked potential audiometry.* Unpublished doctoral dissertation, University of Ottawa, Canada.

Stapells, D. R., Linden, R. D., Suffield, J. B., Hamel, G., & Picton, T. W. (1984). Human auditory steady state potentials. *Ear and Hearing, 5,* 105–113.

Stockard, J. J., Sharbrough, F. W., & Tinker, J. A. (1978). Effects of hypothermia on the human brainstem auditory response. *Annals of Neurology, 3,* 368–370.

Stockard, J. J., Stockard, J. E., & Sharbrough, F. W. (1978). Nonpathologic factors influencing brainstem auditory evoked potentials. *American Journal of EEG Technology, 18,* 177–209.

Tecce, J. J. (1972). Contingent negative variation (CNV) and psychological processes in man. *Psychological Bulletin, 77,* 73–108.

Tecce, J. J., & Hamilton, B. T. (1973). CNV reduction by sustained cognitive activity (distraction). In W. C. McCallum & J. R. Knott (Eds.), Event-related slow potentials of the brain. *Electroencephalography and Clinical Neurophysiology,* Suppl. 33, 229–237.

Ujszaszi, J., & Halasz, P. (1986). Late component variants of single auditory evoked responses during NREM sleep Stage 2 in man. *Electroencephalography and Clinical Neurophysiology, 64,* 260–268.

Walter, W. G., Cooper, R., Aldridge, U. J., McCallum, W. C., & Winter, A. L. (1964). Contingent negative variation: An electric sign of sensorimotor association and expectancy in the human brain. *Nature, 203,* 380–384.

Weitzman, E. E., & Kremen, H. (1965). Auditory evoked responses during different stages of sleep in man. *Electroencephalography and Clinical Neurophysiology, 18,* 65–70.

Williams, H. L., Morlock, H. C., & Morlock, J. U. (1966). Instrumental behavior during sleep. *Psychophysiology, 2,* 208.

Williams, H. L., Tepas, D. I., & Morlock, H. C., Jr. (1962). Evoked responses to clicks and electroencephalographic stages of sleep in man. *Science, 138,* 685–686.

Woldorff, M., Hansen, J. C., & Hillyard, S. A. (1987). Evidence of selective attention in the midlatency range of the human auditory event-related potential. In R. Johnson, J. W. Rohrbaugh, & R. Parasuraman (Eds.), *Current trends in event-related potential research* (pp. 146–154). Amsterdam: Elsevier.

Woods, D. L., & Hillyard, S. A. (1978). Attention at the cocktail party: Brainstem evoked responses reveal no peripheral gating. In D. A. Otto (Ed.), *Multidisciplinary perspectives in event-related brain potential research* (pp. 230–233). Washington, DC: U.S. Government Printing Office.

CHAPTER 4

STIMULUS CONTROL AND SLEEP

JOHN HARSH AND PIETRO BADIA

The transfer of learning from the wake to the sleep state has been the subject of several studies involving conditioned discrimination (e.g., Beh & Barratt, 1965) and operant control procedures (e.g., Williams, Morlock, & Morlock, 1966). These studies show that stimulus control transfers from waking to sleep. The degree to which learned behavior can be controlled, however, has been found to be greatly reduced by sleep. One of the goals of this research was to investigate factors related to the level of control exerted by stimuli presented during sleep. An additional goal was to provide further information about the effects of stimulus control on sleep. Addressing these issues may increase our understanding of brain organization in sleep and may also lead to procedures for controlling sleep-related behavioral disorders.

REINFORCEMENT AND RESPONDING

Because earlier reports suggested that reinforcement affects the probability of responding (e.g., Williams et al., 1966), reinforcement contingencies were varied in our first studies (e.g., Badia et al., 1984; Harsh et al., 1987). Our studies used young adult volunteer subjects who were told while they were awake that tones would be presented repeatedly while they were asleep and that their task would be to respond to the tones by taking a deep breath. Four experimental conditions were studied. In each case, the interstimulus interval averaged 4 min. Further details regarding the procedures, the control conditions, and the rationale for response selection can be found in Badia et al. (1984) and Harsh et al. (1987). The conditions were (a) instructions only, in which subjects were told that their task was to respond to the tone (65 dB of 30-s duration); (b) escape, in which subjects were told to respond to the tone and that responding would terminate the tone (65 dB of 30-s maximum duration); (c) escape/

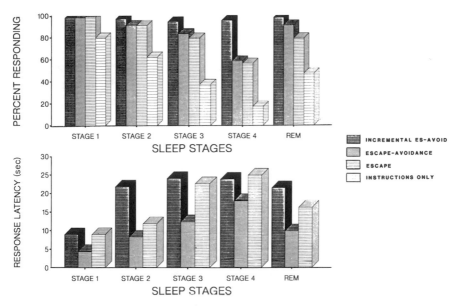

Figure 1   Mean response probability and mean response latency for responses during non-REM (NREM) and REM sleep under different test conditions.

avoidance, in which subjects were told to respond to terminate the tone (65 dB of 30-s maximum duration) and that failure to do so would result in a louder (90 dB) tone; and (d) incremental escape/avoidance, in which subjects were told to respond to terminate the tone that was initially 45 dB but, in the absence of a response, increased in 10 dB increments every 10 s up to 95 dB.

The results of these studies for the first night of testing are shown in Figure 1. Note first the data for the three procedures that involved responding to a fixed intensity (65 dB) tone. In the instructions only group, the percentage of responding varied across sleep stages, with responses during sleep Stages 3 and 4 occurring relatively infrequently (see top of Figure 1). Having subjects respond by terminating the tones (escape group) or avoiding the presentation of louder tones (escape/avoidance group) resulted in an increased likelihood of responding. Responding occurred more quickly in the escape/avoidance group (see bottom of Figure 1). Thus, with these three procedures, responding to a 65-dB tone varied as a function of the consequences of the responding. These findings are consistent with those of earlier studies concerning reinforcement for responding in sleep (cf. Williams et al., 1966).

The incremental escape/avoidance procedure resulted in the greatest control over behavior. Responding occurred on 90–100% of the trials in each stage of sleep. Note that the average response latency with the incremental procedure was 20–25 s during Stages 2, 3, and 4 and during REM sleep. This means that the tone intensity had increased from 45 dB to 65 dB at the time of responding, which was the decibel level of the fixed-intensity tone under the other three procedures. Presumably, the greater behavioral control with the incremental procedure, at the same average decibel level as the other procedures, is attributable to fluctuations in response thresholds during all stages of sleep.

The data from the four experimental procedures demonstrate that reliable control of behavior in all stages of sleep can be obtained with the selective use of reinforcement contingencies. Significantly, the control was obtained with stimuli presented at a high rate (every 4–5 min). Although the data in Figure 1 are from only the first night of testing, reliable responding with the incremental procedure has been maintained across 10 consecutive test nights (Badia, Harsh, & Balkin, 1986). Because the incremental procedure proved to be the most successful in maintaining responding, it was used in subsequent studies.

EFFECTS ON SLEEP

Earlier investigators concerned with behavioral control in sleep studied the electroencephalographic (EEG) record at the time of test stimuli to assess whether subjects had responded while they were asleep or following arousal from sleep (e.g., Williams et al., 1966). Using EEG alpha as evidence of awakening, it has generally been concluded that subjects are able to respond during sleep. Responding without alpha activity has frequently been observed in our studies. However, we approached the question of whether sleep was disturbed by the behavioral control procedure more generally and included subjective sleep reports, physiological measures of variables related to sleep, and measures of daytime sleepiness.

Subject Reports

The morning reports we obtained in early experiments (e.g., Badia et al., 1984; Badia, Harsh, Balkin, O'Rourke, & Burton, 1985; Harsh et al., 1987) assessed subjects' perceptions of sleep quality and also assessed recall of stimulus/response events that occurred in sleep. In these experiments, subjects reliably responded to stimuli presented on an average of once every 4–8 min. When asked to report on the quality of their sleep, subjects typically reported that their sleep was not disturbed or was only minimally disturbed. When asked how many tones were presented during the night, subjects typically reported that only 6–10 tones (up to 100 were actually presented) had been presented. Thus, although behavior was reliably controlled by frequently presented stimuli, there was little awareness of the stimulus presentations and no or minimal sleep disruption was attributed to the behavioral control procedure.

The results were different when subject reports were obtained by waking subjects just after tone presentations. As part of a study of the relation between cognitive activity and response variables (see Burton, Harsh, & Badia, 1988), subjects were awakened 30 s after tones were presented during Stage 2 and REM sleep. The stimulus presentation procedure in this experiment was tailored to provide reports following both response and no response trials. Additionally, the tones were presented relatively infrequently (a variable interval

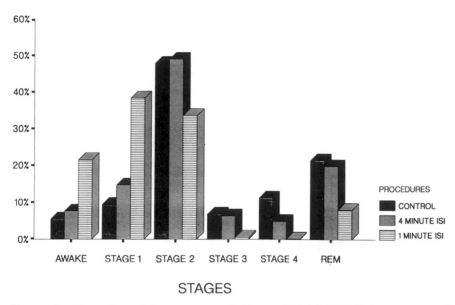

STAGES

Figure 2 Percentage of time spent awake in non-REM (NREM) sleep stages and in REM sleep under control condition and 4-min and 1-min interstimulus interval experimental conditions.

45-min schedule). As with the morning reports, the results support the conclusion that subjects are capable of responding without the perception of waking. That is, subjects responded without reporting awakenings on an appreciable number of trials. However, following approximately 50% of the responses, subjects reported that they had been awakened by the tones. This contrasts with the morning recall of less than 10% of the tones. Thus, subject reports obtained more closely in time to the stimulus/response events were more likely to indicate perceived wakefulness.

Physiological Variables

Electrophysiological data were recorded in each of our experiments. Thirty-second epochs of sleep records were scored following conventional guidelines (Rechtschaffen & Kales, 1968). The results obtained across experiments provide a consistent picture of the effects of behavioral control on sleep structure. Thus, when subjects are tested with an average interstimulus interval of 4 min or more, the only effect on structure is a reduction in Stage 4 sleep (Badia et al., 1984; Badia et al., 1985; Harsh et al., 1987). The observation of minimal change in sleep structure under these test conditions is in accord with the subjects' morning reports (described previously) of minimal sleep disturbance.

Data obtained by Magee, Harsh, and Badia (1987) indicate that interstimulus intervals shorter than 4 min can result in severe sleep disruption. Magee et al. presented stimuli after every 4 min or after every 1 min of sleep. As in previous studies, under the 4-min condition, sleep structure was minimally disturbed. However, when stimuli were presented after every 1 min of sleep, sleep structure was profoundly altered. Figure 2, which is based on data

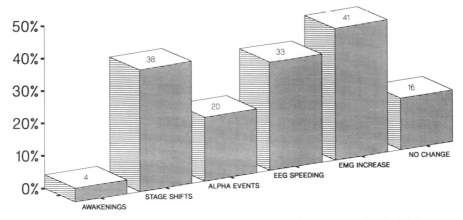

Figure 3   The percentage of trials followed by awakenings, stage shifts, brief changes, and no changes in the sleep record.

from the Badia et al. (1985), Harsh et al. (1987), and Magee et al. (1987) studies, illustrates this outcome. It appears that, with young adults, sleep structure is minimally disturbed with interstimulus intervals of 4 min or more but is greatly disturbed with an interstimulus interval of 1 min. It should be noted that although older adults are as behaviorally responsive, their sleep is much more vulnerable to disruption (Harsh, Purvis, Badia, & Magee, 1989).

The recordings at the time of and just after tone presentations were also examined for evidence of brief electrophysiological changes attributable to stimulus presentation and/or response emission. Figure 3 presents data on the brief electrophysiological changes. Included is the percentage of tones and responses accompanied by awakenings (as scored in 30-s epochs), shifts in sleep stage, alpha events (<15-s bursts), EEG speeding (<15-s increase in EEG frequency), and increases in electromyograph (EMG) recording. Also presented is the percentage of trials accompanied by none of the changes (no change). The data were obtained using the incremental procedure, with tones occurring every 4 min on the average. Tone intensity began at 45 dB and increased in 10 dB increments every 10 s up to 95 dB. It can be seen that awakenings occurred only infrequently, and short bursts of alpha, which are sometimes taken as a sign of brief awakening or arousal, occurred during or following only 20% of the tones. Thus, responding occurred during polygraphically defined sleep on the large majority of trials.

Although awakenings may have been infrequent, some changes were found on all but 16% of the trials. The significance of these changes in relation to the sleep/wake continuum and to overall sleep quality is unclear. It is interesting in this regard that, when tones begin at a higher dB level and increase more rapidly (see Magee et al., 1987), there is a much greater probability of brief electrophysiological changes; however, as long as the interstimulus interval is not less than 4 min, there are minimal effects on sleep structure and daytime sleepiness.

   Data reported by Harsh, Badia, O'Rourke, and Burton (1983) indicate that the effect of behavioral control on sleep includes suppression of sleep spindles. These investigators selected tone/response trials during Stage 2 sleep that did not result in awakenings or stage shifts and studied the distribution of K-complexes and spindles during the 1-min period immediately preceding stimulus presentations and during the 1-min period immediately following stimulus termination. No significant effects were found for the distribution of K-complexes; however, spindle production was very obviously suppressed. The time course of the effect on spindle distribution is very clear, lasting approximately 40 s. As with the measures discussed previously, it is not clear what the suppression of spindles means with regard to the sleep/wake continuum or to sleep quality. Further research is needed to clarify these relations.

Daytime Sleepiness

One index of sleep quality is level of daytime sleepiness. Badia et al. (1985) assessed daytime sleepiness under three test conditions. Under one condition, stimuli were presented with an average interstimulus interval of 8 min. Under a second condition, the average interstimulus interval was 4 min. The third condition was a control condition during which stimuli were not presented and subjects slept without disturbance. The nighttime test conditions were continued for 4 consecutive nights, and daytime sleepiness was assessed in morning and afternoon naps. No evidence was found of differential daytime sleepiness.

   Magee et al. (1987) added to these data. Subjects were tested for 1 night under two experimental conditions, that is, stimuli were presented after every 4 min of sleep or after every 1 min of sleep. Daytime sleepiness was not increased under the 4-min condition relative to the control condition, replicating the findings of Badia et al. (1985). Thus, presenting signal stimuli as frequently as once every 4 min of sleep is not sufficient to disrupt the process underlying sleep's function of minimizing daytime sleepiness. This finding is consistent with the subjects' morning reports (described earlier) that their sleep had been normal or nearly normal. The finding also fits well with the observation that sleep structure is not substantially altered under these conditions. In contrast, under the 1-min condition, subjects were profoundly sleepy. The sleepiness data from this condition are consistent with the finding of a greatly altered sleep structure. This outcome reinforces the conclusion that there are limits on the ability to respond to stimuli without disrupting fundamental processes.

STIMULUS CONTROL AND SLEEP STAGE

The data from the studies reviewed thus far indicate that, with the appropriate contingencies, response probability can be maintained at a high level throughout the night without greatly disrupting sleep. However, variability in response latencies was found in these studies. Some subjects responded far more rapidly than others, and for all subjects, great variability in response latency occurred across the night. At least some of this between-subjects and within-subject variability is associated with sleep stages. Figure 1 depicts the variability in response latencies associated with sleep stage under the escape, escape/avoidance, and incremental escape/avoidance procedures described earlier. As can be seen, sleep stage was more strongly related to response latencies under the escape and escape/avoidance procedure (significant differences were found between all sleep stages; Badia et al., 1984). With the incremental procedure, however, only Stage 1 latencies were reliably different from those of other stages (see Badia et al., 1985; Magee et al., 1987). The absence of stage differences in responsiveness prompted a closer look at the within-night variability under the incremental procedure.

Harsh et al. (1987), using the incremental procedure, examined the average response latencies for each hour of the night and reported that response latencies increased linearly across the night. This function was independent of sleep stage effects. That is, response latencies increased when only Stage 2 or only REM responses were included in the analysis. More recent research examining hour by hour variation in latencies suggests that the time-of-night function is actually curvilinear and is closely related to the body temperature curve (Lammers, Carpenter, Harsh, & Badia, 1989). These data establish that response variability during the night is due to more than sleep stage variation. Several interpretations of the time-of-night functions described have been considered (e.g., Harsh et al., 1987). Although more than one factor may be involved, the curvilinearity observed and the correspondence between responsiveness and body temperature suggest that responsivity is strongly influenced by a circadian process.

Recent analyses have provided a clearer indication of the relation between responsiveness and sleep stage variation. Harsh, Stone, Leiker, and Badia (1989) computed the mean response latencies for successive 10-min periods of the night for each of the subjects tested in the Magee et al. (1987) study and compared the rhythmic variation evident in these time series with the cycling of REM and non-REM (NREM) sleep. Spectral analysis of the response latency time series indicated a periodicity in the range of 100–133 min for several of the subjects. Cross correlation analysis failed to provide evidence of a close relation between response rhythmicity and sleep stages. However, further analysis (see Harsh et al., 1989, for details) indicated that response latency is complexly related to time of night, sleep stage, and the order and duration of REM/NREM cycles. Figure 4 illustrates these relations. The data are from the 6 subjects tested under the 4-min condition who had four identifiable REM/NREM cycles. Mean response latencies are plotted for successive tenths of each REM cycle. The approximate onset and termination of each REM period is indicated. Several effects can be seen in this figure, including (a) an increase in mean response latency across the night, (b) a rhythmic variation in response latencies beginning after the first REM/NREM cycle, and (c) a tendency for REM to occur in the troughs of the response cycles.

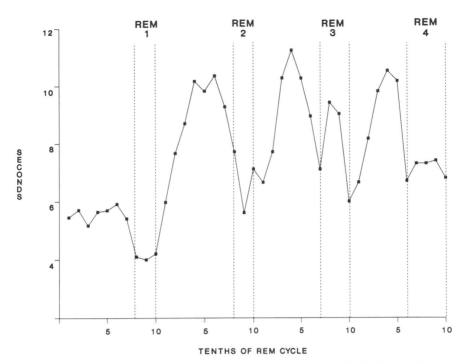

Figure 4 Mean response latencies across consecutive tenths of REM cycles. Means are based on subjects (*N* = 6) with four identifiable REM/NREM cycles during the night.

CONCLUSION

The findings of this research suggest the following conclusions. First, with reinforcement for responding, control of learned behavior can be maintained reliably by stimuli presented during sleep. Second, when stimuli are presented 4 min or more apart, behavioral control results in little or no change in sleep structure, in daytime sleepiness, or in perceptions of sleep quality. Neither perceived wakefulness nor wakefulness as it is scored on the sleep record are necessary for responding, although stimulus/response events typically result in brief EEG or EMG change. Third, within-subject, within-night variance in responsiveness is complexly related to time of night, sleep stage, and REM/NREM cycle.

References

Badia, P., Harsh, J., & Balkin, T. (1986). Behavioral control over sleeping respiration for 10 consecutive nights. *Psychophysiology, 23,* 409–411.

Badia, P., Harsh, J., Balkin, T., Cantrell, P., Klempert, A., O'Rourke, D., & Schoen, L. (1984). Behavioral control of respiration in sleep. *Psychophysiology, 21,* 494–500.

Badia, P., Harsh, J., Balkin, T., O'Rourke, D., & Burton, S. (1985). Behavioral control of respiration in sleep and sleepiness due to signal-induced sleep fragmentation. *Psychophysiology, 22,* 517–524.

Beh, H. C., & Barratt, P. E. H. (1965). Discrimination and conditioning during sleep as indicated by the electroencephalogram. *Science, 147,* 1470–1471.

Burton, S., Harsh, P., & Badia, P. (1988). Cognitive activity in sleep and responsiveness to external stimuli. *Sleep, 11,* 61–68.

Harsh, J., Badia, P., O'Rourke, D., & Burton, S. (1983). K-complexes and sleep spindles in relation to behavioral responses elicited during sleep. *Psychophysiology, 20,* 444.

Harsh, J., Badia, P., O'Rourke, D., Burton, S., Revis, C., & Magee, J. (1987). Factors related to behavioral control by stimuli presented during sleep. *Psychophysiology, 24,* 528–534.

Harsh, J., Purvis, P., Badia, P., & Magee, J. (in press). Behavioral responsiveness in sleeping older adults. *Biological Psychology.*

Harsh, J., Stone, P., Leiker, M., & Badia, P. (1989). *Ultradian rhythms in responsiveness to stimuli presented during sleep.* Manuscript submitted for publication.

Lammers, W., Carpenter, G., Harsh, J., & Badia, P. (1989, June). *Responsivity in sleep, temperature, and time of night.* Paper presented at the annual meeting of the Association of Professional Sleep Societies, Washington, DC.

Magee, J., Harsh, J., & Badia, P. (1987). Effects of experimentally induced sleep fragmentation on sleep and sleepiness. *Psychophysiology, 24,* 528–534.

Rechtschaffen, A., & Kales, A. (Eds.) (1968). *A manual of standardized terminology, techniques, and scoring system for sleep stages of human subjects.* Los Angeles: Brain Information Service/Brain Research Institute, University of California at Los Angeles.

Williams, H. L., Morlock, H. C., & Morlock, J. V. (1966). Instrumental behavior during sleep. *Psychophysiology, 2,* 208–216.

CHAPTER 5

MEMORIES IN SLEEP: OLD AND NEW

PIETRO BADIA

Observations of learning, memory formation, and information processing in sleep have resulted in a confusing body of literature and in contradictory conclusions concerning what does and does not occur. To clarify some of these issues, I distinguish between *forming* new memories in sleep (learning) and *retrieving* old memories in sleep (i.e., information processing). Several questions are considered. Can individuals access established memories and process information in sleep? Are individuals generally or selectively amnesic to new events occurring in sleep? That is, can new memories be formed in sleep? If so, what kind? I conclude with two proposals. One deals with a set of organizing principles for learning in sleep that relate to categories of knowledge: what can be remembered and what cannot—in brief, the limits of memory in sleep. The second proposal deals with a theoretical model of brain (hippocampal) functioning in sleep that may underlie these memory limits.

Individuals interested in information processing and memory in sleep have used different research strategies to approach the problem. The differences relate to the state in which material is presented and the state in which testing takes place. Researchers explicitly interested in memory formation use either a sleep–sleep procedure or a sleep–wake procedure. With a sleep–sleep procedure, material is presented in the sleeping state, and evidence for memory is also tested in the sleeping state. That is, the investigation focuses on whether information can be acquired in the sleep state and can also be altered in the sleep state (acquisition and extinction of conditioning).

With the sleep–wake procedure, information is also presented in the sleeping state but, in this case, tests of retention occur in the waking state. The question asked is whether memories formed in sleep carry over to waking. Of the two, the sleep–wake procedure is the one most commonly used. Two variants of the latter are used. Some researchers test participants when they awaken in the morning after presenting material repeatedly through the night, with the focus on the formation of long-term memory (i.e., learning in sleep). Other researchers awaken the participants immediately or shortly after presenting the material and focus on the duration of short-term memory.

There is a third procedure that relates to the transfer of training and retrieval issues and not to the formation of new memories. Researchers using this procedure present information in the waking state and then test for retention in the sleeping state. With this wake–sleep procedure, the focus is usually on information processing (i.e., on retrieval in sleep of material learned in the waking state). The wake–sleep procedure does not assess the formation of new memories in sleep. It is important to distinguish studies focusing on the retrieval of old memories in sleep (information processing) from those focusing on the formation of new memories in sleep. There is no doubt that information processing occurs in sleep; there is some doubt about the formation of new memories in sleep.

CREATING VERSUS RETRIEVING MEMORIES

Several studies illustrate the distinction between retrieving old memories in sleep and creating new memories in sleep (e.g., Badia, Harsh, Balkin, O'Rourke, & Burton, 1985; Koukkou & Lehmann, 1968). Let me give you an example by taking you through the procedure. We can instruct subjects in the waking state that a tone will be presented while they are sleeping. We instruct them that whenever the tone is perceived they are to make a behavioral response (close a microswitch, take a deep breath). A few practice trials are presented in waking to ensure that they understand and can follow the instructions. We then allow them to sleep and, periodically during the night (e.g., every 4 min), present a series of the tones to them. We find that participants respond to the tone in sleep at a very high level, nearly 100% of the time in some cases, and on most trials they respond without arousing. They demonstrate that instructions given while awake (i.e., learning occurs in waking) can be retrieved while asleep.

The fact that subjects detect the stimulus, recall the instructions, and select the proper response while asleep indicates that information can be processed in sleep and that both short-term memory and long-term memory are functioning. However, when subjects are asked the following morning the number of tones presented and the number to which they responded, they report virtually no memory for hearing the tones or for having responded. It does not matter whether they are questioned in the morning or awakened after the behavioral response at night. Subjects are able to process, in sleep, information acquired in waking, but they cannot remember doing so.

Why are these new events during sleep (hearing tones and responding to them) not reported? One could argue that no new memories were formed in sleep. Subjects heard the tones and were able to retrieve the old memory ("Respond when you hear the tone") that they learned while in the awake state. They were able to process the information and to respond to the tones, but they were not able to form the new memory of having detected the tones and having responded to them.

You may have noted that such findings show a marked similarity to anterograde amnesia, that is, old experiences can be retrieved but new experiences are not remembered. For instance, this deficit closely resembles the memory deficit present in people with hippocampal damage. Indeed, later I will suggest that the basis for "amnesia" in sleep results directly from a hippocampal deficit. Let me return to the literature on memory formation and summarize the findings without giving the details of each study.

To an extent, we are all familiar with the basic findings concerning memory formation (learning) in sleep. This literature is quite consistent. When the material to be learned or remembered is factual (names, numbers, events, etc.), the evidence for learning or for memory in sleep is systematically negative. The conclusions drawn about 30 years ago by Emmons and Simon (1956) and Simon and Emmons (1956) have been confirmed, elaborated, and strengthened, with few exceptions (Aarons, 1976; Eich, 1989). In essence, the conclusions concerning memory formation of factual material relate to the occurrence of an electroencephalographic (EEG) waking pattern or alpha. In brief, the probability of learning in sleep is directly related to the duration of alpha emitted at the time the material is presented.[1] The exact durations of alpha necessary for the formation of long-term memory vary slightly and depend on the delay interval of testing. In general, it is thought that alpha durations less than 5–10 s at the time material is presented will not permit even weak learning to occur (Koukkou & Lehmann, 1968). In addition, studies have indicated that the longer the duration of alpha, the more accurate and longer the memory (Lehmann & Koukkou, 1974; Shimizu et al., 1977). I should note, however, that when short-term memory is of primary interest and subjects are awakened immediately after the information is presented, the findings are less consistent. Some researchers report short-term memory in the absence of alpha (Oltman et al., 1977) and others do not (Shimizu et al., 1977).

The generalization regarding alpha responding applies to the formation of new memories in sleep and does not apply to accessing old memories in

---

[1] I should note a series of experiments conducted by Evans, Gustafson, O'Connell, Orne, and Shor (1970) that seem to conflict with the statements made here. Hypnotizable subjects presented with suggestions and cue words in REM sleep apparently were able to memorize the suggestions in that they followed instructions when given the cue words. They had no memory for doing so in the awake state. The phenomenon described by Evans et al. may be very different from that discussed here because (a) only selective subjects (deeply hypnotizable) demonstrated the phenomenon; (b) responses occurred only when suggestions and cue words were presented in REM; (c) responses to suggestions were very low, varying from 14% to 21% for the various experiments; (d) mean latency to respond was very long, varying from 32 s to 110 s across experiments; and (e) alpha was evoked by the procedure on occasion. In addition, items c and d suggest that the words presented by Evans et al. may have been incorporated into a dream sequence. There is considerable evidence that "incorporation" does occur.

sleep. Subjects can retrieve material already stored in the long-term memory and process the information in short-term (working) memory in the absence of alpha.

How have these findings on memory formation in sleep been interpreted? One interpretation focuses on state dependency and retrieval processes. The argument is that memory is state dependent; if memory occurs in the state of sleep, it cannot be retrieved in the state of awake. In the previous example, a retrieval view would argue that the new memory of responding to the tones in sleep does exist; it simply cannot be retrieved in the waking state. The state-dependency hypothesis has received considerable support in assessments of drug and nondrug states. However, I should note that the transfer of memory from wake to sleep, and not from sleep to wake, suggests that state dependency, if it is operating, is asymmetrical. In addition, other data that I will note shortly are incompatible with the state dependency view.

One could reject the state-dependency and retrieval view and, as noted, argue that new memories in sleep are not formed. We could then theorize about why they are not formed. For example, it could be argued that new memories cannot be formed in sleep because the duration of short-term memory is too brief to permit rehearsal. Without rehearsal, transfer to long-term memory and consolidation cannot occur.

Or one could argue that the link between short-term and long-term memory is severed in sleep. In a sense, the argument is that the brain in sleep is organized in a way that does not permit the formation of memories. Furthermore, the functional state of this organization is partially revealed by the prevailing EEG pattern. For memories to be formed, alpha responding (an EEG awake pattern) must be present during the presentation of the material to be learned (short-term memory trace). I will discuss this later. Let me now turn to some positive findings concerning learning in sleep. These findings involve procedures that require less cognitive loading.

In brief, studies have reported that classical conditioning and habituation (for humans and nonhumans) occur in the sleeping state and that the effects carry over to the waking state. These studies demonstrate that learning, in the absence of alpha, is possible. Interpreting both positive and negative instances of learning in sleep thus becomes a special challenge for emerging theories.

CONDITIONING IN SLEEP

Several well-conducted studies have used classical conditioning in humans to demonstrate learning (memory) in sleep. An elegant study composed of several experiments was reported by Beh and Barratt (1965). In their first experiment, they showed that classical conditioning in the waking state transfers to the sleeping state, a finding that others have since documented. As noted, such findings relate to the transfer of learning from waking to sleep and not to memory formation per se. Beh and Barratt's second study is of greater theoretical interest and relates directly to memory formation in sleep. They presented conditioned stimulus (CS) and unconditioned stimulus (US) trials in Stage 2 of sleep using K complexes as a measure of conditioning. Different tones served as CS+ and CS−, and finger shock served as the unconditioned stimulus. Experimental subjects had CS and US pairings; control subjects had unpaired presentations. Pilot work revealed the shock intensity needed to avoid stage shifts or the elicitation of alpha. The authors emphasized that there were no awakenings for the pairings.

Clear evidence for conditioning in Stage 2 sleep occurred. Once the acquisition of conditioning was demonstrated, Beh and Barratt (1965) tested whether extinction would occur in sleep by giving CS+ alone trials. Extinction of the response was also demonstrated. Then in a later session during waking, they tested whether a CS+ that was conditioned in sleep would result in greater alpha blocking than the CS−. They found that significantly greater alpha blocking occurred to the CS+ than to the CS−. These results provide powerful evidence for the acquisition of learning in sleep and for the transfer of this learning to the waking state. Research in lower animals has also indicated that the acquisition of conditioning can occur in sleep. For example, a study by Maho and Bloch (1983) showed that rats could be conditioned in REM sleep and that the conditioning effects transferred to the waking state.

Other studies with humans, not as complete as the Beh and Barratt (1965) study, provide additional support for memory formation (learning) in sleep. McDonald, Schicht, Frazier, Shallenberger, and Edwards (1975) classically conditioned humans in the waking state and tested them in the sleeping state. They showed that conditioning carried over to the sleeping state and, more important for our interests, that conditioning could be extinguished in sleep. The effects were found with vasoconstriction, heart rate, and K complexes. Conditioning findings very similar to those reported by McDonald et al. (1975) were also reported with cats.

In addition to conditioning, a number of studies have focused on habituation in sleep. Habituation is thought to be a simple form of learning and is used frequently as a learning paradigm. Unfortunately, the findings on habituation with humans are less consistent. Some studies have reported evidence for habituation in sleep, while others have not. This inconsistency may relate to the existence of greater individual variability in sleep than in waking, which may render studies less sensitive to detecting an effect. A description of factors affecting responsivity in sleep was summarized by Bonnet (1982).

In any event, several recent, well-conducted studies provide support for habituation in sleep. Johnson, Townsend, and Wilson (1975) showed that habituation occurred in sleep using vasoconstriction and heart rate responses. They also found that habituation in sleep carried over to the waking state. Similarly, McDonald and Carpenter (1975) found with humans that both habituation and dishabituation occurred in all stages of sleep (vasoconstriction and heart rate response measures). Several other studies using heart rate as a measure have also shown that habituation in sleep occurs (Firth, 1973).

Although the literature on classical conditioning and habituation is not extensive, the studies thus far reviewed provide clear evidence that learning occurs in sleep and that it transfers to the waking state.

Let me summarize the findings on memory in sleep to this point. The evidence for short-term memory in sleep and retrieval from long-term memory is substantial. Material learned while awake can be transferred to sleep, retrieved from long-term memory, and worked upon. There is also evidence that conditioning and habituation occur in sleep and that they transfer to the waking state. However, there is no evidence that factual information (i.e., events, words, and numbers) presented, perceived, and responded to in sleep is converted to long-term memory and remembered in waking.

These data suggest that brain functioning is different in waking and sleeping. The finding that the learning of factual knowledge in sleep depends on the presence of alpha suggests that the neural gateway transmitting this type of knowledge to long-term memory functions only in waking. However, simple conditioning and habituation do occur in sleep and in the absence of alpha. How can we account for these two sets of data? Current hypotheses concerning memory do not adequately organize these data, nor do they provide insights concerning brain functioning in sleep. New organizing principles are needed.

As a prelude to suggesting such principles, let me note the salient findings that must be addressed concerning memory in sleep: (a) short-term (working) memory is functional, (b) long-term memory is accessible, (c) learning such as conditioning and habituation does occur, and (d) learning of new factual material does not occur.

As noted earlier, these findings are strikingly similar to another set of findings related to lesions in the medial temporal region of humans and to the hippocampus in nonhumans. The similarity is especially striking for certain anterograde amnesia patients. This similarity suggests that brain functioning in amnesic patients, and in animals with similar pathology, might serve as a model for brain functioning in sleep (or conversely, brain functioning in sleep could serve as a model for this pathology).

Several benefits will accrue if this model is appropriate: (a) The knowledge gained from the study of this pathology may advance our understanding of brain functioning and learning in sleep; (b) the organizing principles that come with the model may be applied to the positive and negative findings on learning; (c) further, the model may suggest the brain structures that are responsible for the findings; and (d) the model may point to new research directions to pursue.

DECLARATIVE VERSUS PROCEDURAL KNOWLEDGE

To develop the argument, it is necessary to distinguish between two other forms of memory in addition to short-term and long-term memory, namely, declarative and procedural. This distinction has been helpful in understanding the memory deficits in amnesia patients, and it provides an organization for interpreting the data on learning and memory in sleep. I should note that the distinction between declarative and procedural knowledge is also supported by a rich literature involving brain lesioned animals (Isaacson, 1982). The distinction first appeared in the literature on artificial intelligence and was later applied to biological memory by Squire (1987). Other memory distinctions also exist, but they have not achieved the same biological anchoring (see Sherry & Schacter, 1987, for an excellent analysis on the topic).

Generally, the distinction between declarative and procedural knowledge is clear. *Declarative* knowledge is explicit, everyday remembering of factual content, sentences, words, numbers, events, names, and so forth. The information is acquired quickly and is verbalized with ease. The acquisition of declarative knowledge is severely impaired in patients with anterograde amnesia and is dependent on the integrity of the medial temporal region.

In contrast, *procedural* knowledge is implicit, is acquired more slowly, is not easily verbalized, and is closely tied to procedure. It includes skill learning, perceptual learning, classical conditioning, habituation, sensitization, and priming. By its nature, procedural knowledge does not depend on one brain structure or region and is little, if at all, impaired in patients with anterograde amnesia.

THE BRAIN AND MEMORY

Evidence suggesting that the brain is organized in a way compatible with these memory distinctions comes from several sources. One source is the study of patients with amnesia. A particularly well-known patient is referred to as RB. The characteristics of this patient are well-summarized in Squire's informative book (1987) entitled *Memory and Brain.* The descriptions that follow were drawn from this book. In general, there was no discernible impairment of higher cognitive functioning for RB except for his marked incapability to form new memories for factual material.

At age 52, RB had an ischemic episode as a complication of surgery and demonstrated anterograde amnesia after the episode. His IQ was 111, there was no aphasia, and no neuropsychological signs of frontal lobe involvement were evident. No cognitive deficits other than amnesia were ever detected. He was tested over a 5-year period and, during this time, asked the same questions, told the same stories, and did not learn the names or faces of people seen regularly. He also failed to learn paired associates. Both short-term memory and remote long-term memory were intact.

An examination of RB's brain following his death revealed that significant bilateral lesions occurred only in the hippocampal formation. There was also a patchy loss of cerebellar Purkinje cells. The lesions in the hippocampus were limited to the pyramidal cells of the CA1 field. Other surrounding structures on both sides of the brain were normal. This case firmly established that restricted hippocampal damage can result in global anterograde amnesia for factual knowledge.

The different effects of procedural and declarative knowledge on amnesic patients are interesting and informative. Simple classical conditioning and habituation can be demonstrated, without recall of the event predicted by the CS. Similarly, amnesics can show marked improvement on a mirror tracing task yet cannot remember that they had multiple training sessions. Puzzles can also be learned with increasing speed. Priming occurs, despite the failure of recall and recognition, but only when testing is treated as a nonmemory task.

Animals with hippocampal lesions show similar differences between procedural and declarative knowledge. For example, simple classical conditioning occurs with these animals. Thus, procedural knowledge is intact. However, lesioned animals, compared with controls, behave very differently when conditioning involves declarative knowledge. For example, hippocampal-lesioned animals (rats, cats, primates) do not show blocking or overshadowing (e.g., Rickert, Lorden, Dawson, Smyly, & Callahan, 1979), reversal learning (Berger & Orr, 1983), latent inhibition, or conditional discrimination (Squire, 1987). In each of these instances, for learning to occur, the animal must retain factual knowledge concerning the outcomes of past experiences. In short, there are obvious similarities between the memory deficits of normal organisms that are asleep and awake organisms with bilateral damage to the hippocampus.

Let me summarize the salient findings related to memory in sleep and also to hippocampal lesions. The following exists for both: (a) short-term memory is operational; (b) established long-term memory can be accessed; (c) new memories for declarative knowledge (including certain kinds of conditioning) cannot be formed; (d) new memories for procedural knowledge (simple conditioning, habituation, etc.) can be formed. While priming effects occur under certain conditions with amnesics, these effects have not yet been adequately tested in sleep.

These findings, taken together with numerous studies of hippocampal lesions in various species, suggest that declarative knowledge relates directly to a functional hippocampus, while procedural knowledge does not. The distinction between declarative and procedural knowledge characterizes learning in sleep. In sleep, procedural knowledge is stored, and declarative knowledge is not. One implication of this analysis is that the hippocampus, in the presence of an EEG sleep pattern, is not functional for the acquisition of declarative knowledge; that is, it serves its neural gating function of transferring short-term to long-term memory only in the presence of an EEG waking pattern. Evidence supporting hippocampal gating that is contingent on the behavioral state (e.g., awake or asleep) is available in rats (Winson, 1986). Based on his findings, Winson suggested that neural gating in the hippocampal trisynaptic circuit is analogous to an open or closed logic gate in that, depending on the behavioral state, information either flows freely or is almost totally restricted. Others have also noted that the hippocampal contribution to information flow is highly state dependent (Hobson & Schmajuk, 1988).

The analysis presented here provides guidelines for understanding the limits of learning in sleep and suggests some interesting theoretical tests and predictions. The theoretical tests involve the effects of priming while asleep on subsequent responding while awake. They also include the conditions under which complex conditioning should and should not be demonstrated.

However, the analysis also implies that the range of material that can be learned in sleep, while interesting and important, is circumscribed. The broader value of this analysis may be in its focus on brain function in sleep. It may also bear on the related issue concerning the function of sleep. Various theorists (Horne, 1988) have speculated that sleep is a time for central nervous system restoration and for memory consolidation of waking experiences. The latter function may explain why the link between short-term and long-term memory is severed in sleep, that is, why declarative material presented in sleep is not learned. It may be that the hippocampus, in addition to providing a gating function to the long-term memory in waking, also plays the active role during sleep of consolidating previous waking experiences. Perhaps in sleep, gating and consolidating cannot occur concurrently. Thus, the gating of new information and the continued consolidation of old information may be incompatible functions related to waking and sleeping, respectively.

References

Aarons, L. (1976). Sleep assisted instruction. *Psychological Bulletin, 83,* 1–40.

Badia, P., Harsh, J., Balkin, T., O'Rourke, D., & Burton, S. (1985). Behavioral control of respiration in sleep and sleepiness due to signal-induced sleep fragmentation. *Psychophysiology, 22,* 517–524.

Beh, H. C., & Barratt, P. E. H. (1965). Discrimination and conditioning during sleep as indicated by the electroencephalogram. *Science, 147,* 1470–1471.

Berger, T. W., & Orr, W. B. (1983). Hippocampectomy selectively disrupts discrimination reversal learning of the rabbit nictitating membrane response. *Behavioral Brain Research, 8,* 49–68.

Bonnet, M. (1982). Performance during sleep. In W. Webb (Ed.), *Biological rhythms, sleep and performance* (pp. 205–237). New York: Wiley.

Eich, E. (1989). *Learning during sleep.* Paper presented at the Arizona Conference on Sleep and Cognition, Tucson, AZ.

Emmons, W. H., & Simon, C. W. (1956). The non-recall of material presented during sleep. *American Journal of Psychology, 6,* 76–81.

Evans, F. J., Gustafson, L. A., O'Connell, D. N., Orne, M. T., & Shor, R. E. (1970). Verbally induced behavioral responses during sleep. *Journal of Nervous and Mental Disease, 148,* 467–476.

Firth, H. (1973). Habituation during sleep. *Psychophysiology, 10,* 43–51.

Hobson, J. A., & Schmajuk, N. A. (1988). Brain state and plasticity: An integration of the reciprocal interaction model of sleep cycle oscillation with attentional models of hippocampal function. *Archives Italiennes de Biologie, 126,* 209–224.

Horne, J. A. (1988). *Why we sleep.* New York: Oxford University Press.

Isaacson, R. L. (1982). *The limbic system.* New York: Plenum Press.

Johnson, L. C., Townsend, R. E., & Wilson, M. R. (1975). Habituation during sleeping and waking. *Psychophysiology, 12,* 574–584.

Koukkou, M., & Lehmann, D. (1968). EEG and memory storage in sleep experiments with humans. *Electroencephalography and Clinical Neurophysiology, 25,* 455–462.

Lehmann, D., & Koukkou, M. (1974). Computer analysis of EEG wakefulness-sleep patterns during learning of novel and familiar sentences. *Electroencephalography and Clinical Neurophysiology, 37,* 73–84.

Maho, C., & Bloch, V. (1983). Acquisition of classical conditioning during REM sleep in rats. *Sleep Research, 12,* 160.

McDonald, D. G., & Carpenter, F. A. (1975). Habituation of the orienting response in sleep. *Psychophysiology, 12,* 618–623.

McDonald, D. H., Schicht, W. W., Frazier, R. E., Shallenberger, H. D., & Edwards, D. J. (1975). Studies of information processing in sleep. *Psychophysiology, 12,* 624–629.

Oltman, P. K., Goodenough, D. R., Koulack, D., Maclin, E., Schroeder, H. R., & Flannagan, M. J. (1977). Short-term memory during Stage 2 sleep. *Psychophysiology, 14,* 439–444.

Rickert, E. J., Lorden, J. F., Dawson, R., Jr., Smyly, E., & Callahan, M. F. (1979). Stimulus processing and stimulus election in rats with hippocampal lesions. *Behavioral Neural Biology, 27,* 454–465.

Sherry, D. F., & Schacter, D. L. (1987). The evolution of multiple memory systems. *Psychological Review, 94,* 439–454.

Shimizu, A., Takehashi, H., Sumitsiyi, N., Tanaka, M., Yoshida, I., & Kaneko, Z. (1977). Memory retention of stimulations during REM and NREM stages of sleep. *Electroencephalography and Clinical Neurophysiology, 43,* 658–665.

Simon, C. W., & Emmons, W. H. (1956). Responses to material presented during various levels of sleep. *Journal of Experimental Psychology, 51,* 89–97.

Squire, L. R. (1987). *Memory and brain.* New York: Oxford University Press.

Winson, J. (1986). Behaviorally dependent neuronal gating in the hippocampus. In R. L. Isaacson & K. H. Pribram (Eds.), *The hippocampus* (Vol. 4, pp. 77–92). New York: Plenum Press.

CHAPTER 6

BEHAVIORAL RESPONSES
DURING SLEEP

FREDERICK J. EVANS

Cognitive activity during sleep was virtually ignored prior to the discovery of the link between REM sleep and dreaming (Aserinsky & Kleitman, 1953). Freud had rejected hypnotic recall and abreaction in favor of the dream as the royal road to the unconscious. For Freud (1922), the fact that the dream was a product of sleep was quite incidental; indeed, it was a nuisance given the difficulty of eliciting dream recall in some patients.

Historically, cognitive activity during sleep was the basis of the first form of psychotherapy. In the fourth century BC, on the small Turkish island of Cos, the Aesculapian temples were the site of a systematic method of healing centered around suggestions of cure and well-being administered by priests to the sleeping ill. Collison (1988) likened the procedures of the Aesculapians to hypnosis rather than sleep. Certainly, an association between hypnosis and sleep has a long tradition. However, the electroencephalograph (EEG) of hypnosis reveals a waking rather than a sleep state (Evans, 1979b). Nevertheless, this fascination with possible behavioral and subjective similarities between sleeping and hypnotic behavior along with our conviction that cognitive activity during sleep is richer than mere dreaming led a group of us to conduct the studies to be described.

SLEEP-INDUCED BEHAVIORAL RESPONSE

Anecdotal examples support the notion that complex cognitive behavior (in addition to dreaming) can occur during sleep, particularly if an appropriate "set" of instructions has been provided before sleep. One rarely falls out of bed, a remarkable feat considering the amount of bodily activity that occurs throughout the night. Clear territorial boundaries are worked out with our sleeping partners. Loud noises that are repetitive or familiar are less likely to wake the sleeping person than soft, strange, novel, or meaningful noises. Wake/sleep phenomena have been studied in the laboratory. For example, some people claim that they awaken regularly at a preselected time. Oswald (1962) found that, when appropriate waking instructions were given, sleeping subjects woke up only when specified names of friends were spoken. Conditioned responses and discrimination between auditory stimuli may be elicited during sleep if a waking response tendency has been established (Beh & Barratt, 1965; Granda & Hammack, 1961; McDonald, 1966; Weinberg, 1966; Williams, Morlock, & Morlock, 1966; Zung & Wilson, 1961). Sleep/wake phenomena, especially sleep learning, has been studied extensively in Russia and in a few controlled studies in the United States (Simon & Emmons, 1956).

A controversial claim is that hypnoticlike suggestions can be given successfully during sleep (Bernheim, 1889; Bertrand, 1826; Fresacher, 1951; Gill & Brenman, 1959; Schilder & Kauders, 1927). Barber (1956) whispered hypnoticlike suggestions to 22 subjects who were asleep in their rooms. Some subjects responded to the suggestions; physiological and EEG criteria were not used to monitor sleep. Using a sleep/sleep paradigm, Cobb et al. (1965) documented cognitive activity behaviorally in a pilot EEG study with procedures similar to the one described next.

Procedure

For 2 nights, 19 male student nurses slept in a standard sleep laboratory using EEG monitoring techniques. During on-line visual diagnosis of alpha-free REM sleep, suggestions were presented verbally to subjects. Typical suggestions were "Whenever I say the word *itch,* your nose will feel itchy until you scratch it"; "Whenever I say the word *pillow,* your pillow will feel uncomfortable until you move it." The suggestions were tested by saying the cue word (*itch* or *pillow*) once. An attempt was made to test each cue word on at least two separate occasions during the same REM period in which the suggestion was given, during all subsequent REM periods that night, and during REM periods of the second night. The suggestion itself was not readministered on the second night. Suggestions were not repeated after their initial presentation. However, two new suggestions were presented each night whenever possible.

Suggestions were administered and cues were tested only during REM sleep. At least 120 s of alpha-free REM sleep were required between cue-word presentations. It was conservatively assumed that visually detected alpha indicates arousal. During the sleep period, the presence of even minimal alpha (three cycles) was signaled by the technician using a small light outside the line of sight of the subject. Only subjects who displayed an alpha density exceeding 40% during an eyes closed, waking–rest trial were included in the study.

The subject's behavior was observed by the experimenter, who was in the same room. When the subject awakened in the morning, his memory for the session was tested both directly (during an interview) and indirectly (by response to cue words in the context of a word association test). Any behavioral or physiological response to the critical cue word was observed. When the subject awakened after Night 2, a more detailed inquiry was made to evaluate memory for the sleep events.

The subject was not told before either session that suggestions would be given, but he was told that sleep cycles were being studied.

Characteristics of Sleep-Induced Behavior

A detailed parametric description of the important characteristics of sleep-induced behavior is presented elsewhere (Evans, Gustafson, O'Connell, Orne, & Shor, 1969, 1970).

Response Rate

During the 2 nights, 416 cue words were presented during sleep, and 89 correct responses were observed. On the average, the 19 subjects responded to a mean of 21.2% of all cue words; the highest response rate by a subject was 48%.

Stimulation and EEG Alpha

Uninterrupted REM sleep continued for at least 30 s for 71% of all cues administered; that is, alpha activity did not occur before or while the cue word was administered. Many responses were obtained without eliciting alpha activity during the suggestion, after the cue words were administered, or before or after the response.

Specificity of Sleep-Induced Behavior

Once a suggestion was successfully completed (i.e., without eliciting alpha activity), it was not repeated in a subsequent REM epoch, nor was it repeated during Night 2 if it had been administered during Night 1. Cue words were tested in several subsequent REM periods. There are three possible temporal sequences between the administration of a suggestion and the subsequent cue-word testing of it: (a) Immediate testing, with the cue word administered during the same REM period as the suggestion; (b) delayed testing, with the cue word tested the same night but in a REM period following the one in which the suggestion had been administered; and (c) carry-over testing, with the cue word tested during Night 2 (after it had been suggested during Night 1). One day intervened between the administration and testing of these suggestions.

For immediate, delayed, and carry-over conditions, correct responses respectively followed 20%, 23%, and 23% of all cues given. Of the total 89 responses observed, 16 occurred during Night 2 in response to suggestions administered on Night 1. All of these responses were obtained from 6 of the 9 subjects who had been classified as responders based on their Night 1 performance.

Alpha and Response Type

When alpha followed a successful response, it was significantly slower than waking alpha frequency but was not significantly different from the slowed frequency that occurs occasionally (but spontaneously) during unstimulated REM sleep. On those occasions when alpha was elicited to successful responses, it was significantly slower than waking state alpha (10.0 cps vs. 9.01 cps), $t(df = 18) = 2.15, p < .05$.

Response Latency

A successful response tendency was mobilized slowly. The average response latency was 32 s. Latency increased as the temporal dissociation between the administration of the suggestion and the cue word increased. For example, latencies for immediate and carry-over responses were 19 s and 59 s, respectively ($p < .001$). In contrast, a similar suggestion given during hypnosis or tested posthypnotically produces a response latency of only a few seconds.

Subsequent Waking Recall

After the subject awakened, he did not remember the verbally presented material, nor could he remember responding. No difference was found between the latency of cue word associates to which a response had occurred and the latency of control word associates (.92 s vs. .99 s, respectively). This lack of recall involved amnesia rather than forgetting, because the material was still available for future responding during sleep. When the subject returned to sleep the next night, the mere repetition of the relevant cue word (without repetition of the suggestion itself) was sometimes sufficient to elicit the appropriate response. The behavioral response appeared to be specific to sleep in spite of the intervening amnesia.

The behavioral response could not be elicited by repeating the cue word in the waking state. Behavior analogous to posthypnotic suggestion was not observed.

Long-Term Response Specificity

Six subjects returned to sleep for a 3rd night about 5 months after their initial participation. Four of these subjects were responders who had shown carry-over responses on Night 2 to a Night 1 suggestion. Cues for the suggestions given during the initial 2 nights were presented without administering the suggestion again. The 4 subjects responded consistently to the 5-month-old suggestions, even though there was no intervening waking memory about the procedure or the specific suggestions.

Replication Study

A subsequent study (Perry, Evans, O'Connell, Orne, & Orne, 1978) confirmed these characteristics, although a lower response rate (14% vs. 18%) and even longer response latencies were found. Three additional findings confirmed that the motor behavior during sleep was not random but was directly elicited by the suggestions and their associated cue words: (a) Correct videotaped responses were discriminated from random body movement behavior by blind raters; (b) interspersed dummy cue words not associated with suggestions that had been administered did not elicit behavioral responses appropriate to any suggestion; and (c) if a cue word was presented before the suggestion had been given, it did not elicit the specific behavioral response that would later be associated with the suggestion.

SLEEP RESPONSE AND RESPONSIVITY TO HYPNOSIS

Part of the original aim of these studies was to investigate the relation between hypnotizability and sleep-induced response rate. Hypnotizability was assessed several weeks after the two sleep nights by experimenters who were blind to the subjects' rate of responding during sleep. Hypnotic responsiveness was assessed using the Harvard Group Scale of Hypnotic Susceptibility, Form A (HGSHS:A; Shor & Orne, 1962) and the Stanford Hypnotic Susceptibility Scale, Form C (SHSS:C, Weitzenhoffer & Hilgard, 1962).

Those subjects who responded most frequently to sleep-induced suggestions were more responsive to hypnosis. Pearson correlations between susceptibility to hypnosis and the frequencies of cue administration, response, and response rate were positive and consistent for the measures, indicating that sleep-induced response and susceptibility to hypnosis are related in some manner. The relation is complex, however, and several factors influence the interpretation of these correlations.

Response Frequency

Hypnotizable subjects were found to awaken following stimulation less frequently than insusceptible subjects. Consequently, they slept longer, and more cues were tested. The correlations between response-rate percentage (which effectively controls the difference in the frequency of cue administrations) and both HGSHS:A ($r = .42$) and SHSS:C ($r = .39$) were of borderline significance ($p < .10$, two-tailed).

Hypnosis and Temporal Dissociation of Sleep Response

The correlations between sleep suggestibility and responsivity to hypnosis were higher for percentage of delayed responses than for percentage of immediate responses. Responsivity to hypnosis more successfully predicted the ability to respond to sleep-induced suggestion when there was a temporal dissociation between the administration of the suggestion and the cue word, that is, when the response was elicited by a cue word during the second night to a suggestion that had been administered only during the first night. The correlations between the carry-over response rate with HGSHS:A and SHSS:C were .64 ($p < .01$) and .60 ($p < .01$), respectively.

Sleep Response and Type of Hypnotic Phenomena

Neither the frequency of cues nor the frequency of responses correlated with waking suggestibility, hypnotic motor suggestibility, or challenge suggestibility. This is surprising because the sleep behaviors suggested involved motor responses. The correlations with the hallucinatory-reverie and the posthypnotic-dissociative clusters of hypnotic behavior tested by HGSHS:A and SHSS:C were significant for the percentage rate of carry-over (dissociative) responses (rs = .52 and .58, ps < .01) but not for the immediate responses. These two hypnotic clusters include phenomena experienced only by the few subjects who can be deeply hypnotized.

Hypnotizability, Sleep-Induced Response, and Arousal

Subjects who were able to remain asleep while responding to the verbal suggestions administered during sleep were more responsive to hypnosis and slept more soundly than subjects who did not respond. This joint relation reflects the hypnotizable responder's ability to sleep well, both in his verbal claims about his sleeping habits and in his ability to sleep without awakening in the experimental situation. By waking more often, both spontaneously and following stimulation, the unresponsive subject provided himself with less opportunity to respond because fewer cue word administrations were possible. The interesting theoretical question is not so much the extent to which sleep suggestion is analogous to hypnotic phenomena but rather why the hypnotizable subject sleeps better than the more easily aroused insusceptible subject. Ranking subjects by all available hypnosis scores, we found that the 6 subjects who were least susceptible to hypnosis accounted for 48% of all awakenings that occurred during the two experimental nights. In contrast, the 6 subjects who were most hypnotizable accounted for only 26% of the total awakenings (p < .01).

Surprisingly, the relation between hypnotizability and response to sleep-induced suggestions was not significant in the later study by Perry et al. (1978). Whether differences in the presleep set, the complexity of the stimulus discrimination necessary to process suggestions cognitively, or some other factor accounts for this puzzling finding is not known.

SLEEP INDUCED RESPONSE AS A DISSOCIATIVE PROCESS

About 5 months later, 7 of the 19 subjects were invited to sleep another night in the laboratory. In general, the procedures already described were used, combined with various exploratory methods utilizing hypnosis to test the limits of sleep responding.

An attempt was made to hypnotize each subject at the beginning of the sleep session. No special suggestions regarding responding or recall were given to 5 of the 7 subjects. One of these subjects was allowed to fall asleep while hypnotized. The remaining 2 subjects were given strong suggestions to respond during sleep and to recall when awake. During sleep, several cue words were administered that were appropriate to the suggestions of the 2 nights from 5 months previously. New suggestions were also given. Waking recall was tested as before, but each subject was hypnotized in an attempt to elicit further recall. A variety of hypnotic techniques, including regression, was used with the more hypnotizable subjects in an attempt to reverse the amnesia for the sleep experiences (Evans, 1979b).

Some subjects responded much more frequently than they had during the original 2 nights. While the induction of hypnosis and the hypnotic experience gained since the original nights may have contributed to these increases, the evidence indicates that neither hypnotic depth nor the interpersonal variables could account for all of the increases.

Specific presleep suggestions aimed at increasing sleep responsivity may have been helpful. However, hypnotic and/or set influences did not merely affect new suggestions. Many responses were obtained to cue words associated with suggestions that had been neither repeated nor apparently recalled since the first night 5 months before.

Similar problems of interpretation recurred when attempts were made to utilize hypnosis, either before or after the sleep session, to obtain recall of the sleep events. Hypnosis helped, but again the results were not a direct function of hypnotic depth. Some hitherto unrecalled old suggestions were recalled with hypnotic techniques other than regression. This result may indicate that the techniques originally used to probe morning recall were insufficiently sensitive. On the other hand, the possible timeless or contextless effects of hypnosis have been documented by the work on source amnesia (Evans, 1979a; Evans & Thorn, 1966).

HYPNOSIS AND SLEEP LEARNING

Since the carefully controlled EEG studies by Simon and Emmons (1956), learning during sleep has not been seriously considered. Simon and Emmons reported that stimulus material presented during sleep was not recalled later when the subject awakened unless alpha activity occurred simultaneously with the stimulus material. Because alpha during sleep indicates arousal, they felt that any learning occurred in a waking state. In sleep learning studies, the lack of retention upon awakening has been considered as evidence that registration or acquisition did not occur during sleep. However, we have shown that retention (response to cue words) occurs during sleep. The subject not only can respond to sleep-induced suggestions while remaining asleep but also can respond on subsequent nights without repetition of the suggestion and without any apparent waking memory of the suggestions or his responses to them. The problem remaining unsolved is that of the retrieval of sleep-acquired material. In this sense, the problem of the retrieval of sleep-acquired material is similar to the problem of the retrieval of dreams when the subject awakens in the morning.

In Soviet countries, hypnopaedia or sleep learning has been widely practiced, especially in the 1950s and 1960s. Languages have been taught not only to individuals during sleep but also, it has been claimed, to whole villages by radio at night. These studies have been adequately reviewed (Hoskovec, 1966; Rubin, 1968). The concept of hypnopaedia implies hypnosis, and it is typically claimed that learning occurs only with "suggestible" subjects. It is not clear whether "suggestible" implies hypnotizable or whether a strong waking set is induced to convince the person that sleep learning is possible. Simon and Emmons (1956) did not induce such a set.

An attempt was made to maximize the possibility of sleep learning. To obtain waking recall of sleep-acquired material, it was felt that four conditions would have to be fulfilled: (a) subjects must be chosen who could respond during sleep to sleep-administered suggestion, using the procedures described previously; (b) some subjects must be included who were highly responsive to hypnosis; (c) any stimulus presented that was accompanied simultaneously by alpha could not be included or scored (it was, therefore, not possible to replicate the findings by Simon and Emmons, 1956); acquisition during arousal was ruled out by eliminating stimuli presented during alpha; and (d) a strong waking set must establish that sleep learning is possible. The sleep-induced responses were described, and the subjects were told about their own sleep-induced responding during the first sleep session. Soviet hypnopaedia claims were reviewed extensively, and subjects were motivated both by the competitive aim to duplicate Russian studies (during the Cold War era of the early 1960s) and by their special qualifications as likely candidates for successful sleep learning.

Nine subjects were tested in a sleep learning study. They qualified by responding to a sleep-induced suggestion at least twice while remaining asleep. As in the earlier studies, these subjects had no subsequent waking recall of these suggestions. An appropriate presleep set was then established before the sleep learning session. The subjects slept for about 6 hours. Several subjects were included who did not receive this set, although the experimenter was not blind.

Material ("A is for apple"; "P is for palace," etc.) was presented during REM sleep and Stages 2 and 4, defined by standard EEG criteria. Waking recall was tested by asking the subject to check any familiar word on a list of 10 words beginning with the letter A and again from 10 words beginning with the letter P, and so forth. Eight stimulus words, each beginning with a different letter, were presented twice to each subject. Where possible, at least two different letter-word pairs were presented during each stage. After awakening, the subject received the eight appropriate 10-word lists along with two similar dummy lists containing letter-word pairs not used during sleep. Thus, the conservative probability of checking one correct word by guessing was 0.10 for each of the eight relevant lists.

Although recall was partial, it exceeded conservatively estimated chance recall (in fact, none of the dummy list words were ever checked). Of the letter-word combinations administered during the REM stage, 28% of the administered words were correctly checked. In addition, the subject was able to select with certainty the correct letter (without specifying a word) in an additional 17% of all lists. Only those letters were counted that the subject was quite certain he heard. In fact, subjects did not guess a letter unless they were convinced it had been spoken. Although words were rarely recalled from Stages 2 and 4, subjects often recognized letters from these stages. The incidence of guessing, that is, of incorrectly recalled words of letters, was virtually zero. No control subject (without a presleep set) recalled any words correctly.

A secondary result is important theoretically. Although none of the words were presented simultaneously with alpha activity, whenever words presented during the REM stage were subsequently recalled, transient slower frequency alpha (10.25 Hz vs. 9.64 Hz, $p < .01$) had been evoked within 30 s after the presentation of the stimuli during sleep.

A third important finding of this study confirms some of the Russian claims. Of the 9 subjects, 7 had been administered the HGSHS:A and the SHSS: C. The correlations between the total (all stages) recall of words and the HGSHS: A and the SHSS:C were .69 and .42, respectively. The respective rank correlations with REM stage recall were .41 and .49.

It would seem that under optimal conditions in the laboratory, sleep learning of relatively easy material can occur with subsequent waking recall. The practical significance of these results is uncertain. Hypnosis may play a role in further exploration of the theoretically exciting but practically limited phenomenon of sleep learning.

SUMMARY

These studies have documented that meaningful behavioral suggestions can be administered and responded to during sleep, without necessarily evoking arousal from sleep. Although these sleep-induced responses are based on both a subjective experience and a related behavioral response, the repertoire of cognitive activity shown by some subjects is somewhat primitive, as revealed by the slow response latency or the simplistic word association material successfully learned during uninterrupted sleep. The sleep-induced behavior was not remembered using typical recall paradigms in the subsequent waking state but, rather, remained available for recovery on later nights, even up to 5 months later, sometimes in a dramatic and transformed fashion. This amnesia has some similarities to another induced amnesia, posthypnotic amnesia. Posthypnotic amnesia is a temporary failure to utilize temporal sequence cues as an organizational strategy (Evans & Kihlstrom, 1973). However, posthypnotic amnesia differs from the waking state amnesia of the sleep-induced behavior in an important way: Posthypnotic amnesia is easily reversed on cue, but the sleep-induced response to suggestion is not.

The limit of sleep-induced suggestion is not known because there is no way to evaluate whether the failure to respond is intentional or is simply due to a failure of stimulus registration. We have no way of knowing if a subject actually hears the test cue word (or suggestions) or the target words for sleep learning unless (a) there is arousal, which disqualifies the material, or (b) there is a response. The response rates reported must be seen as lower bounds.

The presence of the dissociative sleep response behavior is closely related to other forms of dissociative behavior, especially responsivity to hypnosis. The highly hypnotizable person is able to fall asleep easily, to take naps (Evans,

1977), to respond to sleep administered suggestions without arousal, and to do some learning during sleep. Evans (1989) referred to an individual difference dimension of the ability to (volitionally) control cognitive sets, psychological states, or altered states of consciousness. This dissociative skill is a dimension that is indicated by a cluster of intercorrelated variables, including hypnotic responsivity; napping; ease of falling asleep and the ability to control sleep onset in a variety of circumstances; variable punctuality for appointments; absorption; phobic, stress-related, and bulimic forms of psychopathology; hyperemesis in childbirth and cancer; and the speed of recovery from psychiatric and (probably) medical symptomatology regardless of diagnosis (Evans, 1989).

The 1960s research on the successful response to sleep-induced suggestion and its ramifications for the study of dissociative processes has meaningfully influenced later research on hypnotic behavior and the ability to control states of consciousness. Yet the dramatic nature of individual responses to sleep-induced suggestions may remain the least understood and most difficult area to study. Little progress can be made in studying the limits of cognitive processing of external stimuli during sleep until technology provides a method for measuring arousal during stimulation independently of the presence or absence of the targeted response. In the meantime, perhaps we should judge the Aesculapian method of psychotherapy during sleep a success. At least it deserves a modern test.

References

Aserinsky, E., & Kleitman, N. (1953). Regularly occurring periods of eye modality, and concomitant phenomena, during sleep. *Science, 118,* 273–309.

Barber, T. X. (1956). Comparison of suggestibility during "light sleep" and hypnosis. *Science, 124,* 405.

Beh, H. C., & Barratt, P. E. H. (1965). Discrimination and conditioning during sleep as indicated by the electroencephalogram. *Science, 147,* 1470–1471.

Bernheim, H. (1889). *Suggestive therapeutics: A treatise on the nature and uses of hypnosis.* New York: Putnam.

Bertrand, A. J. F. (1826). *Du magnetisme animal en France et des jugement qu'en ont portes les societes savantes* [On animal magnetism in France and the judgements of the scientific societies]. Paris: Balliere.

Cobb, J. C., Evans, F. J., Gustafson, L. A., O'Connell, D. N., Orne, M. T., & Shor, E. R. (1965). Specific motor response during sleep to sleep-administered meaningful suggestion: An exploratory investigation. *Perceptual and Motor Skills, 20,* 629–636.

Collison, D. R. (1988, August). *A visit to Cos: In search of origins and transitions.* Presidential address at the 11th Triennial Congress of Hypnosis and Psychosomatic Medicine, The Hague.

Evans, F. J. (1977). The subjective characteristics of sleep efficiency. *Journal of Abnormal Psychology, 86,* 561–564.

Evans, F. J. (1979a). Contextual forgetting: Posthypnotic source amnesia. *Journal of Abnormal Psychology, 88,* 556–563.

Evans, F. J. (1979b). Hypnosis and sleep: Techniques for exploring cognitive activity during sleep. In E. Fromm & R. E. Shor (Eds.), *Hypnosis: Research developments and perspective* (rev. ed., pp. 139–183). Chicago: Aldine.

Evans, F. J. (1989). The hypnotizable subject, the hypnotizable patient: Studies in dissociative processes. In A. F. Bennett & K. M. McConkey (Eds.), *Cognition in individual and social processes* (Vol. 3). Amsterdam, Holland: Elsevier Science Publishers, B.V.

Evans, F. J., & Kihlstrom, J. F. (1973). Posthypnotic amnesia as disrupted retrieval. *Journal of Abnormal Psychology, 82,* 317–323.

Evans, F. J., Gustafson, L. A., O'Connell, D. N., Orne, M. T., & Shor, R. E. (1969). Sleep-induced behavioral response: Relationship to susceptibility to hypnosis and laboratory sleep patterns. *Journal of Nervous and Mental Disease, 148,* 467–476.

Evans, F. J., Gustafson, L. A., O'Connell, D. N., Orne, M. T., & Shor, R. E. (1970). Verbally induced behavioral responses during sleep. *Journal of Nervous and Mental Disease, 150,* 171–187.

Evans, F. J., & Thorn, W. A. F. (1966). Two types of posthypnotic amnesia: Recall amnesia and source amnesia. *International Journal of Clinical and Experimental Hypnosis, 14,* 162–179.

Fresacher, L. A. (1951). A way into the hypnotic state. *British Journal of Medical Hypnotism, 3,* 12–13.

Freud, S. (1922). *Introductory lectures on psycho-analysis* (J. Riviere, Trans.). London: Allen & Unwin.

Gill, M. M., & Brenman, M. (1959). *Hypnosis and related states: Psychoanalytic studies in regression.* New York: International Universities Press.

Granda, A. M., & Hammack, J. T. (1961). Operant behavior during sleep. *Science, 133,* 1485–1486.

Hoskovec, J. (1966). Hypnopedia in the Soviet Union: A critical review of recent major experiments. *International Journal of Clinical and Experimental Hypnosis, 14,* 308–315.

McDonald, D. G. (1966, January). *Conditional and unconditional automatic responses during sleep* (Report No. 65-28, Ad. 481520). San Diego, CA: U.S. Navy Medical Neuropsychiatric Research Unit.

Oswald, I. (1962). *Sleeping and waking: Physiology and psychology.* New York: Elsevier.

Perry, C. W., Evans, F. J., O'Connell, D. N., Orne, M. T., & Orne, E. C. (1978). Behavioral response to verbal stimuli administered and tested during REM sleep: A further investigation. *Waking and Sleeping, 2,* 317–329.

Rubin, F. (Ed.). (1968). *Current research in hypnopedia.* New York: Elsevier.

Schilder, P., & Kauders, O. (1927). Hypnosis. In S. Rothenberg (Trans.), *Nervous and Mental Disease Monograph Series* (No. 46).

Shor, R. E., & Orne, E. C. (1962). *The Harvard Group Scale of Hypnotic Susceptibility, Form A.* Palo Alto, CA: Consulting Psychologists Press.

Simon, C. W., & Emmons, W. H. (1956). EEG, consciousness, and sleep. *Science, 124,* 1066–1069.

Weinberg, H. (1966). Evidence suggesting the acquisition of a simple discrimination during sleep. *Canadian Journal of Psychology, 20,* 1–11.

Weitzenhoffer, A. M., & Hilgard, E. R. (1962). *The Stanford Hypnotic Susceptibility Scale, Form C.* Palo Alto, CA: Consulting Psychologists Press.

Williams, H. L., Morlock, H. C., & Morlock, J. V. (1966). Instrumental behavior during sleep. *Psychophysiology, 2,* 208–216.

Zung, W. W. K., & Wilson, W. P. (1961). Response to auditory stimulation during sleep: Discrimination and arousal as studied with electroencephalography. *Archives of General Psychology, 4,* 548–552.

CHAPTER 7

LEARNING DURING SLEEP

ERIC EICH

Is it possible for people to register and retain what is said in their presence while they sleep? If it is possible, is the learning that takes place during sleep efficient enough to be of practical as well as theoretical significance? These are the questions of chief concern in this chapter. To address these issues, research dealing with a number of factors that may have an important influence on sleep learning is summarized in the second section of the chapter, while in the third section, some tentative conclusions concerning the possibility and practicality of learning during sleep are offered, and prospects for future research are outlined. Much of the material covered in both of these sections has been culled from a remarkably thorough and trenchant review of the sleep learning literature by Aarons (1976), which I strongly recommend to interested readers.

As will become apparent in the course of this discussion, solid facts about sleep learning are scarce, and only one of the variables to be considered—the level of electroencephalographic (EEG) activation that accompanies or follows the presentation of a to-be-learned or target item—has been researched in a rigorous manner. Though the present dearth of reliable data is unfortunate, it is also understandable. For many years following the publication of the carefully controlled EEG experiments by Emmons and Simon (1956; Simon & Emmons, 1956), sleep learning was a dead issue. These investigators demonstrated that verbal information presented during sleep was irretrievable upon awakening unless presentation coincided with alpha activity, an EEG indicator of arousal or wakefulness. Their negative results, in combination with a critical commentary (Simon & Emmons, 1955) on the positive results that had been obtained by others (e.g., Fox & Robbins, 1952; Leuba & Bateman, 1952), caused most researchers in the United States and other Western countries to abandon the idea that people may be able to learn while they sleep.

In more recent times, however, there has been a modest revival of interest in the possibility of sleep learning, owing to three developments. First, a number of studies have shown that during slow wave (alpha free) sleep, subjects are able to make complex discriminations between repetitive auditory signals (e.g., Oswald, Taylor, & Treisman, 1960) and to perform, when cued with appropriate sensory stimuli, motor responses that they had learned while awake (e.g., Okuma, Nakamura, Hayashi, & Fujimori, 1966). One implication of these and related results (see Koulack & Goodenough, 1976; Lehmann & Koukkou, 1974) is that, even during deep sleep, short-term storage of new information is possible, as is access to old information in long-term memory. Second, evidence from several sources (see Firth, 1973; Goodenough, 1978) suggests that habituation or conditioning of various physiological responses, such as heart rate and galvanic skin response (GSR), can occur during sleep, albeit at a slower rate than occurs during wakefulness. Because both habituation and conditioning represent forms of learning, this evidence implies that the inability to remember information presented during sleep may be attributable not to problems in storing the information but, rather, to a failure to retrieve the information on waking (Koukkou & Lehmann, 1983; Koulack & Goodenough, 1976). Third, there have been numerous reports from the Soviet Union and other Eastern European nations of success in demonstrating sleep learning (see Hoskovec, 1966; Rubin, 1968, 1971). Though there can be no doubt that learning is dramatically impaired during sleep (see Goodenough, 1978), these reports recommend a reappraisal of the conclusion that sleep learning is impossible and raise a number of interesting questions concerning the conditions under which learning may occur. It is to these conditions that I now turn.

SLEEP LEARNING: METHODOLOGY AND PHENOMENOLOGY

As Aarons (1976) observed, whether or not learning during sleep occurs depends on an intricate interplay of numerous psychological and physiological factors. In this section, I survey those factors that, in my opinion, have the most promise of being important moderators of sleep learning. For ease of exposition, the specific factors to be considered are classified according to four general types: sleep, item, task, and subject.

Sleep Factors

EEG Activation During and Following Item Presentation

The research of Simon and Emmons (1956) revealed that alpha activity during the presentation of a target item is a necessary condition for the later recollection of that item. Evidence also suggests a strong association between memory

This article was prepared with the aid of the National Academy of Sciences (American) and the Natural Sciences and Engineering Research Council (Canadian), and it profited from the insightful comments of Jennifer Campbell and Darrin Lehman.

performance and both the level and the duration of EEG wakefulness or activation patterns that follow item input. Evidence of this sort has been supplied
by a number of studies (e.g., Jus & Jus, 1972; Koukkou & Lehmann, 1968;
Lehmann & Koukkou, 1974; Oltman et al., 1977), one of which is described
next for the purpose of illustration.

In the study by Koukkou and Lehmann (1968), short sentences were
auditorily presented to subjects during slow wave (Stage 2 or 3) sleep, and the
duration of the EEG activation (alpha) pattern produced by the presentation
of each sentence was measured. Upon awakening, the subjects completed a
test of nominally noncued or "spontaneous" recall, which was succeeded by
a test of old/new sentence-recognition memory.

The results showed that the duration of EEG activation that followed
the presentation of a given sentence was quite short ($M = 9$ s) for sentences
that were neither recalled nor recognized, was significantly longer ($M = 26$ s)
for sentences that were recognized but not recalled, and was longer still ($M =
165$ s) for sentences that were spontaneously recalled verbatim (Koukkou &
Lehmann, 1968, Table IIB). Thus, the postsleep recollection of sentences presented during slow wave sleep was systematically related to the duration of
EEG activation that occurred after presentation. (In later work, Lehmann and
Koukkou, 1974, demonstrated an analogous correlation between memory
performance and the level [i.e., EEG wave frequency] of postpresentation activation.) The fact that intermediate durations of activation were associated
with successful recognition but with unsuccessful recall suggests that recognition may be a more sensitive measure of memory for sleep-presented material
than is spontaneous recall, a point to which I will return later.

In an effort to provide a theoretical rationale for their results, Koukkou
and Lehmann (1968) proposed that the duration (and level; see Lehmann &
Koukkou, 1974) of EEG activation that occurs after the presentation of a target item reflects the time available for the long-term storage of that item. This
proposal is reminiscent of the consolidation interpretation of sleep-learning
problems put forth by Hebb (1949), who theorized that there are two distinct
forms of memorial representation: a short-term store in the form of reverberat-
ing neural circuits and a long-term store involving the development of more
permanent neural "knobs." According to this account, it is the transformation
or consolidation of information from a short- to a long-term representation
that is curtailed by the absence of EEG activation.

Several observations are compatible with the consolidation account (see
Goodenough, 1978; Lehmann & Koukkou, 1974). For example, somnambu-
lists can carry out complex motor actions and can respond appropriately to
sensory input during very deep (Stage 4) sleep, but they cannot recall their
actions and responses once they awaken (Jacobson, Lales, Lehmann, & Zweizig, 1965). Also, the apparent accuracy of dream recall is high if sleepers are
awakened during Stage 1 periods of REM sleep (a stage characterized by a
fairly active EEG), but without sleep interruption, dream recall decreases with
increased time spent in slow wave sleep after the end of the REM period (De-

ment & Kleitman, 1957). And a numerical stimulus presented during deep sleep that is not followed by appreciable EEG activation can be recalled if the subject is intentionally and rapidly awakened before the short-term trace of the stimulus ceases to exist (Oltman et al., 1977).

Though much of the difficulty in recalling events that take place during sleep may reflect the impaired consolidation or long-term storage of these events, the possibility that recall difficulties may be due to deficient retrieval should not be overlooked. Within the last 20 years, several retrieval-based accounts of sleep-learning problems have been advanced (see Foulkes, 1966; Goodenough, 1978). One of the more recent of these, the functional state-shift hypothesis of Koukkou and Lehmann (1983), is framed around the concept of *state-specific memory:* the idea that what has been learned in a particular state of mind or brain is best remembered in that state (see Eich, 1989; Overton, 1984). According to Koukkou and Lehmann (1983), the forgetting of events that transpire during sleep (whether internally generated dreams or externally presented items) is a function of the magnitude of the difference between the functional (EEG defined) states in which storage and retrieval of the events take place. Their hypothesis accords well with a number of diverse findings, including the aforementioned fact that if a transient period of wakefulness (as indicated by an increase in EEG activation) occurs soon after the presentation of a target item, then the subsequent recall of that item will be possible during full wakefulness. In addition, the state-shift hypothesis carries the intriguing implication that information acquired during sleep may be accessible for retrieval during later occasions of sleep, though not during intervening periods of wakefulness. Evidence pertinent to this implication will be examined shortly. But first, I would like to make one other point concerning the correlation between EEG activation and memory performance.

As noted earlier, a number of Soviet and Eastern European studies have reported success in producing reliable, sometimes robust, sleep learning effects. In these studies, presentations of the material to be learned are not regulated according to particular EEG patterns (as is customary in Western studies) but are timed to correspond with sleep onset, initial sleep, and early morning sleep, which are optimal times for eliciting EEG activations with alpha waves (Aarons, 1976). Thus it is possible, indeed probable, that participants in these studies are not really asleep when presentation occurs but instead are in a rather drowsy, but nonetheless conscious, state. Is it any wonder, then, that so-called sleep learning is possible under such circumstances? The obvious answer is no, but there is more to it than that. Unlike their Western counterparts, Eastern researchers generally do not find the question of whether subjects are really asleep during presentation of the learning material to be important or meaningful. Their primary concern is not with the theoretical possibility of learning during deep sleep, but with the practical purpose it serves to present learning material to superficially sleeping subjects. This is one of several salient differences (others will be discussed in due course) that distinguishes the prototypical Western study of sleep learning from the prototypical Eastern study. As Aarons (1976) argued, these differences probably account for why Western researchers frequently fail to find evidence of sleep learning, whereas Eastern investigators often succeed.

Sleep-Specific Memory

In 1910, Prince speculated that many people have difficulty remembering their dreams not because they do not *want* to remember, as Freud (1900/1953) and other psychodynamically oriented theorists of the day were claiming, but rather because they *cannot* remember, due to the mismatch between the states of natural sleep and ordinary wakefulness. Intuitively, Prince's idea seems plausible, and so does Koukkou and Lehmann's (1983) hypothesis that failures of waking memory for experimentally devised materials (such as sentences) presented during sleep are attributable to the shift from sleeping to waking states. Plausibility is one thing, however, and proof is quite another. What empirical evidence is there to support the proposition that memory for events occurring during sleep is specific to the sleep state?

To my knowledge, only one study—described briefly by Evans, Gustafson, O'Connell, Orne, and Shor (1966) and more elaborately by Evans (1972) and Evans et al. (1969, 1970)—has sought to secure such evidence.

In this study, 18 student nurses slept in a laboratory for 2 or 3 nights. During the first night, suggestions (e.g., "Whenever I say the word *itch,* your nose will feel itchy until you scratch it") were auditorily presented to subjects while they were in alpha-free Stage 1 sleep. The suggestions were then tested immediately by saying a cue word (e.g., itch) and observing the subjects' behavioral responses. Of the 18 subjects tested, 11 were able to perform the suggested responses while remaining in Stage 1 sleep. After the subjects awakened, they did not remember the verbally presented suggestions, nor did they remember responding to them. In addition, when presented with the same cue words that had elicited an appropriate response during sleep, the subjects did not respond behaviorally when awake. Thus, the subjects appeared to have a dense waking amnesia for events that had occurred during the prior night's sleep.

That the absence of waking memory reflected transient amnesia rather than permanent forgetting is implied by the observation that, of the 11 subjects who had responded to cue words during the first night, 7 responded to the same cues during the second night. Thus, in the majority of cases, successful second-night responding to cue words during sleep occurred even though (a) the suggestions themselves were not readministered and (b) the subjects had no intervening waking recollection of the suggestions or of their responses during sleep.

After an interval of approximately 5 months, 7 subjects were retested on a third sleep night. None of these subjects remembered the events of either earlier evening, and 5 of the 7 had responded on both prior nights to the cue words of the initial night. These 5 subjects responded, while in Stage 1 sleep, to cue words from the first night's sleep, despite the fact that the suggestions had neither been readministered nor recalled in the intervening months.

To summarize, the results reported by Evans et al. (1966) suggest that at least some subjects can respond to suggestions for specific motor actions while they remain in Stage 1 sleep. Further, these responses can be elicited during Stage 1 sleep of a following night and even in the same sleep stage several months later, without further reinstatement of the suggestion. This retention occurs even though the subjects, when awake, are unable to either verbalize their sleep experiences or to perform the sleep-acquired responses.

As noted earlier, the Evans et al. (1966) experiment is the only one of which I am aware that directly examined whether memory for events experienced during sleep is specific to the sleep state. Accordingly, their results, though strongly suggestive of sleep specific memory, should be viewed with caution. Why no efforts have been made to replicate and extend these results remains a mystery.

There is one other aspect of the relation between state specificity and sleep learning that deserves attention, and it concerns the asymmetric form in which state-specific effects sometimes appear. In several studies involving alcohol or other depressant drugs (e.g., Eich, Weingartner, Stillman, & Gillin, 1975; Goodwin, Powell, Bremer, Hoine, & Stern, 1969), it has been shown that, although events encoded in an intoxicated state are difficult to retrieve under conditions of sobriety, events experienced in the drug-free state tend not to be state specific and can often be accessed as efficiently in the presence of alcohol as in its absence. An analogous pattern of results has been obtained in research involving stimulant drugs, such as nicotine (Peters & McGee, 1982), as well as in experiments entailing alterations of affect or mood. Bartlett and Santrock (1979), for example, found that if preschoolers learned narrative material while they were feeling especially happy, they remembered more of this material when tested for recall in a happy than in a neutral mood. However, stories studied in a neutral affective state were equally well recalled regardless of whether the children were tested in a neutral or a happy mood. The implication of these and other studies (see Eich, 1989; Overton, 1984) is that information transfers more completely from an ordinary or typical state of mind or brain (such as sobriety or neutral affect) to an altered or atypical state (such as alcohol intoxication or extreme happiness) than it does in the reverse direction. The main point I want to make now is that asymmetric state-specific memory may also be involved in sleep. That is to say, while it is evident that knowledge acquired during wakefulness is expressible during sleep—we do, after all, tend to dream about things we perceived while awake—events experienced during sleep are difficult, if not impossible, to access during wakefulness. Why asymmetric state specificity should occur in conjunction with sleep, or any other experiential state (such as intoxication or happiness) for that matter, is an open issue. One possible reason relates to the concept of *cue overload,* the idea that the effectiveness of a given retrieval cue is inversely related to the number of discrete events it subserves (Watkins, 1979). Because the vast majority of our perceptual experiences occur while we are awake, the state of wakefulness cannot act as an effective cue for the retrieval of these experiences:

It is simply too overloaded. Sleep, in contrast, may constitute a much more salient or distinctive context for encoding and, thus, may serve as a powerful cue for the retrieval of events that were encoded in the sleep state. It remains to be seen whether this reasoning can be developed into a satisfying account of asymmetric state-specific memory as it occurs in sleep or other experiential states.

Item Factors

Methods of Item Presentation
Though analyses of dream reports indicate that sleep mentation can be reliably and systematically modified by the external presentation of either visual or tactual stimuli (Arkin & Antrobus, 1978), it is principally through audition that sleepers maintain contact with the external environment (Aarons, 1976). For this reason, and in the interest of practicality, audition has been the sensory channel of choice in studies of sleep learning.

Two methods of transmitting auditory information are available to the sleep-learning researcher: air conduction (loud speaker; e.g., Lehmann & Koukkou, 1974; Simon & Emmons, 1956) and bone conduction (pillow speaker; e.g., Bruce, Evans, Fenwick, & Spencer, 1970; Zukhar, Kaplan, Maksimov, & Pushkina, 1965/1968). Though the former method has been used more often in past research, the latter may be more conducive to the demonstration of sleep-learning effects. As Aarons (1976) noted, bone transmits mainly in the low-frequency range of speech, which includes the fundamental frequency of the speaker's voice, and may therefore enhance the fidelity of the spoken message. Moreover, bone conduction has the curious effect of shifting the phenomenal source of speech from the outside to the inside of one's head. That this may be beneficial for sleep learning is suggested by the idea (Foulkes, 1966) that the extent to which external stimuli are ignored during sleep is reciprocally related to the sleepers' preoccupation with their own internal mentation. Thus, it is possible that sleepers may be more receptive to, and hence more retentive of, information that seems to originate in their own minds rather than in the outside world. Whether this possibility is real or remote is a matter that merits serious consideration.

Characteristics of the Target Items
The list of variables that have a significant impact on the learning of verbal items in the waking state is extremely long and includes such factors as the frequency and spacing of item presentations as well as the meaningfulness and familiarity of the items themselves (see Adams, 1980; Baddeley, 1976). Unfortunately, the effect that these and other variables have on the efficiency of verbal learning during sleep is virtually unknown.

In regard to the frequency of item presentation, Simon and Emmons (1955) asserted that sleep learning, if it is to occur at all, may require that a massive number of item presentations take place, but they did not offer any clear empirical evidence to back their claim. Bliznitchenko (1968; also cited in Aarons, 1976), a pioneer in applied Soviet research on sleep learning, argued that repeated item presentations in the same sequence are a prerequisite to improvements in learning during sleep, but he too supplied no solid supporting data.

With respect to the spacing of item presentations, an early experiment by Coyne, which is described in detail by Simon and Emmons (1955), indicated that distributed repetitions of the material to be learned (number–word pairs) produced better sleep learning than did massed repetitions. However, Coyne's results are hopelessly confounded by the fact that the distributed repetitions occurred during the period just preceding wakefulness (typically a light, drowsy state), while the massed repetitions occurred during deeper and possibly less receptive stages of sleep (see Simon & Emmons, 1955).

The conflicting results revealed by several studies involving nonsense syllables, common words, simple sentences, and even Chinese–English paired associates prompted Simon and Emmons (1955) to conclude that meaningfulness is not a critical determinant of sleep learning. However, as Aarons (1976) commented, in no sleep learning study have the semantic or denotative dimensions of the learning material been systematically manipulated. Aarons also remarked that, apart from whatever role that semantic meaningfulness may play in sleep learning, the personal meaningfulness or affective significance of the learning material may be important. Indeed, hand movements and electrographic (K complex) responses occur more frequently when subjects are presented, during deep sleep, with their own rather than with someone else's name (Oswald et al., 1960), and emotionally toned words, in contrast to neutral items (e.g., *dumb, sin* vs. *drum, sit*), provoke more pronounced eye movements and cardiovascular changes when presented during sleep than during wakefulness (Minard, Loiselle, Ingledue, & Duatlich, 1968). Given that personally or affectively meaningful material is more apt to be registered during sleep, it would be interesting to know whether such material is also more likely to be retained upon awakening.

Earlier I pointed out that a salient difference between Western and Eastern studies of sleep learning is that in the former, material is presented only during EEG-defined sleep, whereas in the latter, presentation occurs at the beginning and the end of the normal sleep cycle. Another significant difference concerns the learner's familiarity with the material. In most Western studies, subjects do not know what it is they will hear while they sleep, and they usually participate in only a single sleep-learning session. In contrast, Eastern investigators have developed a "hypnopaedic tutorial system" (see Rubin, 1970) in which the presentation of material during superficial sleep is coordinated with ongoing audiovisual presleep and postsleep instruction that lasts for several weeks. Though it has been claimed that this system accelerates the learning of telegraphy, foreign-language vocabulary, and other types of practical knowledge (see Aarons, 1976; Bliznitchenko, 1968; Rubin, 1971), the absence of appropriate controls makes it impossible to determine how much of the learning is attributable to waking instruction alone. Still, the possibility exists that the presentation of learning material during sleep improves performance in the waking state, provided that the material is familiar to the learners prior to its presentation.

Preliminary support for this possibility has been provided by Tilley (1979). Subjects in his experiment examined a set of 20 pictures of common objects at bedtime. Later that night, a tape-recorded list of 10 words—the names of half of the pictures in the original set—was presented 10 times during either Stage 2 or REM sleep. The following morning, the subjects were tested for free recall and recognition of the complete set of 20 picture names.

In comparison with items that had been studied at bedtime only, those that had been presented both before and during sleep were significantly better recalled and recognized. Curiously, the beneficial effect of repetition during sleep was much more evident in the morning retention of items that had been repeated during Stage 2 sleep than those that had been repeated during REM. This finding is curious in that REM, which is characterized by low-amplitude EEG activity and the periodic appearance of alpha frequencies, would seem to be more conducive to the processing of incoming information than would non-REM (in this case, Stage 2) sleep. At any rate, Tilley's (1979) results are clearly consistent with the Soviet claim that presleep learning can be strengthened or reinforced through within-sleep repetition. It is equally clear, however, that Tilley's results need to be replicated and, if possible, extended to other types of learning materials and retention tasks.

Task Factors

Recall Versus Recognition

Although a few studies have used savings in relearning to assess the retention of sleep-presented materials (often with contradictory outcomes; compare, for instance, the positive results obtained by Fox and Robbins, 1952, with the negative findings of Bruce et al., 1970), most have employed tests of recall, recognition, or both (see Aarons, 1976, Table 2).

Recognition may be a more sensitive measure of memory than recall for events experienced during sleep. As noted earlier, Koukkou and Lehmann (1968; see also Lehmann & Koukkou, 1974) found that items whose presentation during slow wave sleep was followed by an intermediate duration and level of EEG activation were subsequently recognized but were not spontaneously recalled. In addition, Levy, Collidge, and Stabb (1972) observed that, although subjects were unable to recall Russian–English paired associates that had been presented during either Stage 1 or Stage 4 sleep, recognition of the response or target words was slightly but significantly above chance for both sleep stages. And a study by Johnson, Kahan, and Raye (1984) showed that the probability of recalling a dream that had been immediately reported upon awakening fell to below .20 after a 2-week retention interval, whereas the probability of recognizing the dream was an impressive .80 after the same interval.

Why events experienced during sleep should be more readily recognized than recalled remains to be determined. However, basic memory research involving more conventional materials suggests that how readily information is comprehended and organized may matter more for recall than for recognition (see Kintsch, 1970). Conceivably, then, events that occur during sleep may be particularly difficult to recall either because sleep is not conducive to the coherent organization of ongoing events or because the events themselves are incomprehensible (as often appears to be the case for dreams).

Implicit Versus Explicit Memory

Evidence from several sources suggests that memory for past events can influence present actions even if one is not aware of remembering the earlier experiences. As an example, prior presentation of a word makes it more likely that college students can report that word when later it is briefly exposed in a perceptual identification task, regardless of whether or not they recognize the word as one that had been presented before (Jacoby & Dallas, 1981). Similarly, amnesic patients reveal the effects of practice in their subsequent performance of a cognitive, perceptual, or motor skill, even though they cannot remember ever having practiced that skill (Schacter & Tulving, 1982). These and other observations suggest that it is possible to distinguish the implicit effects of memory for prior episodes or experiences on a person's current behavior from the person's explicit awareness that he or she is remembering events of the past (Richardson-Klavehn & Bjork, 1988; Schacter, 1987; Schacter & Kihlstrom, 1989).

The point I wish to make is that it may be useful to apply the distinction between implicit and explicit memory to the question of whether events that occur during sleep can be registered and retained. As noted previously, most earlier experiments examining this question have focused on the individual's ability to recall or recognize a specific item (e.g., a spoken number, word, or sentence) as having occurred in a specific situation, namely, while the individual was superficially or soundly asleep. Memory as measured in these experiments is explicit in that the person must necessarily be aware that he or she is remembering a particular past event. Given that most people appear profoundly amnesic when tested for the deliberate recall or recognition of events to which they had been exposed while asleep, it is reasonable to infer that events that are denied conscious attention are ordinarily not amenable to conscious reflection or accessible through explicit forms of remembering. The inference need not be drawn, however, that events occurring during sleep leave no lasting impression in memory and exert no enduring effect on behavior. The possibility remains that even though the effects of memory for sleep-experienced events may not be revealed via tests of recall or even of recognition, such effects might become evident in situations that do not demand explicit recollection.

How might this possibility be explored? One way of doing so is suggested by Jacoby and Witherspoon (1982). Participants in their study were 5 university students and 5 Korsakoff alcoholics, clinically diagnosed as amnesic. In the first phase of the study, subjects answered questions such as: "Name a musical instrument that employs a *reed*." As implied by this example, the intent of the question-answering task was to encourage the subjects to encode homophones, such as *reed*, in relation to their low-frequency or less common interpretations.

In the second phase of the study, the subjects were read a list that consisted in part of equivalent numbers of old and new homophones (i.e., words that either had or had not appeared in the context of biasing questions), and were asked to spell each word aloud. Jacoby and Witherspoon (1982) reasoned that if the first presentation of a "biased" homophone is remembered and influences its later interpretation, more of the old than the new homophones should be spelled in keeping with their less common interpretations. They further reasoned that an influence of memory on the spelling of a word would not necessarily require the subjects to be aware that they were remembering the first presentation of that word but rather that such explicit recollection would be required in the test of old/new recognition memory that was given in the third and final phase. To the extent, then, that the processes or systems underlying implicit and explicit memory are distinct, performance on a test (viz., recognition) that requires awareness of earlier events and performance on a test (viz., spelling) that does not demand explicit recollection should be independent of one another, in that performance on one type of test should not be predictable on the basis of performance on the other type.

Evidence of such independence was revealed in two ways. First, in comparison with the students, the amnesic patients recognized far fewer old homophones (25% vs. 76%, with neither group of subjects generating any false positives) but spelled more of these items in line with their less common, experimentally biased interpretations (63% vs. 49%, with approximately 21% of the new homophones spelled in their low frequency forms by both groups). Thus, the disadvantage of the amnesic patients was restricted to recognition memory, an explicit form of remembering. Second, for both patients and students, the conditional probability of recognizing an old homophone in the third phase of the study, given that its spelling had been biased by memory in the second phase, p(recognition | spelling), did not differ significantly from the unconditional probability of correct recognition, p(recognition). Thus, for neither type of subject was recognition memory associated with or enhanced by an effect of memory on spelling.

In short, it seems that the prior presentation of a word has a substantial impact on its subsequent interpretation and spelling, regardless of whether or not the word is correctly classified as old in a later test of recognition memory. Though this dissociation of spelling and recognition performance was especially striking among the amnesics (who outperformed the students on the former test and were themselves outperformed by the students on the latter), it was demonstrated by the nonamnesics as well, as evidenced by the students' statistically equivalent values of p(recognition | spelling) and p(recognition).

Recognition and spelling thus seem to reflect different forms or functions of memory, whether intact or organically impaired. Whereas recognition of an old word requires the recognizer to be aware of its prior presentation, an influence of memory on the spelling of a word does not necessarily demand explicit remembering (see Eich, 1984; Jacoby, 1982).

Approached from the standpoint of sleep learning, the idea that recognition and spelling tap different memory processes or systems raises an interesting question for research. Specifically, suppose that during sleep, subjects are presented with a series of short, descriptive phrases, each consisting of a homophone and one or two words that bias the homophone's less common interpretation (e.g., *war and* PEACE; *deep* SEA). Suppose further that, upon awakening, the subjects are read a list composed chiefly of old and new homophones on two successive occasions. On one occasion, the subjects are simply asked to spell each list item aloud; on the other occasion, the subjects are asked to state aloud which list items they recognize as having been presented during sleep. Might the subjects spell significantly more old than new homophones in line with their less common interpretations and yet fail to discriminate reliably between the two types of items in the test of recognition memory—a test, unlike that of spelling, which would presumably require the subject to consciously reflect upon events that had occurred during a state of unconsciousness? More broadly stated, is it possible that people implicitly know something about events that take place during sleep but do not explicitly know that they know? The answer to this question might be of interest from an applied as well as a theoretical perspective.

Subject Factors

Age

Several authors have speculated about whether the ability to learn during sleep is dependent on age, but no one has provided any telling data. Svyadoshch (1962/1968), for example, employed subjects ranging in age from 10 to 60 years in a series of studies concerning the reproduction of stories presented during sleep. Though Svyadoshch asserted that the majority of his subjects, regardless of their age, demonstrated a high level of text reproduction (arbitrarily defined as 66% or more of the story material), he did not provide a breakdown of reproduction scores by age group. Svyadoshch also offered no hard numbers to support a second, seemingly contradictory assertion concerning the relation between sleep learning and age: specifically, that the ability to assimilate speech during sleep can be acquired artificially by means of suggestions delivered in the context of either deep hypnosis or ordinary wakefulness and that children and adolescents, being more suggestible by nature than older adults, are especially adept at developing sleep-learning abilities.

Interestingly, the idea that an optimal period for learning how to learn during sleep may arise at an early age also occurred to Aarons (1976), but for different and more defensible reasons. These include the observation that (a) even as early as 3 days after birth, the human voice and its fundamental frequency are more effective than other sounds in eliciting behavioral and physiological reactions during alert, relaxed, and somnolent states (Hutt, Hutt, Lenard, Bernuth, & Muntjewerff, 1968); (b) children appear to acquire second languages more readily than do adults, which suggests a greater facility in phonetic processing during wakefulness that could conceivably carry over to sleep; and (c) in comparison with older children, younger children devote more attention to and are more likely to remember auditorily rather than visually presented information (Hallahan, Kauffman, & Ball, 1974). Though the foregoing observations are compatible with the developmental hypothesis advanced by Aarons (1976), more direct evidence is needed.

Health

Given that (a) between 5% and 10% of otherwise healthy medical students suffer from chronic sleep disturbances that range from mild to moderate in severity (Johns, Gay, Goodyear, & Masterton, 1971), (b) emotional stress disrupts the natural sleep cycles of men and women alike (Breger, Hunter, & Lane, 1971), and (c) both mentation and physiological processes during sleep are influenced by menstruation in women (Sheldrake & Cormack, 1974), the need to screen subjects for sleep-learning research on the basis of specific criteria related to their physical and psychological health seems clear. Yet apart from the research of Zukhar' et al. (1965/1968) in which people with histories of sleep disturbance were specifically excluded from participation, health-related variables have not been taken into account in prior studies of sleep learning. Instead, researchers have simply assumed that their subjects are in generally good health and have normal hearing. As Aarons (1976) remarked, information on personal health and sleep habits would help investigators determine the suitability of a particular person to a particular sleep-learning intervention, and it is therefore hoped that the gathering of such information will become a standard practice in future studies of sleep learning.

Capacity to Learn While Awake

According to Simon and Emmons (1955), sleep-learning researchers would be well-advised to select as their subjects people who are particularly proficient at learning in the waking state, since the effect of presenting material during sleep may be so subtle that its benefits will be evident only in highly intelligent individuals. In consideration of Simon and Emmon's (1955) conjecture, four points are worth making. First, there is no a priori reason to assume that general intelligence plays a more prominent role in learning during sleep than it does in wake instruction (Aarons, 1976). Second, it seems plausible that positive effects of sleep learning might be more readily demonstrated in individuals who are deficient rather than proficient in wake-state acquisition, in much the same manner as the memory-enhancing effects of nootropic drugs, such as oxiracetam (Itil, Menon, Bozak, & Sangor, 1982), may be more readily demonstrated in memory-impaired patients (e.g., those with senile dementia of the Alzheimer's type) than in cognitively intact controls. Third, there is no empirical evidence to support Simon and Emmon's (1955) position, and fourth, what little evidence does exist runs counter to Simon and Emmon's conjecture. The pertinent evidence comes from an early experiment by Elliott (1947/1968). All 40 of the subjects in Elliott's study first learned one list of words (List A) to criterion in the waking state. Subsequently, a second list (List B) was presented to 20 subjects while they slept (the experimental group) but not to the other 20 subjects (the control group). The following morning, all 40 subjects learned List B to criterion. The key finding was that the percentage of savings in learning List B, that is, $S = (A - B/A) \times 100$, where A and B designate the number of trials required by a given subject to learn Lists A and B and S designates percentage of savings, was significantly greater for experimental than for control subjects, a finding that Elliott interpreted as evidence of sleep learning. For the present purpose, a more interesting finding concerns the correlation between the values of A and S for each group of subjects. For purely statistical reasons, one would expect to observe a positive correlation between these measures for either group (because if any 2 subjects take the same number of trials to learn List B, the one who required more trials to learn List A will necessarily obtain a higher savings score). However, if Simon and Emmon's (1955) speculation that the benefits of sleep learning are more likely to be detected in good than in poor wake-state learners, then one would also expect to find a smaller correlation between the A and S scores of experimental subjects than between those of control subjects. That is to say, good learners in the experimental group (those who required relatively few trials to master List A) ought to show more savings in their learning of List B than should poor learners in the same group (those who required relatively many trials to learn List A). In fact, the correlation between A and S was somewhat greater among the experimental subjects ($r = .37$) than it was among the control subjects ($r = .21$). (These correlations were calculated from the data presented in Table III of Elliott, 1968, p. 13.) Thus, the advantage of having been presented with List B during sleep on the later learning of that list *appears* to have accrued more to the poor than to the good wake-state learners, the opposite of what would have been anticipated on the basis of Simon and Emmon's account. I emphasize the word *appears* because Elliott's experiment was not free of methodological flaws (e.g., he did not continuously monitor sleep using EEG; see Simon & Emmons, 1955). More rigorous research will need to be performed before the relation between learning capacities in waking and sleeping states can be stated with any degree of precision.

Suggestibility: Hypnotic Susceptibility and Learning Set

By several Soviet accounts (e.g., Svyadoshch, 1962/1968; Zavalova, Zukhar, & Petrov, 1964/1968; see also Aarons, 1976; Hoskovec, 1966), learning during sleep is possible provided that the learners are suggestible. As a rule, however, Russian researchers have been neither clear nor consistent in their usage of the term *suggestible:* At times the term appears to imply susceptibility to hypnosis, at other times it refers to a strong waking set that is induced in the subjects to convince them that sleep learning is a bona fide phenomenon, and on still other occasions it connotes both of these senses. In addition, the evidence these researchers have presented to support their position cannot be regarded as compelling.

Consider, for example, the work of Kulikov (1964/1968). Subjects in his studies included 21 grade school and 15 college students, all of whom were highly susceptible to hypnosis (as tested by the method of hand gripping). The subjects were separated into three groups of 12, each composed of 7 children and 5 adults; random assignment of subjects to groups was not specifically noted by the author.

Subjects in the first group were repeatedly presented during natural sleep with a narrative (a Tolstoy story for the children; a description of nervous system functions for the adults) and were tested for recall of the text when they awoke. These subjects were not, as Kulikov (1964/1968) put it, "prepared" for sleep learning; that is, they had received no specific suggestions for assimilation and retention of the text prior to its presentation. Kulikov did not specify the number of times the text was presented, the precise form of the recall test (i.e., whether it was spontaneous or prompted), or the duration of the retention interval. Further, it is not clear from Kulikov's account exactly when the text was presented; on procedure, he remarked only that the text was presented, via tape recorder, at a volume that was below the threshold of hearing in the waking state and that sleep was monitored by activity records (assessing the absence of motor movements) and pneumographic tracings (assessing the absence of marked respiratory reaction). Be that as it may, Kulikov found that only 1 of the 12 subjects in this group had any waking recollection of the text, and the 1 exceptional subject was a boy who had taken part in previous studies in which hypnopaedic suggestions had been delivered.

Kulikov began testing of subjects in the second group by establishing contact with them while they slept. After the subjects had been sleeping for 1 or 2 hours, tape-recorded suggestions were presented (e.g., "You are sleeping peacefully, do not wake up" and "Your breathing is becoming deeper and deeper"). Having made contact with the sleeping subjects in this manner, the suggestion was given, "Now you will hear a story, listen to what is said, try and memorize it as much as possible, you will remember this all your life, and whenever wanted you will be able to relate it." The text was then presented (an unspecified number of times) and was followed by additional suggestions to remember the text and to sleep soundly.

The impact these suggestions had on the subjects' waking-recall performance appears to have been profound. Among the 12 subjects in the second group who had been prepared with a suggested set to learn while asleep, the percentage of idea units contained in the text that were recalled averaged 64% and ranged from 47% to 87%; there was no appreciable difference in the performance of the children and the adults. These figures are remarkably similar to those yielded by the third group of subjects, who were awake at the time of text presentation (mean recall of 66%, range from 44% to 80%).

Taken at face value, Kulikov's (1964/1968) data indicate that learning during sleep is possible in hypnotically suggestible subjects when a suggested set to register and retain the learning material is involved. Moreover, his data suggest that the capacity to learn during sleep is comparable to that of the waking state.

Kulikov's (1964/1968) results are not beyond reproach, however. First, the suggestions ("preparations") that were imparted to subjects in the second group were evidently not imparted to subjects in the third group, thus precluding a valid comparison of the effectiveness of sleep versus wake learning. Second, it is possible that the striking difference in recall performance found between the first and second groups does not demonstrate the importance of preparing subjects for sleep learning but rather reflects the fact that only the second group of subjects received any suggestions at all. A more meaningful contrast would have been between groups receiving suggestions that either were or were not relevant to the specific learning task at hand.

Though Kulikov's (1964/1968) studies have some serious shortcomings, his contention that sleep learning is possible in hypnotically susceptible subjects who have acquired an appropriate set to learn, which is shared with other Soviet researchers (see Hoskovec, 1966), finds support in a small study by Evans (1972), an American-based investigator. Nine of the subjects in Evans' experiment were people of varying levels of hypnotic susceptibility who could respond while they remained asleep to suggestions for specific motor actions (e.g., "Whenever I say the word *pillow,* your pillow will feel uncomfortable until you move it") without a presleep "set" to perform these actions; none of the subjects had any waking recollection of the suggestions. A strong waking set was then instilled that sleep learning is possible. Specifically, subjects were told that, unlike most people, they were able to respond to suggestions presented during sleep and that this made them particularly promising candidates for sleep learning. Further, subjects were informed about successful Soviet demonstrations of sleep learning and thus were motivated both by their own special qualifications and by the competitive aim to duplicate the Russian results. In addition to these 9 subjects, several others were included who did not receive the suggested set.

Material of the form "A is for Apple, P is for Palace," was presented to the subjects during REM sleep and Stages 2 and 4. Any letter–word pair whose presentation was accompanied simultaneously by alpha was excluded from subsequent analyses of retention. Eight target words, each beginning with a different letter, were presented twice to each subject; at least two words were presented during each sleep stage.

Waking retention was tested by having subjects check any familiar word on a list of 10 words beginning with the letter A and again from 10 words beginning with the letter P, and so forth; two similar "dummy" lists, containing words that had not been presented during sleep, were also administered. Thus, the conservative probability of recognizing a target word by guessing was .10 for each of the eight relevant lists.

Three main findings emerged from the recognition test. First, subjects who had not received the set to learn during sleep recognized none of the target words from any sleep stage. Second, subjects who had received the set recognized, on the average, .28, .10, and .00 of the words that had been presented during Stages REM, 2, and 4, respectively; none of these subjects ever claimed to recognize a word that was not a true target. Thus, only those words that had been presented to suggested-set subjects during REM sleep were recognized at a better-than-chance level. Third, among the suggested-set subjects, those who had a relatively high level of hypnotic susceptibility (as indexed by the Stanford Hypnotic Susceptibility Scale, among other instruments) tended to recognize more REM stage targets than did subjects who had a relatively low level ($r = .49$).

Viewed as a whole, the results of Evans' (1972) experiment seem to square with the Soviet position that sleep learning is possible in hypnotically susceptible subjects in whom a strong set to learn has been established. As such, Evans' results illuminate a number of interesting issues for future research. Consider first the concept of a suggested set. Intuitively, it seems reasonable to suppose that the induction of a set will increase the subjects' motivation to learn while they sleep. If motivation is indeed one of the keys to successful sleep learning, then the odds of observing significant sleep-learning effects should be improved by offering subjects a substantial monetary reward for good retention performance (e.g., Levy et al., 1972), by ensuring that the material to be learned during sleep is pertinent to the subjects' personal needs or educational goals (e.g., Balkhasov, 1965/1968), or by restricting the subject sample to individuals who have a strong interest in the research (e.g., Svyadoshch, 1962/1968).

Examination of the role of hypnotic susceptibility in sleep learning, (reviewed by Hilgard, 1979) indicates that high hypnotizables are able to process information outside of conscious awareness more effectively and completely than are low hypnotizables. A striking example of this "splitting" of consciousness, a process termed *dissociation,* is shown when a person discovers that he or she is reacting, in an apparently automatic or involuntary manner, to a suggestion implanted previously under hypnosis. Owing to their greater dissociative abilities, high hypnotizables may be able to attend and process incoming information selectively, without consciousness awareness, after they have fallen asleep. Lacking this ability, low hypnotizables have to awaken to process similar information and are therefore incapable of learning while they sleep. Though this hypothesis is as speculative as it is sketchy, it does seem to fit with the findings that, in comparison with low hypnotizables, high hypnotizables are (a) less likely to awaken either spontaneously or following verbal stimulation (Evans, 1972), (b) more likely to respond to behavioral suggestions administered during sleep (Evans et al., 1966, 1969), and (c) more adept at changing their dream experiences to conform with specific presleep instructions (Belicki & Bowers, 1982). These findings, in addition to the others mentioned earlier in this section, suggest that the relations among hypnotizability, dissociability, and sleep learning comprise an inviting target for future research.

CONCLUSION

Whether it is possible and practical for people to learn while they sleep is a question to which Western and Eastern researchers have given different answers. Little, if any, learning has been revealed in most Western studies, wherein novel verbal material has been presented to randomly selected subjects during a single session of EEG-defined sleep. The learning that has materialized in these studies has frequently been found to be correlated with both the duration and the level of EEG wakefulness patterns that coincide with or closely follow presentation of the learning material. In contrast, evidence of substantial sleep learning has emerged in numerous Eastern studies, wherein familiar material was presented to suggestible subjects who had received a strong presleep instruction set to learn and were willing to participate in a lengthy training regimen. No attempt has been made in these studies to input information during deep stages of sleep; instead, presentations have been timed to correspond with sleep onset, initial sleep, and early morning sleep, periods in which significant EEG activations are likely to occur. Any improvements in performance obtained under these conditions would thus appear to reflect a composite of wake and sleep experience and not pure, unadulterated "sleep learning."

Although it appears clear that information presented during sleep that is not accompanied by EEG activation is not retained upon awakening, it would be interesting to know, for theoretical as well as for applied reasons, whether there is any substance to the Soviet claim that substantial improvements in learning can be achieved by a systematic program of combined wake/sleep instruction. It would also be informative to discover whether such improvements are dependent (a) on the learner's age, health, capacity to acquire knowledge in the waking state, susceptibility to hypnosis, and motivation to learn; (b) on the nature of the learning materials (e.g., whether they are affectively intoned or personally insignificant) and the methods of material presentation (e.g., air- vs. bone-conducted transmission); and (c) on the means by which retention of the material is measured (e.g., whether the test taps implicit vs. explicit memory). These are among the many issues that remain to be settled in future research aimed at investigating both the possibility and the practicality of learning during sleep.

References

Aarons, L. (1976). Sleep-assisted instruction. *Psychological Bulletin, 83,* 1–40.
Adams, J. A. (1980). *Learning and memory: An introduction.* Homewood, IL: Dorsey Press.

Arkin, A. M., & Antrobus, J. S. (1978). The effects of external stimuli applied prior to and during sleep on sleep experiences. In A. M. Arkin, J. S. Antrobus, & S. J. Ellman (Eds.), *The mind in sleep: Psychology and psychophysiology* (pp. 351–391). Hillsdale, NJ: Erlbaum.

Baddeley, A. D. (1976). *The psychology of memory.* New York: Basic Books.

Balkhasov, I. (1968). The rapid teaching of a foreign language by lessons heard during sleep. In F. Rubin (Ed.), *Current research in hypnopaedia* (A. Scott, Trans.) (pp. 160–163). New York: Elsevier. (Originally published in 1965)

Bartlett, J. C., & Santrock, J. W. (1979). Affect-dependent episodic memory in young children. *Child Development, 50,* 513–518.

Belicki, K., & Bowers, P. (1982). The role of demand characteristics and hypnotic ability in dream change following a presleep instruction. *Journal of Abnormal Psychology, 91,* 426–432.

Bliznitchenko, L. (1968). Hypnopaedia and its practice in the USSR. In F. Rubin (Ed.), *Current research in hypnopaedia* (pp. 202–209). New York: Elsevier.

Breger, L., Hunter, I., & Lane, R. W. (1971). *The effect of stress on dreams.* New York: International Universities Press.

Bruce, D. J., Evans, C. R., Fenwick, P. B. C., & Spencer, V. (1970). Effects of presenting novel verbal material during slow-wave sleep. *Nature, 225,* 873–874.

Dement, W. C., & Kleitman, N. (1957). The relation of eye movements during sleep to dream activity: An objective method for the study of dreaming. *Journal of Experimental Psychology, 53,* 339–346.

Eich, E. (1984). Memory for unattended events: Remembering with and without awareness. *Memory and Cognition, 12,* 105–111.

Eich, E. (1989). Theoretical issues in state dependent memory. In H. L. Roediger III & F. I. M. Craik (Eds.), *Varieties of memory and consciousness: Essays in honor of Endel Tulving* (pp. 331–354). Hillsdale, NJ: Erlbaum.

Eich, J. E., Weingartner, H., Stillman, R. C., & Gillin, J. C. (1975). State-dependent accessibility of retrieval cues in the retention of a categorized list. *Journal of Verbal Learning and Verbal Behavior, 14,* 408–417.

Elliott, C. R. (1968). Extracts from an experimental study of the retention of auditory material presented during sleep. In F. Rubin (Ed.), *Current research in hypnopaedia* (pp. 6–27). New York: Elsevier. (Original work published 1947)

Emmons, W. H., & Simon, C. W. (1956). The non-recall of material presented during sleep. *American Journal of Psychology, 69,* 76–81.

Evans, F. J. (1972). Hypnosis and sleep: Techniques for exploring cognitive activity during sleep. In E. Fromm & R. E. Shor (Eds.), *Hypnosis: Research developments and perspectives* (pp. 43–83). Chicago: Aldine/Atherton.

Evans, F. J., Gustafson, L. A., O'Connell, D. N., Orne, M. T., & Shor, R. E. (1966). Response during sleep with intervening amnesia. *Science, 152,* 666–667.

Evans, F. J., Gustafson, L. A., O'Connell, D. N., Orne, M. T., & Shor, R. E. (1969). Sleep-induced behavioral response: Relationship to susceptibility to hypnosis and laboratory sleep patterns. *Journal of Nervous and Mental Disease, 148,* 467–476.

Evans, F. J., Gustafson, L. A., O'Connell, D. N., Orne, M. T., & Shor, R. E. (1970). Verbally induced behavioral responses during sleep. *Journal of Nervous and Mental Disease, 150,* 171–187.

Firth, H. (1973). Habituation during sleep. *Psychophysiology, 10,* 43–51.

Foulkes, D. (1966). *The psychology of sleep.* New York: Scribners.

Fox, B. H., & Robbins, J. S. (1952). The retention of material presented during sleep. *Journal of Experimental Psychology, 43,* 75–79.

Freud, S. (1953). The interpretation of dreams. In J. Strachey (Ed. and Trans.), *The standard edition of the complete psychological works of Sigmund Freud* (Vol. 4–5). London: Hogarth Press. (Original work published 1900)

Goodenough, D. R. (1978). Dream recall: History and current status of the field. In A. M. Arkin, J. S. Antrobus, & S. J. Ellman (Eds.), *The mind in sleep: Psychology and psychophysiology* (pp. 113–140). Hillsdale, NJ: Erlbaum.

Goodwin, D. W., Powell, B., Bremer, D., Hoine, H., & Stern, J. (1969). Alcohol and recall: State dependent effects in man. *Science, 163,* 1358–1360.

Hallahan, D. P., Kauffman, J. M., & Ball, D. W. (1974). Developmental trends in recall of central and incidental auditory material. *Journal of Experimental Child Psychology, 17,* 409–421.

Hebb, D. O. (1949). *The organization of behavior: A neuropsychological theory.* New York: Wiley.

Hilgard, E. R. (1979). Divided consciousness in hypnosis: The implications of the hidden observer. In E. Fromm & R. Shor (Eds.), *Hypnosis: Developments in research and new perspectives.* New York: Aldine.

Hoskovec, J. (1966). Hypnopaedia in the Soviet Union: A critical review of recent major experiments. *International Journal of Clinical and Experimental Hypnosis, 14,* 308–315.

Hutt, S. J., Hutt, C., Lenard, H. G., Bernuth, H., & Muntjewerff, W. J. (1968). Auditory responsivity in the human neonate. *Nature, 218,* 888–890.

Itil, T. M., Menon, G. N., Bozak, M., & Sangor, A. (1982). The effects of oxiracetam (ISF 2522) in patients with organic brain syndrome. *Drug Development Research, 2,* 447–461.

Jacobson, A., Lales, A., Lehmann, D., & Zweizig, J. (1965). Somnambulism: All night electroencephalographic studies. *Science, 148,* 975–977.

Jacoby, L. L. (1982). Knowing and remembering: Some parallels in the behavior of Korsakoff patients and controls. In L. S. Cermak (Ed.), *Memory and amnesia.* Hillsdale, NJ: Erlbaum.

Jacoby, L. L., & Dallas, M. (1981). On the relationship between autobiographical memory and perceptual learning. *Journal of Experimental Psychology: General, 110,* 306–340.

Jacoby, L. L., & Witherspoon, D. (1982). Remembering with and without awareness. *Canadian Journal of Psychology, 36,* 300–324.

Johns, M. W., Gay, T. J. A., Goodyear, M. D. E., & Masterton, J. P. (1971). Sleep habits of healthy young adults: Use of sleep questionnaire. *British Journal of Preventative and Social Medicine, 25,* 236–241.

Johnson, M. K., Kahan, T. L., & Raye, C. L. (1984). Dreams and reality monitoring. *Journal of Experimental Psychology: General, 113,* 329–344.

Jus, K., & Jus, A. (1972). Experimental studies on memory disturbances in pathological and physiological conditions. *International Journal of Psychobiology, 2,* 205–208.

Kintsch, W. (1970). Models of free recall and recognition. In D. A. Norman (Ed.), *Models of human memory* (pp. 331–373). New York: Academic Press.

Koukkou, M., & Lehmann, D. (1968). EEG and memory storage in sleep experiments with humans. *Electroencephalography and Clinical Neurophysiology, 25,* 455–462.

Koukkou, M., & Lehmann, D. (1983). Dreaming: The functional state-shift hypothesis. *British Journal of Psychiatry, 142,* 221–231.

Koulack, D., & Goodenough, D. R. (1976). Dream recall and dream recall failure: An arousal-retrieval model. *Psychological Bulletin, 83,* 975–984.

Kulikov, V. N. (1968). The question of hypnopaedia. In F. Rubin (Ed.), *Current research in hypnopaedia* (A. Scott, Trans.) (pp. 132–144). New York: Elsevier. (Original work published 1964)

Lehmann, D., & Koukkou, M. (1974). Computer analysis of EEG wakefulness-sleep patterns during learning of novel and familiar sentences. *Electroencephalography and Clinical Neurophysiology, 37,* 73–84.

Leuba, C., & Bateman, D. (1952). Learning during sleep. *American Journal of Psychology, 65,* 301–302.

Levy, C. M., Collidge, F. L., & Stabb, L. V. (1972). Paired associate learning during EEG-defined sleep: A preliminary study. *Australian Journal of Psychology, 24,* 219–225.

Minard, J., Loiselle, R., Ingledue, E., & Duatlich, D. (1968). Discriminative electrooculogram deflections (EGDs) and heart rate (HR) pauses elicited during maintained sleep by stimulus significance. *Psychophysiology, 5,* 232.

Okuma, T., Nakamura, K., Hayashi, A., & Fujimori, M. (1966). Psychophysiological study on the depth of sleep in normal human subjects. *Electroencephalography and Clinical Neurophysiology, 21,* 140–147.

Oltman, P. K., Goodenough, D. R., Koulack, D., Maclin, E., Schroeder, H. R., & Flanagan, M. J. (1977). Short-term memory during Stage 2 sleep. *Psychophysiology, 14,* 439–444.

Oswald, I., Taylor, A. M., & Treisman, M. (1960). Discriminative responses to stimulation during human sleep. *Brain, 83,* 440–453.

Overton, D. A. (1984). State dependent learning and drug discriminations. In L. L. Iverson, S. D. Iverson, & S. H. Snyder (Eds.), *Handbook of psychopharmacology* (Vol. 18, pp. 59–127). New York: Plenum Press.

Peters, R., & McGee, R. (1982). Cigarette smoking and state-dependent memory. *Psychopharmacology, 76,* 232–235.

Prince, M. (1910). The mechanism and interpretation of dreams. *Journal of Abnormal Psychology, 19,* 137–195.

Richardson-Klavehn, A., & Bjork, R. A. (1988). Measures of memory. *Annual Review of Psychology, 39,* 475–543.

Rubin, F. (1968). *Current research in hypnopaedia.* New York: Elsevier.

Rubin, F. (1970). Learning and sleep. *Nature, 226,* 477.

Rubin, F. (1971). *Learning and sleep.* Bristol, England: Wright.

Schacter, D. L. (1987). Implicit memory: History and current status. *Journal of Experimental Psychology: Learning, Memory, and Cognition, 13,* 501–518.

Schacter, D. L., & Kihlstrom, J. F. (1989). Functional amnesia. In F. Boller & J. Grafman (Eds.), *Handbook of neuropsychology.* Amsterdam: Elsevier.

Schacter, D. L., & Tulving, E. (1982). Memory, amnesia, and the episodic/semantic distinction. In R. L. Isaacson & N. E. Spear (Eds.), *The expression of knowledge.* New York: Plenum Press.

Sheldrake, P., & Cormack, M. (1974). Dream recall and the menstrual cycle. *Journal of Psychosomatic Research, 18,* 347–350.

Simon, C. W., & Emmons, W. H. (1955). Learning during sleep? *Psychological Bulletin, 52,* 328–342.

Simon, C. W., & Emmons, W. H. (1956). Responses to material presented during various levels of sleep. *Journal of Experimental Psychology, 51,* 89–97.

Svyadoshch, A. M. (1968). The assimilation and memorization of speech during natural sleep. In F. Rubin (Ed.), *Current research in hypnopaedia* (A. Scott, Trans.) (pp. 91–117). New York: Elsevier. (Original work published 1962)

Tilley, A. J. (1979). Sleep learning during Stage 2 and REM sleep. *Biological Psychology, 9,* 155–161.

Watkins, M. J. (1979). Engrams as cuegrams and forgetting as cue overload: A cueing approach to the structure of memory. In C. R. Puff (Ed.), *Memory organization and structure.* New York: Academic Press.

Zavalova, N. D., Zukhar, V. P., & Petrov, Y. A. (1968). The question of hypnopaedia (preliminary communication). In F. Rubin (Ed.), *Current research in hypnopaedia* (A. Scott, Trans.) (pp. 145–151). New York: Elsevier. (Original work published 1964)

Zukhar', V. P., Kaplan, Y. Y., Maksimov, Y. A., & Pushkina, I. P. (1968). A collective experiment on hypnopaedia. In F. Rubin (Ed.), *Current research in hypnopaedia* (A. Scott, Trans.) (pp. 152–159). New York: Elsevier. (Original work published 1965)

CHAPTER 8

LUCID DREAMING:
PSYCHOPHYSIOLOGICAL STUDIES OF CONSCIOUSNESS DURING REM SLEEP

STEPHEN LaBERGE

Although we are usually not explicitly aware that we are dreaming while we are dreaming, at times a remarkable exception occurs, and we become conscious enough to realize that fact. "Lucid" dreamers (the term derives from van Eeden, 1913) report being able to remember the circumstances of waking life freely, to think clearly, and to act deliberately upon reflection, all while experiencing a dream world that seems vividly real (Green, 1968; LaBerge, 1985; Gackenbach & LaBerge, 1988). This contrasts with the usual characterization of dreams as states that typically evince no reflective awareness or true volition (Rechtschaffen, 1978).

Lucid dreaming is normally a rare experience. Though most people report having had a lucid dream at least once in their lives, only about 20% of the population reports having lucid dreams once a month or more (Snyder & Gackenbach, 1988).

Although most people have experienced lucid dreams, some theoreticians have considered them impossible and even absurd (e.g., Malcolm, 1959). In the absence of empirical evidence, most sleep researchers have been inclined to accept Hartmann's (1975) "impression" that lucid dreams are "not typical parts of dreaming thought, but rather brief arousals" (p. 74; see also Berger, 1977). Schwartz and Lefebvre (1973) noted that frequent transitory arousals are common during REM sleep and proposed that these "microawakenings" are the physiological basis for lucid dream reports. Although no one has found any evidence for this mechanism, their proposal has been the predominant opinion (cf. Foulkes, 1974) until the last few years.

LUCID DREAMING PHYSIOLOGICALLY VERIFIED

Empirical evidence began to appear in the late 1970s suggesting that lucid dreams occur during REM sleep. Based on standard sleep recordings of 2 subjects who reported a total of three lucid dreams upon awakening from REM periods, Ogilvie, Hunt, Sawicki, and McGowan (1978) cautiously concluded that "it may be that lucid dreams begin in REM." However, no proof was given that the reported lucid dreams had in fact occurred during the REM sleep immediately preceding the awakenings and reports. What was needed to establish the physiological status of lucid dreams unambiguously was a behavioral response that would signal to the experimenter the exact time at which the lucid dream was taking place.

LaBerge, Nagel, Dement, and Zarcone (1981) provided the necessary verification by instructing subjects to signal the onset of lucid dreams with specific dream actions that would be observable on a polygraph (i.e., eye movements and fist clenches). Using this approach, they reported that the occurrence of lucid dreaming during unequivocal REM sleep had been demonstrated for 5 subjects. After being instructed in the method of lucid dream induction (MILD) described by LaBerge (1980c), subjects were each recorded from 2 to 20 nights. In the course of the 34 nights of the study, 35 lucid dreams were reported subsequent to spontaneous awakening from various stages of sleep as follows: REM sleep, 32 times; non-REM (NREM) Stage 1 sleep, 2 times; the transition from NREM Stage 2 to REM sleep, 1 time. The subjects reported signaling during 30 of these lucid dreams. After each recording, the reports mentioning signals were submitted along with the respective polysomnograms to a judge uninformed of the times of the reports. In 24 cases (90%), the judge was able to select the appropriate 30-s epoch on the basis of correspondence between reported and observed signals. All signals associated with lucid dream reports occurred during epochs of unambiguous REM sleep scored according to the conventional criteria (Rechtschaffen & Kales, 1968).

A later analysis extending these data with 2 additional subjects and 20 more lucid dreams produced identical results (LaBerge, Nagel, Taylor, Dement, & Zarcone, 1981). LaBerge et al. argued that their investigations demonstrated that lucid dreaming usually (though perhaps not exclusively) occurs during REM sleep. This conclusion was supported by research carried out in several other laboratories (Dane, 1984; Fenwick et al., 1984; Hearne, 1978; Ogilvie, Hunt, Kushniruk, & Newman, 1983).

Ogilvie et al. (1983) reported that the physiological state preceding 14 spontaneous lucidity signals was unqualified REM in 12 (86%) of the cases; of the remaining 2 cases, 1 was reported to be "ambiguous" REM and the other was reported to be wakefulness. Hearne and Worsley collaborated on a pioneering study of lucid dreaming in which the latter spent 50 nonconsecutive

I am grateful to Ronald Hertel, the Institute for Human Development, the Mericos Foundation, and the Reality Foundation for financial support and to Lynne Levitan for editorial assistance.

nights in the Hull University sleep laboratory while the former monitored the polygraph. Worsley reported signaling in 8 lucid dreams, all of which were described by Hearne (1978) as having occurred during REM sleep.

However, demonstrations that the signaling of lucid dreams occurs during REM sleep raise another kind of question: What exactly do we mean by the assertion that lucid dreamers are "asleep?" Perhaps these "dreamers" are not really dreamers, as some have argued in the last century; or perhaps this "sleep" is not really sleep, as some have argued in this century. How do we know that lucid dreamers are really asleep when they signal? If we consider perception of the external world as a criterion of being awake (to the external world), we can conclude that they are actually asleep (to the external world) because, although they know they are in the laboratory, this knowledge is a matter of memory, not perception. Upon awakening, lucid dreamers report total immersion in the dream world and no sensory contact with the external world.

One might object that lucid dreamers are simply not attending to the environment; rather than being asleep, perhaps they are merely absorbed in their private fantasy worlds as are those, for example, who are deeply immersed in a novel or daydream. However, according to the reports of lucid dreamers (LaBerge, 1980b, 1985), if they deliberately attempt to feel the bedcovers they know they are sleeping in or try to hear the ticking of the clock they know is beside their bed, they fail to feel or hear anything except what they find in their dream worlds. Lucid dreamers are conscious of the absence of sensory input from the external world; therefore, on empirical grounds, they conclude that they are asleep.

Conversely, if subjects claim to have been awake while showing physiological signs of sleep (or vice versa), we might have cause to doubt their subjective reports. However, when the subjective accounts and objective physiological measures are in clear agreement (as they are here), it is embarrassingly awkward to assert (as some critics have done) that subjects who report being certain that they were asleep while showing physiological indications of unequivocal sleep were actually awake (cf. LaBerge, Nagel, Dement, & Zarcone, 1981).

Some critics have suggested that demand characteristics might account for our results. It is true that our subjects were under demand to have, signal, and report lucid dreams, but could demand alone account for their actions if they were not lucid in the first place? If they merely unconsciously signaled, we would have found REM periods with signals without subsequent reports of lucidity, but we did not. If they merely reported having signaled without actually having done so, we would have found reports without signals, which we did not. Further, by this account, where would the reported and observed signals have come from?

The evidence is clear: Lucid dreaming is an experiential and physiological reality; though perhaps paradoxical, it is clearly a phenomenon of sleep.

PHYSIOLOGICAL CHARACTERISTICS OF LUCID DREAMING

The preceding studies have shown that lucid dreams typically occur in REM sleep. However, REM sleep is a heterogeneous state that exhibits considerable variations in physiological activity, ordinarily distinguished by two distinct phases. In its most active form, REM is dominated by a striking variety of irregular and short-lived events such as muscular twitching, including the rapid eye movements that give the state one of its most common names. This variety of REM is referred to as *phasic,* whereas the relatively quiescent state remaining when rapid eye movements and other phasic events temporarily subside is referred to as *tonic.* On first thought, one might expect lucid dreams to be associated with decreased phasic activity (Pivik, 1986). However, research described later has shown lucid dreaming to be associated instead with increased phasic activity.

LaBerge, Levitan, and Dement (1986) analyzed physiological data from 76 signal-verified lucid dreams (SVLDs) of 13 subjects. The polysomnograms corresponding to each of the SVLDs were scored for sleep stages, and every SVLD REM period was divided into 30-s epochs aligned with the lucidity onset signal. For each epoch, sleep stage was scored, and rapid eye movements (EMs) were counted; if scalp skin-potential (SP) responses were observable as artifacts in the electroencephalograph (EEG), these were also counted. Heart rate (HR) and respiration rate (RR) were determined for SVLDs recorded with these measures.

For the first lucid epoch, beginning with the initiation of the signal, the sleep stage was unequivocal REM in 70 cases (92%). The remaining 6 SVLDs were less than 30-s long and, hence, were technically unscorable according to standard criteria (Rechtschaffen & Kales, 1968). For these cases, the entire SVLD was scored as a single epoch; with this modification, all SVLDs qualified as REM. The lucid dream signals were followed by an average of 115 s (range = 5–490) of uninterrupted REM sleep. Physiological comparisons of EM, HR, RR, and SP for lucid versus nonlucid epochs revealed that the lucid epochs of the SVLD REM periods had significantly higher levels of physiological activation than the preceding epochs of nonlucid REM from the same REM period. Similarly, H reflex amplitude was lower during lucid than nonlucid REM (Brylowski, Levitan, & LaBerge, 1989).

To study the temporal variations of physiology as they correlated with the development and initiation of lucidity, for each SVLD REM period, the physiological variables were converted to standard scores and averaged across dreams and subjects. Figure 1 shows the resultant mean standard scores for the 5 min before and the 5 min after the initiation of lucidity. Note the highly significant increases in physiological activation during the 30 s before and after lucidity onset.

Physiological data (EM, RR, HR, and SP) were also collected for 61 control nonlucid REM periods, derived from the same 13 subjects, to allow comparison with SVLDs. Mean values for EM and SP were significantly higher for REM periods with lucid dreams than nonlucid control REM periods (RR and HR did not differ).

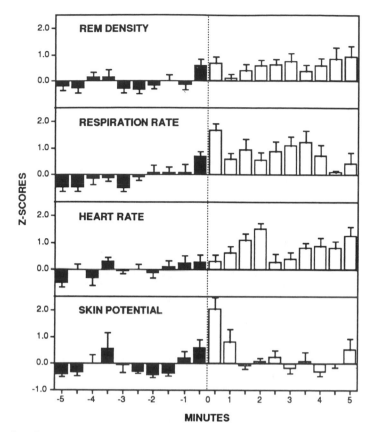

Figure 1   Grand mean z-scores and standard errors for REM density (EM), respiration rate (RR), heart rate (HR), and scalp skin potential responses (SP) during the 5 min before the onset of lucidity (black bars) and the 5 min after the onset of lucidity (white bars). Epochs are 30 s in length and the dotted line represents the signaled onset of lucidity. Sample sizes vary with variable and epoch, but all values are averaged across lucid dreams and subjects.

Given the finding that lucid dreams reliably occur during activated (phasic) REM, measures of central nervous system activation, such as eye movement density, should contribute something to the pattern of lucid dream distribution. Because it has been observed that eye movement density starts at a low level at the beginning of REM periods and increases until it reaches a peak after approximately 5–7 min (Aserinsky, 1971), we (LaBerge et al., 1986) hypothesized that lucid dream probability should follow a parallel development. Accordingly, we found that mean eye movement density correlated positively and significantly with lucid dream probability ($r = .66, p < .01$).

Lucid dreams have most commonly been reported to occur late in the sleep cycle (Green, 1968). LaBerge et al. (1986) tested this hypothesis by first determining for each of their 12 subjects the time of night that divided their total REM time into two equal parts. All but 1 of the subjects had more lucid dreams in the second half of their REM time than in the first half (binomial

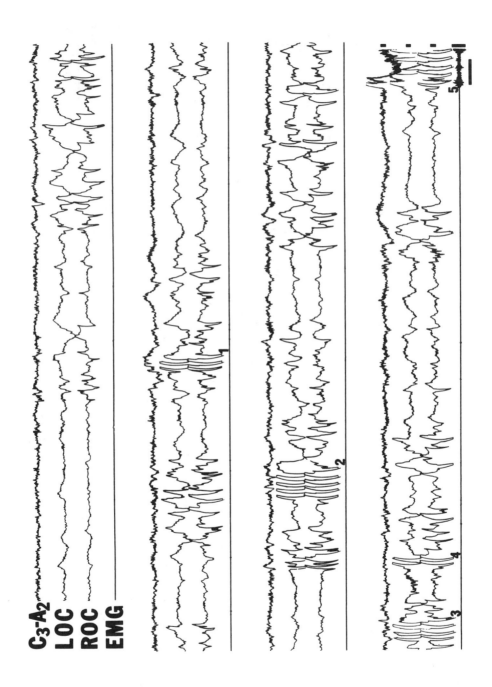

test, $p < .01$). For the combined sample, relative lucidity probability was calculated for REM Periods 1–6 of the night by dividing the total number of lucid dreams observed in a given REM period by the corresponding total time in the REM stage for the same REM period. A regression analysis clearly demonstrated that relative lucidity probability was a linear function of ordinal REM period number ($r = .98$, $p < .0001$).

Lucid dreams are initiated in two distinct ways. Subjects usually report having been in the midst of a dream when a bizarre occurrence causes sufficient reflection to yield the realization that they are dreaming. Less frequently, subjects report having briefly awakened from a dream and then, falling back asleep, directly entering the dream with no (or very little) break in consciousness (Green, 1968; LaBerge, 1985). Here is an example of a wake-initiated lucid dream:

> I was lying awake in bed late in the morning listening to the sound of
> running water in the adjoining bathroom. Presently an image of the
> ocean appeared, dim at first like my usual waking imagery. But its
> vividness rapidly increased while, at the same time, the sound of running
> water diminished; the intensity of the internal image and external sound
> seemed to alter inversely (as if one changed a stereo balance control from
> one channel to the other). In a few seconds, I found myself at the seashore
> standing between my mother and a girl who seemed somehow familiar. I
> could no longer hear the sound of the bath water, but only the roar of the
> dream sea. (LaBerge, 1980b, p. 85)

Note that the subject was continuously conscious during the transition from wakefulness to sleep. This fact suggests that Foulkes (1985) was overstating the case by claiming that it is "a necessary part of the experience we call 'sleep' that we lose a directive and reflective self. You can't fall asleep, or be asleep, if your waking self is still regulating and reflecting upon your conscious mental state" (p. 42).

Because lucid dreams initiated in these two ways ought to differ physiologically in at least one respect (i.e., an awakening preceding one but not the other), the SVLDs were dichotomously classified as either wake-initiated (WILD) or dream-initiated (DILD), depending on whether or not the reports

---

Figure 2 A typical dream-initiated lucid dream (DILD). Four channels of physiological data (central EEG [C_3-A_2], left and right eye-movements [LOC and ROC], and chin muscle tone [EMG]) from the last 8 min of a 30 min REM period are shown. Upon awakening, the subject reported having made five eye movement signals (labeled 1–5 in figure). The first signal (1, LRLR) marked the onset of lucidity. Note the skin potential artifacts in the EEG at this point. During the following 90 s the subject "flew about" exploring his dream world until he believed he had awakened, at which point he made the signal for awakening (2, LRLRLRLR). After another 90 s, the subject realized he was still dreaming and signaled (3) with three pairs of eye movements. Realizing that this was too many, he correctly signaled with two pairs (4). Finally, upon awakening 100 s later he signaled appropriately (5, LRLRLRLR). Calibrations are 50 μV and 5 s.

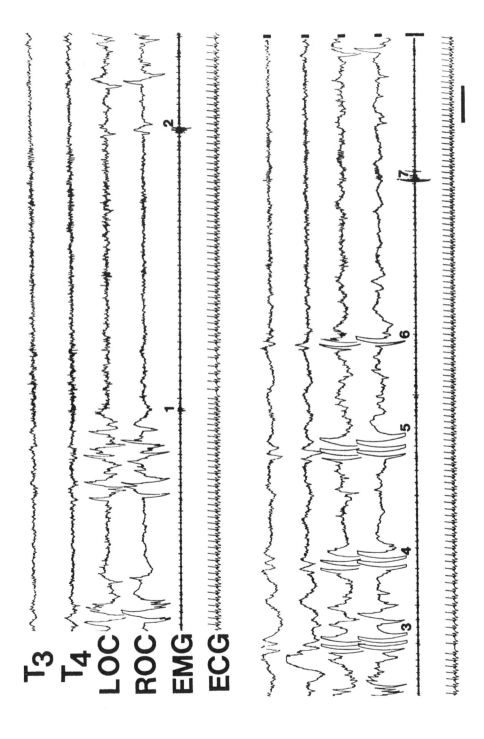

mentioned a transient awakening in which the subject consciously perceived the external environment before reentering the dream state.

Fifty-five (72%) of the SVLDs were classified as DILDs, and the remaining 21 (28%) were classified as WILDs. For all 13 subjects, DILDs were more common than WILDs (binomial test, $p < .0001$). As expected, compared with DILDs, WILDs were more frequently immediately preceded by physiological indications of awakening, $\chi^2(1, N = 76) = 38.3, p < .0001$, establishing the validity of classifying lucid dreams in this manner. See Figures 2 and 3 for illustrations of these two types of lucid dream.

As was mentioned earlier, momentary intrusions of wakefulness occur very commonly during the normal course of REM sleep, and Schwartz and Lefebvre (1973) proposed that lucid dreaming occurs during these microawakenings. However, LaBerge, Nagel, Taylor, Dement, & Zarcone's (1981) and LaBerge et al.'s (1986) data indicate that, while lucid dreams do not take place during interludes of wakefulness within REM periods, a minority of lucid dreams (WILDs) are initiated from these moments of transitory arousal and continue in subsequent undisturbed REM sleep.

To summarize, an elevated level of central nervous system (CNS) activation seems to be a necessary condition for the occurrence of lucid dreams. Evidently, the high level of cognitive function involved in lucid dreaming requires a correspondingly high level of neuronal activation. In terms of Antrobus's (1986) adaptation of Anderson's (1983) ACT* model of cognition to dreaming, working memory capacity is proportional to cognitive activation, which in turn is proportional to cortical activation. Becoming lucid requires an adequate level of working memory to activate the presleep intention to recognize that one is dreaming. This level of cortical and cognitive activation is apparently available only during phasic REM.

PSYCHOPHYSIOLOGICAL RELATIONS DURING REM SLEEP

Psychologists attempting to apply rigorous scientific methodology to the study of such phenomena as mental imagery, hallucinations, dreaming, and conscious processes in general face a major challenge: The most direct account available of the private events occurring in a person's mind is his or her own

---

Figure 3 A typical wake-initiated lucid dream (WILD) following a transient awakening during REM. Six channels of physiological data (left and right temporal EEG [T_3 and T_4; C_z reference], left and right eye-movements [LOC and ROC], chin muscle tone [EMG], and electrocardiogram [ECG]) from the last 3 min of a 14 min REM period are shown. The subject awoke at 1 and after 40 s returned to REM sleep at 2, realized he was dreaming 15 s later, and signaled at 3. Next he carried out the agreed-upon experimental task in his lucid dream, singing between signals 3 and 4, and counting between signals 4 and 5. This allowed comparison of left and right hemisphere activation during the two tasks (LaBerge & Dement, 1982b). Note the heart-rate acceleration–deceleration pattern at awakening (1) and at lucidity onset (3), and the skin potential artifacts in the EEG (particularly T_4) at lucidity onset (3). Calibrations are 50 μV and 5 s.

subjective report. Unfortunately, subjective reports are difficult to verify objectively, and introspection is far from an unbiased and direct process of observation. Two strategies are likely to increase our confidence in the reliability of subjective reports: (a) the use of highly trained (and in the context of dream research, lucid) subjects who are skillful reporters, and (b) the use of the psychophysiological approach, which proposes that the convergent agreement of physiological measures and subjective reports provides a degree of validation to the latter (Stoyva & Kamiya, 1968).

Indeed, the psychophysiological approach was responsible for the golden age of dream research in the decades following the discovery of REM sleep (Aserinsky & Kleitman, 1953) and the subsequent association of REM with dreaming (Dement & Kleitman, 1957). Although the psychophysiological paradigm of dream research has yielded an abundant harvest for many years (see Arkin, Antrobus, & Ellman, 1978), it possesses a fatal flaw: As long as the subjects are nonlucid, the researcher has no way of making certain that the subjects will dream about what the researcher might like to study. Presleep manipulations producing reliable effects on dream content have not been highly successful (Tart, 1988). One can only wait and hope that, eventually, a dream report will unearth what one is looking for. This is really no better than a shot-in-the-dark approach, and some researchers have proposed abandoning the psychophysiological method in favor of a purely psychological approach. Foulkes (1981) wrote that "psychophysiological correlation research now appears to offer such a low rate of return for effort expended as not to be a wise place for dream psychology to continue to commit much of its limited resources" (p. 249). This conclusion may well be justified, but only insofar as it refers to the psychophysiological approach as it is traditionally practiced, using nonlucid subjects. The use of lucid dreamers overcomes the basic difficulty of the old methodology and may revitalize the psychophysiological approach to dream research.

The fact that lucid dreamers can remember to perform predetermined actions and can signal to the laboratory suggested to LaBerge (1980b) a new paradigm for dream research: Lucid dreamers, he proposed, "could carry out diverse dream experiments marking the exact time of particular dream events, allowing the derivation of precise psychophysiological correlations and the methodical testing of hypotheses" (LaBerge, Nagel, Dement, & Zarcone, 1981, p. 727). This strategy has been put into practice in a number of studies that are summarized later.

How long do dreams take? This question has intrigued humanity for many centuries. A traditional answer is that dreams take very little or no time at all, as in the case of Maury's famous dream in which he somehow got mixed up in a long series of adventures during the French Revolution and finally lost his head on the guillotine, at which point he awoke to find that the headboard had fallen on his neck. He therefore supposed that the lengthy dream had been produced in a flash by the painful stimulus. The idea that dreams occur in the moment of awakening has found supporters over the years.

We have straightforwardly approached the problem of dream time by asking subjects to estimate 10-s intervals (by counting "one thousand and one, one thousand and two," etc.) during their lucid dreams. Signals marking the beginning and end of the subjective intervals allowed comparison with objective time. In all cases, time estimates during the lucid dreams were very close to the actual time between signals (LaBerge, 1980b, 1985). However, this finding does not rule out the possibility of time distortion effects under some circumstances.

The data reported by LaBerge, Nagel, Dement, and Zarcone (1981) and LaBerge, Nagel, Taylor, Dement, and Zarcone (1981) indicate that there is a very direct and reliable relation between the gaze shift reported in lucid dreams and the direction of polygraphically recorded eye movements. The results obtained for lucid dreams (see also Dane, 1984; Fenwick et al., 1984; Hearne, 1978; Ogilvie, Hunt, Tyson, Lucescu, & Jeakins, 1982) are much stronger than the generally weak correlations obtained by previous investigators testing the hypothesis that the dreamer's eyes move with his or her hallucinated dream gaze, who relied on the chance occurrence of a highly recognizable eye movement pattern that was readily matchable to the subject's reported dream activity (e.g., Roffwarg, Dement, Muzio, & Fisher, 1962).

LaBerge (1985) reported related experiments in which 2 subjects tracked the tip of their fingers moving slowly from left to right during four conditions: (a) awake, eyes open; (b) awake, eyes closed, mental imagery; (c) lucid dreaming; and (d) imagination ("dream eyes closed") during lucid dreaming. The subjects showed saccadic eye movements in the two imagination conditions (b and d) and smooth tracking eye movements during dreamed or actual tracking (a and c).

In another study, LaBerge and Dement (1982b) demonstrated the possibility of voluntary control of respiration during lucid dreaming. They recorded 3 lucid dreamers who were asked either to breathe rapidly or to hold their breath (in their lucid dreams), marking the interval of altered respiration with eye movement signals. The subjects reported successfully carrying out the agreed-upon tasks a total of nine times and, in every case, a judge was able to predict correctly on the basis of the polygraph recordings which of the two patterns had been executed (binomial test, $p < .002$).

Evidence of the voluntary control of other muscle groups during REM was found by LaBerge, Nagel, Dement, and Zarcone (1981) while testing a variety of lucidity signals. They observed that a sequence of left and right dream-fist clenches resulted in a corresponding sequence of left and right forearm twitches as measured by electromyograph (EMG). However, the amplitude of the twitches bore an unreliable relation to the subjective intensity of the dreamed action. Because all skeletal muscle groups except those that govern eye movements and breathing are profoundly inhibited during REM sleep, it is to be expected that most muscular responses to dreamed movements will be feeble. Nonetheless, these responses faithfully reflect the motor patterns of the original dream. Similar observations were made by Fenwick et al. (1984).

Following reports of cognitive task dependency of lateralization of EEG alpha activity in the waking state by many researchers, LaBerge and Dement (1982a) undertook a pilot study to demonstrate the feasibility of similar investigations in the lucid dream state. The two tasks selected for comparison were dreamed singing and dreamed counting, activities expected to result in relatively greater engagement of the subjects' left and right cerebral hemispheres, respectively.

Integrated alpha band EEG activity was derived from electrodes placed over right and left temporal lobes while 4 subjects sang and estimated 10 s by counting in their lucid dreams (marking the beginning and end of each task by eye movement signals). The results supported the hypothesized lateralization of alpha activity: The right hemisphere was more active than the left during singing; during counting, the reverse was true. These shifts were similar to those observed during actual singing and counting. In contrast, a control condition with imagined singing and counting showed no significant laterality shifts. Because of the small number of subjects, the conclusions of this study must be regarded as suggestive at best.

LaBerge and Dement (1982a, 1982b) noted an important implication of their results for the interpretation of EEG alpha activity during REM sleep. Because continuous alpha activity occurs when a subject awakens, sleep researchers have usually assumed that increased alpha activity in the context of sleep is always a sign of wakefulness or relative cortical activation. The findings just discussed suggest the contrary: Alpha activity during REM sleep is, as in waking, inversely related to cortical activation. When a person awakens from a vivid dream to a dark room, his cortical (at least occipital) activation has decreased, not increased, with the resultant appearance of elevated alpha power.

In this view, it is a straightforward prediction that occipital alpha power during REM sleep will correlate negatively with subsequently reported dream vividness. This could provide the proper explanation for the finding that awakenings following REM periods with high levels of alpha activity are more likely to yield "thinking" reports than awakenings from low-alpha REM periods which yield more "dreaming" reports (Antrobus, Dement, & Fisher, 1964).

Sexual activity is a rather commonly reported theme of lucid dreams (LaBerge, 1985; Garfield, 1979). LaBerge, Greenleaf, and Kedzierski (1983) undertook a pilot study to determine the extent to which subjectively experienced sexual activity during REM lucid dreaming would be reflected in physiological responses.

Sixteen channels of physiological data, including EEG, electrooculogram (EOG), EMG, respiration, skin conductance level (SCL), heart rate, vaginal EMG (VEMG), and vaginal pulse amplitude (VPA), were recorded from a single subject. The experimental protocol called for her to make specific eye movement signals at the following points: When she realized she was dreaming (i.e., the onset of the lucid dream), when she began sexual activity (in the dream), and when she experienced orgasm.

The subject reported a lucid dream in which she carried out the experimental task exactly as agreed upon. Data analysis revealed a significant correspondence between her subjective report and all but one of the autonomic measures; during the 15-s orgasm epoch, mean levels for VEMG activity, VPA, SCL, and respiration rate reached their highest values and were significantly elevated compared with means for other REM epochs. Contrary to expectation, heart rate increased only slightly and nonsignificantly.

IMPLICATIONS FOR RESEARCH ON SLEEP AND COGNITION

Lucid dreaming presents conceptual difficulties for certain traditional beliefs about sleep and about the presumed limitations of dream mentation. In a certain sense, the anomalous appearance of lucid dreaming parallels that of the state that has been called "paradoxical sleep." The discovery of REM sleep required the expansion of our concept of sleep. The evidence we have reviewed associating lucid dreaming with REM sleep seems to require a similar expansion of our concept of dreaming as well as a clarification of our concept of sleep.

Fenwick et al. (1984) showed that a subject was able to perceive and respond to environmental stimuli (electrical shocks) without awakening from his lucid dream. This result raises a theoretical issue: If we take perception of the external world to be the essential criterion for wakefulness, then Worsley must have been at least partially awake. On the other hand, when environmental stimuli are incorporated into dreams without producing any subjective or physiological indications of arousal, it seems that the perception must have occurred during sleep.

Furthermore, it may be possible, as LaBerge (1980a) suggested, for one sense to remain functional and awake while others fall asleep. Similarly, Antrobus, Antrobus, and Fisher (1965) argued that "the question—awake or asleep—is not a particularly useful one. Even though we have two discrete words—sleep and wakefulness—this does not mean that the behavior associated with the words can be forced into two discrete categories. . . . not only do sleeping and waking shade gradually into one another but there is only limited agreement among the various physiological and subjective operations that discriminate between sleeping and waking. At any given moment, all systems of the organism are not necessarily equally asleep or awake." (pp. 398–399)

As long as we continue to consider wakefulness and sleep a simple dichotomy, we will lie in a Procrustian bed that is bound at times to be most uncomfortable. There must be degrees of being awake, just as there are degrees of being asleep (i.e., the conventional sleep stages). Before we find our way out of this muddle, we will probably need to characterize a wider variety of states of consciousness than the few that are currently distinguished (e.g., dreaming, sleeping, waking, etc.).

It may be helpful to consider lucidity from a cognitive–developmental perspective. According to Piaget (1926), children pass through three stages of understanding of the concept *dream*. In the first stage, they believe that dreams take place in the same external world as all other experiences. In the second stage, children treat dreams as if they were partially external and partially internal. This transitional stage gives way to the third stage in which children recognize the dream is entirely internal in nature, a purely mental experience.

These foregoing developmental stages refer to how children think about dreams when they are awake. While asleep and dreaming, children, and also adults, tend to remain at the first stage, implicitly assuming that the dream events are external reality. Out-of-body experiences, with a contradictory mixture of material and mental (external and internal), may provide examples of the second stage (LaBerge, Levitan, Brylowski, & Dement, 1988). In the fully lucid dream, the dreamer attains the third stage, realizing that the dream world is distinct from the physical world.

Foulkes (1982, 1985) has emphasized the idea that the growth of the mind, whether dreaming or awake, shows parallel degrees of development: "there are 'stages' of dream development which individual children reliably pass through one after the other, and that the precise age at which they reach a new stage is at least partially predictable from independent measures of their waking mental development" (1985, p. 137).

In this view, lucid dreaming represents what ought to be a normal ability in adults. If this is correct, why are lucid dreams so rare, especially in cases such as nightmares, where lucidity would be extremely helpful and rewarding? A possible answer may be found by comparing lucid dreaming with another cognitive skill, language acquisition. All normal adults speak and understand at least one language. But how many would do so if they were never taught? Unfortunately, in this culture, with few exceptions, we are not taught to dream.

LaBerge (1980c) demonstrated that lucid dreaming is a learnable skill and that there are a variety of techniques available for inducing lucid dreams (LaBerge, 1985; Price & Cohen, 1988). LaBerge and colleagues have experimented with methods for helping dreamers realize that they are dreaming by means of external cues applied during REM sleep, which, if incorporated into dreams, can remind dreamers that they are dreaming (LaBerge, 1980b). They have tested a variety of stimuli, including tape recordings of the phrase "this is a dream" (LaBerge, Owens, Nagel, & Dement, 1981), conditioned tactile stimuli (Rich, 1985), olfactory stimuli (LaBerge, Brylowski, & Levitan, unpublished data, 1986), and light (LaBerge, Levitan, Rich, & Dement, 1988). The most promising results so far have resulted from light stimuli.

The psychophysiological studies reviewed here all support the following picture: During REM dreaming, the events we experience (or seem to experience) are the results of patterns of CNS activity that produce in turn effects on our autonomic nervous systems (ANS) and bodies, which are to some extent modified by the specific conditions of active sleep but are still homomorphic to the effects that would occur if we were actually to experience the corresponding events while awake.

This conclusion may need further qualification and explanation. Although the events we appear to perceive in dreams are illusory, our feelings in response to dream content are real. Indeed, most of the events we experience in dreams are real; when we experience feelings like anxiety or ecstasy in dreams, we really do feel anxious or ecstatic at the time. When we think in dreams, we really do think (whether clearly or not is another matter). If we think in our dreams that Monday comes before Sunday, it is not the case, as some philosophers (e.g., Malcolm, 1959) assert, that we have only dreamed we thought; we may have thought incorrectly (to the usual way of thinking), but we thought nonetheless.

If we vividly imagined a detailed sequence of movements, like walking around the room, it is probable that motor areas of the brain would be activated in the same pattern that is activated in actual walking. However, they would presumably be less activated than when walking. Otherwise, what would prevent us from actually walking when we imagined doing so?

In REM sleep, a spinal paralysis causes the muscles of locomotion and vocalization to fail to completely execute the action orders programmed by the brain. Thus, in REM, unlike the waking state, nothing impedes the brain from issuing sequences of motor commands at normal levels of activation, and this probably contributes to the experienced reality of dreamed action.

As for the afferent side of the equation, a great deal of evidence suggests that imagery uses the same neural systems as perception in the corresponding sensory mode (e.g., see Farah, 1988; Finke, 1980). In this view, the essential difference between a perception and a corresponding image is how the identical neural system acquires sufficient activation to produce a conscious experience. In the case of perception, neural excitation (and the resultant experience) is generated by external input, driving activation of the particular schema to-be-perceived in a largely bottom-up process. In the case of imagining (likewise, hallucinating or dreaming), the experienced image is generated internally by top-down processes activating the appropriate neural network (schema).

Imaginations and perceptions are normally distinguishable by the fact that images are usually much less vivid than perceptions. Normally, perceptions seem real and images seem imaginary. How real something appears depends mainly on its relative vividness, and experienced vividness is probably a function of the intensity of neural activation. Thus, we may conjecture that images usually involve a lesser degree of neural activation than the corresponding perceptions, and this results in a lesser degree of experiential reality for imagination. At least two factors contribute to this state of affairs: One is that, while we are awake, sensory input produces much higher levels of activation than imaginary input. Imagination interferes with perception in the same modality (Perky, 1910; Segal, 1971), and we may suppose the reverse is true as well. Another more speculative factor favoring perceptual processes over imagination in the waking state is the existence of a neural system to inhibit the activation (vividness) of memory images while perception is active. Evolutionary considerations make such a system likely; it would obviously be extremely maladaptive for an organism to mistake a current perceptual image of a predator for the memory of one (LaBerge, 1985). Mandell (1980) implicated serotonergic neurons as part of a system that normally inhibits vivid images (hallucinations) but is itself inhibited in REM sleep, allowing dreamed perceptions (i.e., images) to appear as vividly real as perceptions. In REM, sensory input is also actively suppressed to prevent competition from perceptual processes.

Perhaps this explains in part why we are so inclined to mistake our dreams for reality: To the functional systems of neuronal activity that construct our experiential world (model), dreaming of perceiving or doing something is equivalent to actually perceiving or doing it.

References

Anderson, J. R. (1983). *The architecture of cognition.* Cambridge, MA: Harvard University Press.

Antrobus, J. S. (1986). Dreaming: Cortical activation and perceptual thresholds. *Journal of Mind and Behavior, 7,* 193–212.

Antrobus, J. S., Antrobus, J. S., & Fisher, C. (1965). Discrimination of dreaming and nondreaming sleep. *Archives of General Psychiatry, 12,* 395–401.

Antrobus, J. S., Dement, W., & Fisher, C. (1964). Patterns of dreaming and dream recall: An EEG study. *Journal of Abnormal and Social Psychology, 69,* 244–252.

Arkin, A., Antrobus, J., & Ellman, S. (Eds.). (1978). *The mind in sleep.* Hillsdale, NJ: Erlbaum.

Aserinsky, E. (1971). Rapid eye movement density and pattern in the sleep of young adults. *Psychophysiology, 8,* 361–375.

Aserinsky, E., & Kleitman, N. (1953). Regularly occurring periods of eye motility and concomitant phenomena during sleep. *Science, 118,* 273–274.

Berger, R. (1977). Psyclosis: *The circularity of experience.* San Francisco: Freeman.

Brylowski, A., Levitan, L., & LaBerge, S. (1989). H-reflex suppression and autonomic activation during lucid REM sleep: A case study. *Sleep, 12,* 374–378.

Dane, J. (1984). *An empirical evaluation of two techniques for lucid dream induction.* Unpublished doctoral dissertation, Georgia State University.

Dement, W., & Kleitman, N. (1957). Cyclic variations in EEG during sleep and their relation to eye movements, body motility, and dreaming. *Electroencephalography and Clinical Neurophysiology, 9,* 673–690.

Farah, M. J. (1988). Is visual imagery really visual? Overlooked evidence from neurophysiology. *Psychological Review, 95,* 307–317.

Fenwick, P., Schatzman, M., Worsley, A., Adams, J., Stone, S., & Baker, A. (1984). Lucid dreaming: Correspondence between dreamed and actual events in one subject during REM sleep. *Biological Psychology, 18,* 243–252.

Finke, R. A. (1980). Levels of equivalence in imagery and perception. *Psychological Review, 87,* 113–132.

Foulkes, D. (1974). [Review of Schwartz and Lefebvre (1973)]. *Sleep Research, 3,* 113.

Foulkes, D. (1981). Dreams and dream research. In W. Koella (Ed.), *Sleep 1980* (pp. 246–257). Basel, Switzerland: Karger.

Foulkes, D. (1982). A cognitive-psychological model of dream production. *Sleep, 5,* 169–187.

Foulkes, D. (1985). *Dreaming: A cognitive-psychological analysis.* Hillsdale, NJ: Erlbaum.

Gackenbach, J., & LaBerge, S. (1988). *Conscious mind, sleeping brain.* New York: Plenum Press.

Garfield, P. (1979). *Pathway to ecstasy.* New York: Holt, Rhinehart, & Winston.

Green, C. (1968). *Lucid dreams.* London: Hamish Hamilton.

Hartmann, E. (1975). Dreams and other hallucinations: An approach to the underlying mechanism. In R. K. Siegal & L. J. West (Eds.), *Hallucinations* (pp. 71–79). New York: Wiley.

Hearne, K. M. T. (1978). *Lucid dreams: An electrophysiological and psychological study.* Unpublished doctoral dissertation, University of Liverpool.

LaBerge, S. (1980a). Induction of lucid dreams. *Sleep Research, 9,* 138.

LaBerge, S. (1980b). Lucid dreaming: An exploratory study of consciousness during sleep (Doctoral dissertation, Stanford University, 1980). *Dissertation Abstracts International, 41,* 05B-1966. (University Microfilms International No. 80-24, 691).

LaBerge, S. (1980c). Lucid dreaming as a learnable skill: A case study. *Perceptual and Motor Skills, 51,* 1039–1042.

LaBerge, S. (1985). *Lucid dreaming.* Los Angeles: Tarcher.

LaBerge, S., & Dement, W. C. (1982a). Lateralization of alpha activity for dreamed singing and counting during REM sleep. *Psychophysiology, 19,* 331–332.

LaBerge, S., & Dement, W. C. (1982b). Voluntary control of respiration during REM sleep. *Sleep Research, 11,* 107.

LaBerge, S., Greenleaf, W., & Kedzierski, B. (1983). Physiological responses to dreamed sexual activity during lucid REM sleep. *Psychophysiology, 20,* 454–455.

LaBerge, S., Levitan, L., Brylowski, A., & Dement, W. (1988). "Out-of-body" experiences occurring during REM sleep. *Sleep Research, 17,* 115.

LaBerge, S., Levitan, L., & Dement, W. C. (1986). Lucid dreaming: Physiological correlates of consciousness during REM sleep. *Journal of Mind and Behavior, 7,* 251–258.

LaBerge, S., Levitan, L., Rich, R., & Dement, W. (1988). Induction of lucid dreaming by light stimulation during REM sleep. *Sleep Research, 17,* 104.

LaBerge, S., Nagel, L., Dement, W. C., & Zarcone, V., Jr. (1981). Lucid dreaming verified by volitional communication during REM sleep. *Perceptual and Motor Skills, 52,* 727–732.

LaBerge, S., Nagel, L., Taylor, W., Dement, W. C., & Zarcone, V., Jr. (1981). Psychophysiological correlates of the initiation of lucid dreaming. *Sleep Research, 10,* 149.

LaBerge, S., Owens, J., Nagel, L., & Dement, W. (1981). "This is a dream": Induction of lucid dreams by verbal suggestion during REM sleep. *Sleep Research, 10,* 150.

Malcolm, N. (1959). *Dreaming.* London: Routledge.

Mandell, A. J. (1980). Toward a psychobiology of transcendence: God in the brain. In J. M. Davidson & R. J. Davidson (Eds.), *The psychobiology of consciousness.* New York: Plenum Press.

Ogilvie, R., Hunt, H., Kushniruk, A., & Newman, J. (1983). Lucid dreams and the arousal continuum. *Sleep Research, 12,* 182.

Ogilvie, R., Hunt, H., Sawicki, C., & McGowan, K. (1978). Searching for lucid dreams. *Sleep Research, 7,* 165.

Ogilvie, R., Hunt, H., Tyson, P. D., Lucescu, M. L., & Jeakins, D. B. (1982). Lucid dreaming and alpha activity: A preliminary report. *Perceptual and Motor Skills, 55,* 795–808.

Perky, C. W. (1910). An experimental study of imagination. *American Journal of Psychology, 21,* 422–452.

Piaget, J. (1926). *The child's conception of the world.* New York: Harcourt, Brace.

Pivik, R. T. (1986). Sleep: Physiology and psychophysiology. In M. G. H. Coles, E. Donchin, & S. Porges (Eds.), *Psychophysiology: Systems, processes, and applications* (pp. 378–406). New York: Guilford Press.

Price, R. F., & Cohen, D. B. (1988). Lucid dream induction: An empirical evaluation. In J. Gackenbach & S. LaBerge (Eds.), *Conscious mind, dreaming brain* (pp. 105–154). New York: Plenum Press.

Rechtschaffen, A. (1978). The single-mindedness and isolation of dreams. *Sleep, 1,* 97–109.

Rechtschaffen, A., & Kales, A. (Eds.). (1968). *A manual of standardized terminology, techniques and scoring system for sleep stages of human subjects.* Bethesda, MD: HEW Neurological Information Network.

Rich, R. (1985). *The induction of lucid dreams by tactile stimulation during REM sleep.* Unpublished honors thesis.

Roffwarg, H., Dement, W. C., Muzio, J., & Fisher, C. (1962). Dream imagery: Relationship to rapid eye movements of sleep. *Archives of General Psychiatry, 7,* 235–238.

Schwartz, B. A., & Lefebvre, A. (1973). Contacts véille/P.M.O.: II. Les P.M.O. morcelées [Conjunction of waking and REM sleep: II. Fragmented REM periods]. *Revue d'Electroencephalographie et de Neurophysiologie Clinique, 3,* 165–176.

Segal, S. J. (1971). Processing of the stimulus in imagery and perception. In S. J. Segal (Ed.), *Imagery: Current cognitive approaches* (pp. 73–100). New York: Academic Press.

Snyder, T., & Gackenbach, J. (1988). In J. Gackenbach & S. LaBerge (Eds.), *Conscious mind, dreaming brain* (pp. 221–259). New York: Plenum Press.

Stoyva, J., & Kamiya, J. (1968). Electrophysiological studies of dreaming as the prototype of a new strategy in the study of consciousness. *Psychological Review, 75,* 192–205.

Tart, C. (1988). From spontaneous event to lucidity: A review of attempts to consciously control nocturnal dreaming. In J. Gackenbach & S. LaBerge (Eds.), *Conscious mind, dreaming brain* (pp. 67–103). New York: Plenum Press.

van Eeden, F. (1913). A study of dreams. *Proceedings of the Society for Psychical Research, 26,* 431–461.

CHAPTER 9

COGNITIVE PROCESSING AND GENERAL ANESTHESIA

LES GOLDMANN

In this chapter, I will (a) draw comparisons between sleep and general anesthesia and (b) present evidence for cognitive processing under general anesthesia. To those familiar with general anesthesia, it may be puzzling that this topic is included in a conference devoted to sleep and cognition. Although anesthetists and surgeons speak of putting the patient "to sleep," the two states are worlds apart, both physiologically and psychologically.

Before noting these differences, let me explain why cognitive processing under general anesthesia may be of interest to this audience. First, because it is difficult, if not impossible, to know whether a sleeper or an anesthetized patient is phenomenally aware, research in each area provides ideas and methods that are of mutual benefit. Second, many authors have referred (I believe mistakenly) to instances of the recall of perioperative events as dreams. Although these instances may or may not be dreams, it is possible that they are influenced in a manner similar to dream recall. And finally, increasing evidence shows that patients under general anesthesia continue to hear, process, and respond to auditory input. Responses to this input bear comparison to those displayed by sleeping subjects.

GENERAL ANESTHESIA AND SLEEP

General anesthesia is not sleep. Lunn (1982, p. 66) defined *sleep* as a physiological coma and *general anesthesia* as a pharmacological coma. Physiologically, anesthesia resembles non-REM (NREM) sleep, with increased activity in the sympathetic nervous system and cortical depression. Electroencephalograph (EEG) and electromyograph (EMG) recordings during anesthesia bear some resemblances to NREM sleep. However, EEG recordings are dramatically effected by differing drug combinations, which makes it difficult or impossible both to assess the depth of anesthesia and to make consistent comparisons with sleep. A flat EEG, as might be found with barbiturate induction, for example, does not change the auditory evoked response to a stimulus at the cortex.

Patients are often given anticholinergics that interfere with the transition from NREM to REM sleep. These factors may explain why patients almost uniformly report that no time has passed and that REM-like dreams are rare. In addition to changes in time perception, patients often report feelings of being another person or being dissociated from their bodies when they awaken. They do not report feeling rested or having dreamt, and they do not remember moving. They are usually awakened by someone calling their name and asking them to open their eyes, which is clearly different from a usual awakening from sleep. Finally, the reasons for sleep and general anesthesia are unquestionably different, and the contexts in which they occur are relevant.

AWARENESS UNDER ANESTHESIA

Crawford (1971) defined awareness under anesthesia as the recall of an event that is neither a dream nor a hallucination. Although this definition appears to be quite sensible, he did not suggest how instances of awareness might be differentiated, nor did he consider the possibility of recall via dreams or hallucinations. In addition to these problems, patients often fall asleep after their operations, if not immediately afterward, usually before they are interviewed about perioperative events. It is therefore possible that reports of awareness could be mixed with sleep mentation occurring after the operation. Most people are skilled at separating sleep, dreams, daydreams, and normal waking reality from each other, and these skills are probably carried into the operating room. Most important, however, is that patients may recollect perioperative events that they were unaware of at the time they occurred. In addition, the possibility exists that patients are phenomenally aware under general anesthesia but that anterograde or retrograde amnesia is sufficiently dense to make recollection improbable.

COGNITIVE PROCESSING UNDER GENERAL ANESTHESIA

The cognitive processing under investigation is the ability of patients, either during or after their operation, to respond to auditory stimuli, while under the influence of a properly administered general anesthetic. In the case of verbatim recall, the cognitive process is obvious. However, more often than not, the process is subtle and open to interpretation. The following statements can be made about information processing under general anesthesia:

1. Patients do process information under general anesthesia. The results of this processing can be detected by orienting responses, classical conditioning (in animals), postoperative nonverbal responses, recognition, and recall.
2. Evidence for the recollection of perioperative events decreases as the intentionality of retrieval strategies increases.

3. Recall is, in general, a poor indicator of cognitive processing under general anesthesia.
4. General anesthesia disrupts the encoding and retrieval of memories. Retrieval can be enhanced through strategies, such as hypnosis, that supply cues and contextual elements or improve rapport.
5. Recollection occurs with and without phenomenal awareness.

Support for the occurrence of information processing under anesthesia can be found in stimuli presentations that result in (a) orienting responses (Goldmann & Levey, 1986; Levinson, 1965); (b) nonverbal responses that relate to recovery (Evans & Richardson, 1988); affective responses (Blacher, 1975) and specific behavioral responses (i.e., ear pulling; Bennett, Davis, & Giannini, 1985; Goldmann, Shah, & Hebden, 1987); (c) conditioning (in animals) demonstrated by response suppression (Weinberger, Gold, & Sternberg, 1984); (d) the recognition of words in a signal detection task (Millar & Watkinson, 1983); and (e) the recall of operative events through dreamlike processes (Federn, 1953) and verbatim recall (Cheek, 1979; Goldmann, 1986; Goldmann et al., 1987; Levinson, 1965).

In examining the evidence, the reader should bear in mind that the phenomenon of cognitive processing under anesthesia and subsequent recollection occurs in a very particular environment, that of the operating room and the hospital. Patients may not wish to remember or to report. They may feel constrained by staff–patient relationships and by their desire to appear compliant and grateful. In addition, patients may have been told that they will be asleep and unconscious and, thus, may have every reason to doubt their perceptions. This doubt is often reinforced, both by the staff and by the patients' desire to believe that they were not in any way observers at their own operations. Consequently, recollections that bypass conscious recall or occur outside the patient's phenomenal awareness are more likely to present evidence for cognitive processing under anesthesia. Unfortunately, these same responses may be the most difficult to detect.

One anecdote illustrates this latter point: During the induction of anesthesia, an anesthetist explained the observed contractions of different muscle groups to a medical student. He said that it reminded him of writhing bodies on funeral pyres in India. The next morning, I questioned the patient about his operation. He had no recall of events, even with the aid of hypnosis. However, he emphatically stated that he had had a hot, uncomfortable, restless, and altogether miserable night's sleep. Whether there is a connection between these two events is difficult to ascertain. However, it is suggestive of the plausible connections that could be made between perioperative events and later nonconscious recollections.

Orienting
The orienting response can be seen as behavioral, perceptual, or physiological efferent activity that can be elicited by a particular stimulus and occurs in close

temporal proximity to the eliciting stimulus. Only two orienting responses have been investigated for general anesthetics, the EEG and the galvanic skin responses (GSR). Studies of orienting responses have not yielded consistent results. This may be due, in part, to the collative variables (probability, novelty, etc.) of the stimuli. In one successful study, Goldmann and Levey (1986) found that a majority of premedicated, spontaneously breathing patients receiving a volatile anesthetic agent showed an orienting response (GSR) when the name Arthur Scargill (the leader of the National Union of Mineworkers) was mentioned. The study was conducted in the United Kingdom during the mineworkers' strike, and a similar response may not have occurred had the strike not been in effect at that time. Names other than Scargill's, including the patient's own name, did not elicit orienting responses. This result differs from the result found with sleepers. In addition, conversation pertinent to the operation did not elicit an orienting response as readily as unusual conversation, such as a joke. Salience appears to be a key variable, and studies that do not provide meaningful or significant stimuli are unlikely to present evidence supportive of awareness.

Postoperative Nonverbal Responses

Several researchers (Bonke, Schmitz, Verhage, & Zwaveling, 1986; Bonnett, 1966; Evans & Richardson, 1988; Pearson, 1961, 1965) have investigated the influence of intraoperative suggestions on the patient's postoperative course. Evans and Richardson's study is most notable for its striking results, including significant decreases in hospital stay, pyrexia, and gastrointestinal problems.

Other authors have concentrated on highly specific postoperative behavioral responses. Bennett et al. (1985) found that patients instructed under general anesthesia to pull on their ears during a postoperative interview did so significantly more often than a control group. Goldmann et al. (1987) found similar results with cardiac patients who were asked to touch their chins. None of the patients in either study recalled the suggestion, even with the aid of hypnosis. Goldmann et al. (1987) enhanced the salience of the message by recording the patient's name at the beginning and included additional suggestions for an easy and comfortable recovery. All patients were seen preoperatively and were told that they might hear a tape during their operation. The preoperative interview as well as the specific nature of the intraoperative suggestions were designed to enhance expectancy and patient motivation.

Recognition

Several researchers have examined the recognition of words or phrases played under anesthesia, with differing results. Dubovsky and Trustman (1976) gave obstetric patients letter-word pairs to remember under anesthesia (e.g., "G is for game"). The experimental group did not do significantly better than the control group on simple correct pairings. However, in a more sophisticated study, Millar and Watkinson (1983) found that when the "false alarm" rate was taken into account, significant differences occurred on recognition of the target words. Loftus, Schooler, Loftus, and Glauber (1985) conducted a similar (if slightly less rigorous) experiment with only a single, highly knowledgeable and motivated subject (one of the authors). No significant results were found on three recognition tests. As an afterthought, the authors tested one of the doctors present at the operation and found that her recognition scores also did not differ from chance. The authors concluded that the results "still leave open the possibility that information presented under anesthesia leaves some lasting impression that cannot be revealed in tests of retention that require remembering to be deliberate or intentional."

Goldmann (1986) gave two groups of patients a preoperative "general information" questionnaire. This included questions such as "What is the blood pressure of an octopus?" The experimental group listened to the answers during anesthesia. Both groups received suggestions for an easy recovery as well as a suggestion of the patient's own choosing. None of the patients recalled hearing the answers, but the experimental group performed significantly better on a postoperative recognition test. As with the source amnesia experienced with hypnosis, patients acquired new knowledge but were uncertain about where or how they had learned it. Unlike hypnotic source amnesia, neither hypnosis nor a posthypnotic cue aided the patients in recalling how they had learned the new facts.

Recall

Reports of recall in the anesthetic literature are rare. Retrospective studies have often reported an incidence of recall around 2% (Hutchinson, 1960). Recall has been associated with the absence of premedication and volatile anesthetics, light anesthesia, equipment failures, poor anesthetic technique (Breckenridge & Aitkenhead, 1983), and highly salient events. For many reasons, cases have been difficult to verify. As with dreaming, patients may feel as if something happened but have no specific recall of the event.

If evidence of dreaming were based solely on recall, we might conclude that dreams are rare. However, most people believe that we dream far more than we can remember and that the failure to recall does not suggest that dreaming did not occur. The failure is considered to be one of retrieval. Several factors associated with dream recall are when and how a subject is awakened; the setting of the awakening; the motivation, personality, and cognitive style of the subject; the demand characteristics of the interview; the rapport between subject and interviewer; and the characteristics of the dream itself. The characteristics of the dream include aspects of dream content that relate to salience and intrapsychic conflict.

If factors that influence the recall of dreams also influence the recall of awareness under anesthesia, then perioperative events will most likely be recalled if the patient is awakened quickly after the operation, after hearing something highly salient (that will not cause intrapsychic conflict) during the operation, achieves good rapport with the interviewer, and is both motivated and interested in reporting.

When prospective studies have been conducted (with the exception of Levinson, 1965), intraoperative stimuli have not been highly salient. Levinson's study is perhaps the most famous in the literature: Levinson created a mock perioperative crisis, telling patients under deep ether anesthesia that he did not like their color and that something was wrong with their breathing. Under hypnosis, 40% had specific recall, and 40% became highly anxious. Other researchers, for ethical reasons, have used much less salient material. For example, McIntyre (1966) repeatedly played a tape about a cleaning woman who had been robbed of $15 to women undergoing gynecological or obstetric operations. Patients had no recall of the tape. Other authors have used music (Brice, Hetherington, & Utting, 1970) or words (Eisele, Weinreich, & Bartle, 1976; Trustman, Dubovsky, & Titley, 1977) and have found little evidence supportive of recall. The use of highly salient stimuli are likely to create intrapsychic conflict, anxiety, or an unwillingness to report, thus rendering recall more difficult.

Because recall is more affected by drugs, context, mood, and the conduct of the interview than forms of remembering that are less intentional, such as recognition (Godden & Baddeley, 1975), evidence for awareness based on recall is slim. Two studies (Goldmann, 1986; Goldmann et al., 1987) provide additional support for the notion that evidence for recall, even when efforts are made to maximize its occurrence, is both difficult to find and may be uncovered at the risk of psychological distress to the patient.

Returning to the study of cardiac patients mentioned earlier (Goldmann et al., 1987), 7 of the 30 patients (23%) reported recall. Three reports (10%) included verbatim recall of conversations that were later corroborated. High postoperative anxiety was significantly associated with patients reporting recall. These patients had not been more anxious than the rest when tested preoperatively. All patients who reported recall became anxious during their interviews and believed that they had been conscious during the incidents they reported. Memories were both verbal and kinesthetic. Several were enhanced with hypnosis.

In a double blind trial with premedicated spontaneously breathing patients, little evidence for recall was found when intraoperative stimuli of low and moderate salience were played to the patients. Information thought to be salient to the patient was gleaned during the preoperative interview and was used in making the intraoperative tape. Of 25 patients, 3 reported images under hypnosis that could be associated with the taped message. Two of these incidents follow:

Taped message: You have a lovely garden.
Interviewer: Does anything else come to mind?
Patient: Tomatoes and lettuce.
Interviewer: Anything about tomatoes and lettuce?
Patient: We are trying to grow them in our garden.

Taped message: You left nursing to have a lovely little girl.

> Interviewer: Does anything come to mind that was said to you or about you in theater [the operating room]?
>
> Patient: No. I am just thinking about my family.

These messages were designed not to stress the patient. Because the patient's hearing was not completely occluded, intraoperative events that were of greater salience may have overshadowed the prerecorded messages.

Finally, in a study designed to maximize recall, the experimenter was not blind to the intraoperative stimulus. All patients were women, and all were good hypnotic subjects. The same suggestion was used throughout: "When you awaken from your anesthetic, you will believe for a moment that you have green hair." The statements of 3 patients are suggestive of the taped message. Only the excerpt from the first interview occurred under hypnosis.

Patient A
Interviewer: Anything at all. Anything come to mind?
Patient: Well, I dreamt of green strands.

Patient B
Interviewer: Does anything come to mind when you think about your operation?
Patient: No.
Interviewer: What about now. Anything at all?
Patient: I keep thinking about green things.

Patient C
Interviewer: How are you this morning?
Patient: Pretty good.
Interviewer: Everything went well?
Patient: Great. I'm leaving this morning. I can't wait to wash my hair.

Even the use of an informed interviewer, good hypnotic subjects, and hypnosis does not supply incontrovertible evidence for recall. The connections, however, are intuitive and plausible.

CONCLUSION

It is clear from the previous evidence that recollection of perioperative events decreases as the intentionality of retrieval strategies increases. Eich (1984) wrote that "events that occur while a person is asleep, anesthetized, or selectively attending to other ongoing events . . . are rarely revealed in tests of retention that require remembering to be deliberate or intentional." Similar findings have been found with Korsakoff patients (Graf, Squire, & Mandler, 1984). Evidence for learning can be found where otherwise it might not have been when methods such as spelling, puzzle completion, or word recognition are used. These methods supply cues and contextual elements. Hypnosis may enhance remembering by reinstating contextual elements, by allowing the patient to supply particular affective cues, and by improving rapport. However, even with the aid of hypnosis, only a tiny fraction of the events that occur under anesthesia may be available for recall, although they may perhaps be remembered in another way. It is possible that cognitive processing under general anesthesia occurs outside conscious awareness.

Evidence from subliminal perception, blindsight, and dichotic listening as well as research with amnesic patients (Dixon, 1981; Eich, 1984; Marcel, 1983) suggests that information processing occurs both consciously and nonconsciously. Nonconsciously processed events are not available for recall, although they may influence behavior (Mattis & Kovner, 1984, p. 118). Consequently, a careless remark by a surgeon may result in a longer hospital stay or slower healing. Conversely, a patient's recovery may be improved by the judicious use of suggestions. As with hypnosis, the suggestion may not be recalled, but its influence on the patient's subsequent behavior may nevertheless be important and valuable as a tool in the aid of healing.

References

Bennett, H. L., Davis, H. S., & Giannini, J. A. (1985). Nonverbal response to intraoperative conversation. *British Journal of Anaesthesia, 57,* 174–179.

Blacher, R. S. (1975). On awakening paralyzed during surgery: A syndrome of traumatic neurosis. *Journal of the American Medical Association, 234,* 67–68.

Bonke, B., Schmitz, P. I. M., Verhage, F., & Zwaveling, A. (1986). Clinical study of so-called unconscious perception during general anaesthesia. *British Journal of Anaesthesia, 58,* 957–964.

Bonnett, O. T. (1966). Effects of positive suggestions on surgical patients. *Pacific Journal of Medicine and Surgery,* 297–300.

Breckenridge, J. L., & Aitkenhead, A. R. (1983). Awareness during anaesthesia: A review. *Annals of the Royal College of Surgeons, 65,* 93–96.

Brice, D. D., Hetherington, R. R., & Utting, J. E. (1970). A simple study of awareness and dreaming during anaesthesia. *British Journal of Anaesthesia, 42,* 535–541.

Cheek, D. B. (1962). Importance of recognizing that surgical patients behave as though hypnotized. *American Journal of Clinical Hypnosis, 4,* 227–236.

Cheek, D. B. (1964). Surgical memory and reaction to careless conversation. *American Journal of Clinical Hypnosis, 6,* 237–240.

Cheek, D. B. (1979, November). *Awareness of meaningful sounds under general anesthesia: Considerations and a review of the literature 1959–1979.* Paper presented at the Annual Scientific Meeting of the American Society of Clinical Hypnosis.

Crawford, J. S. (1971). Awareness during operative obstetrics during general anaesthesia. *British Journal of Anaesthesia, 43,* 179–182.

Dixon, N. (1981). *Preconscious processing.* New York: Wiley.

Dubovsky, E. L., & Trustman, R. (1976). Absence of recall after general anesthesia. *Anesthesia and Analgesia, 55,* 696–671.

Eich, E. (1984). Memory for unattended events: Remembering with and without awareness. *Memory and Cognition, 12*(2), 105–111.

Eisele, V., Weinreich, A., & Bartle, S. (1976). Perioperative awareness and recall. *Anesthesia and Analgesia, 55,* 513–518.

Evans, C., & Richardson, P. H. (1988). Improved recovery and reduced postoperative stay after therapeutic suggestions during general anaesthesia. *Lancet II:* 491–493.

Federn, P. (1953). A dream under general anesthesia. In P. Federn (Ed.), *Ego psychology and the psychoses* (pp. 100–103). London: Littlemore.

Godden, D. R., & Baddeley, A. D. (1975). Context dependent memory in two natural environments: On land and underwater. *British Journal of Psychology, 66,* 325–331.

Goldmann, L. (1986). *Awareness under general anaesthesia.* Unpublished doctoral dissertation, Cambridge University, London, U.K.

Goldmann, L., & Levey, A. B. (1986). Orienting under anaesthesia. *Anaesthesia, 41,* 1056–1057 (letter).

Goldmann, L., Shah, M. V., & Hebden, M. W. (1987). Memory of cardiac anaesthesia: Psychological sequelae in cardiac patients of intra-operative suggestions and operating room conversation. *Anaesthesia, 42,* 596–603.

Graf, P., Squire, L. R., & Mandler, G. (1984). The information that amnesic patients do not forget. *Journal of Experimental Psychology, 10,* 164–178.

Huchinson, R. (1960). Awareness during surgery: A study of its incidence. *British Journal of Anaesthesia, 33,* 463–469.

Levinson, B. W. (1965). States of awareness during general anaesthesia. *British Journal of Anaesthesia, 37,* 544–546.

Loftus, E., Schooler, J., Loftus, G., & Glauber, D. (1985). Memory for events occurring under anaesthesia. *Acta Psychology, 59,* 123–128.

Lunn, J. N. (1982). *Lecture notes on anaesthetics* (2nd ed.). Blackwell: Oxford.

Marcel, A. J. (1983). Conscious and unconscious perception: An approach to the relations between phenomenal experience and perceptual processes. *Cognitive Psychology, 15,* 238–300.

Mattis, S., & Kovner (1984). Amnesia is as amnesia does: Toward another definition of anterograde amnesias. In L. Squire & N. Butters (Eds.), *Neuropsychology of memory* (pp. 115–121). London: Guilford Press.

McIntyre, J. W. R. (1966). Awareness during general anesthesia: Preliminary observations. *Canadian Anaesthetists Society Journal, 13,* 495–499.

Millar, K., & Watkinson, N. (1983). Recognition of words presented during general anaesthesia. *Ergonomics, 26,* 585–594.

Pearson, R. E. (1961). Response to suggestions given under general anaesthesia. *American Journal of Clinical Hypnosis, 4,* 106–114.

Pearson, R. E. (1965). Response to suggestions given under general anaesthesia. *British Journal of Anaesthesia, 37,* 544–546.

Trustman, R., Dubovsky, S., & Titley, R. (1977). Auditory perception during general anesthesia—myth or fact? *International Journal of Clinical and Experimental Hypnosis, 25,* 88–105.

Weinberger, N. M., Gold, P. E., & Sternberg, D. B. (1984). Epinephrine enables Pavlovian fear conditioning under anaesthesia. *Science, 223,* 605–606.

PART THREE

COGNITION BEFORE AND AFTER SLEEP

CHAPTER 10

INSOMNIA:
THE PATIENT AND THE PILL

WALLACE B. MENDELSON

In one sense, we have learned a great deal about patients with chronically disturbed sleep; in another sense, we know very little. A major advance in the last decade has been the growing recognition that poor sleep is often a symptom of a series of diagnosable, treatable conditions. Complaints of poor quality sleep may result, for instance, from sleep apnea, nocturnal myoclonus, depressive illness, and many other causes (Mendelson, 1987). On the other hand, there remains a core of patients with chronically disturbed sleep in whom none of these disorders are found. In this article, I shall use the term *insomniacs* to refer to these unhappy individuals. I would like to suggest that the study of insomniacs leads to knowledge of how hypnotics act and that, conversely, the study of hypnotics provides insight into the nature of insomnia. In summary, I will argue that the clinical effects of hypnotics cannot be well-understood if they are assessed only in terms of enhancing sleep defined by the electroencephalogram (EEG). On the contrary, hypnotic efficacy may involve alterations in the patient's perception of his or her state of consciousness. Similarly, the development of tolerance may be influenced not only by pharmacologic issues, but also by a learned process. Before we look at these issues, however, let us briefly review some general thoughts about insomnia.

Insomnia is a complaint, a symptom and not an illness. In the Association of Sleep Disorder Centers nosology (1979), a variety of causes of poor sleep are listed. After eliminating the many physiological (e.g., sleep apnea), psychiatric (e.g., depression) and chronobiologic (e.g., phase lag) problems, at least two major categories remain. The first of these is subjective disorder of initiating and maintaining sleep (DIMS) without objective findings. Although the exact terminology for this condition will probably change in forthcoming

139

revisions, the thought remains the same, that is, that many insomniacs complain strongly about poor sleep while showing minimal disturbances during polysomnography. Thus, there can be a substantial disparity between patients' subjective reports of their sleep and objective measures from the same night.

A second form of insomnia is persistent psychophysiological DIMS. In these patients, internal cues (ruminative worries about not sleeping) and external cues (the bedroom environment) lead to poor sleep. Their EEG measures of sleep may be relatively normal or disturbed. In either event, however, patients' morning estimates of their sleep are relatively consistent with the EEG findings. In clinical situations, the distinction between subjective and persistent psychophysiological insomnia is often unclear, because conditioned elements may be superimposed on the subjective disorder. Nonetheless, the basic principle that insomnia may involve a dissociation of subjective experience from objective measures, as well as conditioned responses, sets the background for the discussion of hypnotics. Let us now look at sleep studies of insomnia and at data on possible physiological differences between insomniacs and control subjects.

NOCTURNAL SLEEP AND DAYTIME WAKEFULNESS OF INSOMNIACS

From the 1950s through the late 1970s, many laboratories reported sleep data from insomniacs (Institute of Medicine, 1979). However, these studies are difficult to assess because patients were selected on the basis of history and not on the basis of complete polysomnography to rule out other disorders (e.g., sleep apnea). Not surprisingly, later studies that did include polygraphic screening found objective sleep disturbance in insomniacs to be relatively small. One study of 10 insomniacs reported that they had increased intermittent waking time and lower sleep efficiency compared with control subjects (Mendelson, Garnett, Gillin, & Weingartner, 1984). The only significant difference in another study was more early morning waking time for insomniacs, with trends toward lower sleep efficiency and less total sleep (Mendelson, James, Garnett, Sack, & Rosenthal, 1986). Gillin and Mendelson (1981) reviewed 25 hypnotic efficacy studies and found that baseline total sleep was 383 min in insomniacs. This is similar to normal control values of 389 min and 383 min in the two previously cited studies. Similarly, Reynolds et al. (1984) reported that patients with persistent psychophysiological DIMS had a sleep efficiency of 81.5% and total sleep of 359.8 min.

Many studies of insomnia have reported decreased slow wave sleep (e.g., Gillin, Duncan, Pettigrew, Frankel, & Snyder, 1979), which has been suggested to play a crucial role in insomnia (Gaillaird, 1978). Although this is possible, such a theory would have to encompass the many other disorders characterized by decreased slow wave sleep, such as depression and schizophrenia (Mendelson, 1987). Moreover, it is difficult to rationalize this view with the observation that benzodiazepine hypnotics decrease slow wave sleep and yet result in improved subjective reports of sleep. Finally, electronic analyses of sleep EEGs in insomniacs have not confirmed a decrease in either slow wave or total EEG power (Mendelson, in press). In summary, EEG sleep studies of insomnia have found relatively few changes in the sleep of insomniacs. This may reflect the measures that we use; perhaps more subtle measures would reveal differences. On the other hand, this may resemble the Sherlock Holmes story in which a mystery was solved on the basis of the absence of a dog's bark. The important point might be the absence of substantial differences between the EEG sleep of insomniacs and normal subjects.

Insomniacs traditionally complain not only of disturbed sleep but also of daytime fatigue or sleepiness. An objective measure of daytime wakefulness may be obtained from the Multiple Sleep Latency Test (MSLT), which records the mean latency to sleep during four or five 20-min periods in which a patient is placed in bed in a darkened room (Mendelson, 1987). Interestingly, MSLT studies in both young and older insomniacs have shown normal daytime wakefulness (Dement, Seidel, & Carskadon, 1982, 1984; Mendelson et al., 1984, 1986; Stepanski, Zorick, Roehrs, Young, & Roth, 1988). There are at least two possible interpretations of these observations. First, given the relatively mild sleep disturbance shown in EEG studies, the normal MSLTs may confirm that insomniacs are not really sleep deprived. And second, insomniacs may indeed suffer from some degree of chronic mild sleep deprivation, but they may respond differently from normals in terms of how this affects their daytime wakefulness. At least two observations support this latter view. One comes from a study by Stepanski, Lamphere, Badia, Zorick, and Roth (1984), which assessed the relation of nocturnal sleep disturbance and daytime wakefulness in patients with sleep apnea, nocturnal myoclonus, and insomnia. In the first two groups, the number of nocturnal arousals correlated with decreased daytime wakefulness. In normal control subjects (who had few arousals), there was no significant relation. In the insomniacs, however, the number of nocturnal arousals was positively associated with increased daytime wakefulness. The type of arousal was also critical: Very brief arousals (increased EEG frequency and electromyograph [EMG] amplitude) were associated with daytime wakefulness, whereas more substantial awakenings were associated with sleepiness. A later study by Stepanski et al. (1988) also found that shorter sleep times in insomniacs correlated with increased daytime wakefulness.

A second line of evidence suggesting that insomniacs may respond to sleep deprivation differently than normal subjects comes from Bonnet (1986), who compared recovery sleep after 64 hours of total sleep loss in older insomniacs and control subjects. In both groups, sleep efficiency was very high (about 97%) on the first recovery night. In the normal subjects, values returned toward baseline by the second recovery night, whereas for the insomniacs this did not take place until the fourth night. Thus, the issue of whether insomniacs are not sleep deprived or whether they suffer from some form of mild chronic sleep deprivation to which they respond abnormally remains to be settled.

THE PERCEPTION OF SLEEP

Another question that arises is whether insomniacs differ from normals in their perception of the experience of sleeping. This idea was first expressed by Rechtschaffen (1968), who awakened poor sleepers and control subjects 10 min after the first sleep spindle and asked them whether they had been awake or asleep. The normal subjects tended to report that they had been asleep; the insomniacs reported that they had been awake. Coates et al. (1983) reported a similar phenomenon. Mendelson et al. (1984, 1986) found no differences in responses between insomniacs and control subjects when they were awakened by an 80 dB tone but did find a disparity after arousal by a tone of gradually increasing intensity. In the periods between the forced awakenings, the insomniacs and control subjects fell asleep at about the same rate and had equal amounts of sleep. The subjective estimates of the insomniacs, however, were only about half as long as the estimates of the control subjects. These data, taken together, raise the possibility that an important aspect of insomnia might be a misperception of the insomniac's state of consciousness vis-à-vis the EEG.

THE ACTIONS OF HYPNOTICS

Having reviewed the sleep and wakefulness of insomniacs, we will now examine the effects of hypnotics. Clinically used hypnotics comprise many different pharmacologic classes; indeed, an intriguing mystery is how drugs of such disparate biochemical qualities can have such similar effects. We will consider hypnotic actions on both individual sleep stages and on total sleep.

Until the 1960s, the dominant clinical hypnotics were the barbiturates, which greatly suppress REM sleep. They were reported variously to not affect (Baekeland, 1967; Kay, Jasinski, Eisenstein, & Kelly, 1972) or to decrease (Feinberg, Wender, Koresko, Gottlieb, & Piehuta, 1969) slow wave sleep. Since that time, benzodiazepines have become the most widely prescribed hypnotics. In general, they have minimal effects on REM sleep but profoundly decrease slow wave sleep (Mendelson, 1987). Because it has traditionally been thought that slow wave sleep is particularly deep and restful, it seems somewhat paradoxical that drugs which suppress slow wave sleep result in subjectively improved sleep. This dilemma may be resolved if slow wave sleep is not necessarily associated with a subjective sense of deep or good quality sleep. When arousal thresholds to relatively meaningless stimuli such as electronic tones are measured, slow wave sleep does indeed seem to be the "deepest" stage. On the other hand, the amount of Stage 4 sleep in normal volunteers has been positively associated with morning reports of light sleep (Saletu, 1975). Volunteers reported having previously been awake in 56% of forced awakenings from Stage 2 sleep compared with 77% of forced awakenings from slow wave sleep (Sewitch, 1984). In both insomniacs and control subjects, slow wave sleep has been associated with retrospectively poorer quality sleep on a morning questionnaire (Mendelson et al., 1986). However, data also suggest the opposite. Healthy older women (but not men) have been found to associate slow wave sleep with reported soundness of sleep (Hoch et al., 1987). The issue remains open, but it seems possible that slow wave sleep is not necessarily experienced subjectively as the deepest or most restful sleep.

Studies of the effects of hypnotics on total sleep mirror the data on base-line sleep among insomniacs: Just as the deficit in total sleep in insomniacs is small, the enhancement of sleep by hypnotics is also modest. Gillin and Mendelson (1981), in a review of hypnotic efficacy studies, found that the mean increase in total sleep time was 35 min. An often-cited study of flurazepam (which at the time was the most widely prescribed hypnotic) reported an increase in total sleep of only 6–8% over 1 month (Kales, Kales, Bixler, & Scharf, 1975), with sleep latency significantly decreased only during Nights 11–13. Thirty milligrams of flurazepam given to insomniacs over 5 weeks enhanced total sleep by a mean of 21 min (Mitler, Seidel, Van Den Hoed, Greenblatt, & Dement, 1984). Roehrs, Zorick, Kaffeman, Sicklesteel, and Roth (1982) reported an increase in total sleep of 29 min in a study using 15 mg of flurazepam. In spite of these relatively modest improvements in EEG-defined sleep, approximately 20 million prescriptions are written for hypnotics every year, and another 3% or 4% of the population takes over-the-counter sedatives. Thus, it seems that many people feel they are helped by these agents. Studies of subjective responses to hypnotics bear this out. Rickels (1983) found that, in six of seven studies of flurazepam, patients reported that the drug was more beneficial than a placebo. Significantly improved quality of sleep was also subjectively described in five of the seven studies. One possible interpretation is that insomniacs suffer from a long-term form of sleep deprivation and that the modest increase of total sleep from hypnotics corrects this problem. An alternative view is that the subjective benefit of hypnotics is very disproportionate to the small hypnotic-induced improvement in sleep (in much the same way that the subjective distress of insomniacs is disproportionately greater than their modest decrements in sleep). If the latter is the case, several interesting hypotheses need to be considered:

1. *Hypnotics improve sleep in polygraphic measures that are more subtle than those used to date.* Evidence increasingly suggests that sleep continuity, rather than total sleep, may be more important for the restorative value of sleep. On the other hand, careful studies of sleep disruption in insomniacs have shown less discontinuity than might have been expected. Stepanski et al. (1984) found that, in three of four categories of sleep interruption, insomniacs actually had fewer arousals than patients with sleep apnea or myoclonus and, indeed, had amounts similar to those of control subjects. Insomniacs reported more disturbance only in shifts to a lighter stage of sleep. Insofar as the sleep of insomniacs may not be substantially more disrupted than that of control subjects, the argument that hypnotic therapeutic effects derive from improved continuity is weakened.
2. *Hypnotics alter a physiological process not measured by clinical polysomnography.* Such a measure might be core temperature. The

early studies of Monroe (1967) and more recent work (Mendelson et al., 1984) have reported that insomniacs have higher mean rectal temperatures at sleep onset and throughout the night. It seems unlikely that this merely reflects increased waking time during the night. In the first 2 hr after sleep onset, insomniacs had the same or less waking time than control subjects, yet their temperatures remained higher. Hypnotics are known to lower core temperature (Pleuvry, Maddison, Odeh, & Dodson, 1980). Slow wave sleep can be enhanced by increasing core temperature (Horne, Moore, Reid, & Shackell, 1985). One might speculate that the benzodiazepine-induced decrease in slow wave sleep results from drug-induced changes in temperature. This view differs from the speculation that the minimal slow wave sleep among insomniacs results from their relative lack of decline in core temperature after sleep onset (Sewitch, 1987). Another confounding variable in studying this system is that sleep is very sensitive to ambient temperature (Haskell, Palca, Walker, Berger, & Heller, 1981; Muzet, Libert, & Candas, 1984). Exploration of this area must continue.

3. *Hypnotics alter processes not susceptible to physiological measurement.* It is conceivable that hypnotics change the insomniac's memory of sleep. This might occur through two types of mechanisms. First, a direct pharmacologic action might affect episodic memory. Benzodiazepines can decrease the ability to learn new material, although opinions differ on whether the ability to retrieve and use previously learned information is affected (Mendelson, Weingartner, Greenblatt, Garnett, & Gillin, 1982; Roehrs, Kribbs, Zorick, & Roth, 1986). Thus, hypnotics may alter the patient's ability to remember his or her experience. There is also increasing evidence that an anterograde amnesia occurs for the time immediately before sleep onset. These observations have been used to explain the complaints of memory trouble made by narcoleptics. Similarly, Carskadon et al. (1976) found that, although insomniacs exaggerated most aspects of their sleep compared with EEG data, they actually underreported the number of awakenings throughout the night. These awakenings may not have been remembered as clearly because of an anterograde amnesia after the return to sleep. This hypothesis must be assessed very carefully. For instance, word lists learned at night by subjects receiving 0.25 mg triazolam are remembered better the next morning than those by subjects receiving a placebo (Mendelson et al., 1989). Such an effect may result from the drug-induced sedation that minimizes the amount of subsequent distracting material.

As we have just mentioned, hypnotics affect memory processes and the ability to perform a variety of tasks. These effects have been studied extensively because of the concern that patients might be more susceptible to automobile accidents (Betts & Birtle, 1983; Binnie, 1983; Linnoila, 1978). Indeed, it could be argued that no clinical hypnotic exists that does not produce cognitive alterations. Although cognitive changes have traditionally been viewed as side effects, they may be a daytime manifestation of the therapeutic effect, that is, alterations in the patients' experiences of whether they are awake or asleep. A number of studies have shown that benzodiazepines alter auditory arousal during sleep. Preliminary evidence suggests that, during forced awakenings 10 min after the first sleep spindle, insomniacs are more likely to report having been asleep after receiving flurazepam than placebo (Mendelson et al., 1987). Certainly this area appears to be ripe for exploration.

TOLERANCE TO HYPNOTICS

We have previously described how conditioned responses might result in the complaint of insomnia, either in persistent psychophysiological DIMS or as a complication to subjective insomnia. Conditioned responses may also play a role in clinical tolerance to hypnotics. Just as the efficacy of hypnotics must be measured both physiologically and subjectively, tolerance may be a combination of traditional pharmacologic issues (i.e., pharmacokinetics and dynamics) and learned responses. Classical conditioning theory could be applied to suggest that environmental cues associated with drug administration may result in conditioned responses that are opposite to the unconditioned effect of the drug (Siegel, 1975; Spielman, Caruso, & Glovinsky, 1987). These "compensatory" responses, which contrast with those resembling the unconditioned drug response, have been described in a number of studies. King, Bouton, and Musty (1987), for instance, gave the sedative benzodiazepine midazolam to rats at 48-hr intervals until tolerance was established. When they gave saline to the rats in the same environment used for drug injection, animals tested 2 min after administration became hyperactive. Similar compensatory responses have been demonstrated for motor behavior after chlordiazepoxide (File, 1982) and for the hypothermic effect of ethanol (Melchior & Tabakoff, 1985). These observations have a number of interesting clinical implications. As Spielman et al. (1987) pointed out, the conditioning theory of tolerance predicts that the occasional administration of placebo (which is in effect an extinction trial) would be superior to continuous drug administration in maintaining efficacy. Occasional placebos might also be more beneficial than drug holidays. The clinical utility of this principle has not yet been established. However, it exemplifies once again the complexity of the relation between the patient and the pill.

References

Association of Sleep Disorder Centers. (1979). Diagnostic classification of sleep and arousal disorders. *Sleep, 2,* 1–137.

Baekeland, F. (1967). Phenobarbital and dextroamphetamine sulfate: Effects on the sleep cycle in man. *Psychopharmacologia, 11,* 388–396.

Betts, T. A., & Birtle, J. (1983). Effect of two hypnotic drugs on actual driving performance next morning. *British Medical Journal, 285,* 852.

Binnie, G. A. (1983). Psychotropic drugs and accidents in a general practice. *British Medical Journal, 287,* 1349–1350.

Bonnet, M. H. (1986). Effect of 64 hours of sleep deprivation upon sleep in geriatric normals and insomniacs. *Neurobiology of Aging, 7,* 89–96.

Carskadon, M. A., Dement, W. C., Mitler, M. M., Guilleminault, C., Zarcone, V. P., & Spiegel, R. (1976). Self-reports versus sleep laboratory findings in 122 drug-free subjects with complaints of chronic insomnia. *American Journal of Psychiatry, 133,* 1382–1383.

Coates, T. J., Killen, J. D., Silberman, S., Marchini, J., Hamilton, S., & Thoresen, C. E. (1983). Cognitive activity, sleep disturbance, and stage specific differences between recorded and reported sleep. *Psychopharmacology, 20,* 243.

Dement, W. C., Seidel, W., & Carskadon, M. A. (1982). Daytime alertness, insomnia and benzodiazepines. *Sleep, 5,* 528–545.

Dement, W. C., Seidel, W., & Carskadon, M. A. (1984). Issues in the diagnosis and treatment of insomnia. *Psychopharmacology, 2*(Suppl.), 11–43.

Feinberg, I., Wender, P. H., Koresko, R. L., Gottlieb, F., & Piehuta, J. (1969). A differential effect of chlorpromazine and phenobarbital on EEG sleep patterns. *Journal of Psychiatric Research, 7,* 101–109.

File, S. E. (1982). Development and retention of tolerance to the sedative effects of chlordiazepoxide: Role of apparatus cues. *European Journal of Pharmacology, 81,* 637–643.

Gaillaird, J. M. (1978). Chronic primary insomnia: Possible physiopathological involvement of slow wave sleep deficiency. *Sleep, 1,* 133–147.

Gillin, J. C., Duncan, W., Pettigrew, K. D., Frankel, B. L., & Snyder, F. (1979). Successful separation of depressed, normal, and insomniac subjects by EEG sleep data. *Archives of General Psychiatry, 36,* 85–90.

Gillin, J. C., & Mendelson, W. B. (1981). Sleeping pills: For whom? When? How long? In G. C. Palmer (Ed.), *Neuropharmacology of central nervous system and behavioral disorders* (pp. 285–316). New York: Academic Press.

Haskell, E. H., Palca, J. W., Walker, J. M., Berger, R. J., & Heller, H. C. (1981). The effects of high and low ambient temperature on human sleep stages. *Electroencephalography and Clinical Neurophysiology, 51,* 494–501.

Hoch, C. C., Reynolds, C. F., Kupfer, D. J., Berman, S. R., Houck, P. R., & Stack, J. A. (1987). Self-report versus recorded sleep in healthy seniors. *Psychophysiology, 24,* 293–299.

Horne, J. A., Moore, V. J., Reid, A. J., & Shackell, B. S. (1985). Waking body temperature manipulation and subsequent sleep (SWS). *Sleep Research, 14,* 15.

Institute of Medicine. (1979). *Sleeping pills, insomnia and medical practice* (Publication No. 10M-79-04). Washington, DC: National Academy of Sciences.

Kales, A., Kales, J. D., Bixler, E. O., & Scharf, M. B. (1975). Effectiveness of hypnotic drugs with prolonged use: Flurazepam and pentobarbital. *Clinical Pharmacology and Therapeutics, 18*(3), 356–363.

Kay, D. C., Jasinski, D. R., Eisenstein, R. B., & Kelly, O. A. (1972). Quantified human sleep after pentobarbital. *Clinical Pharmacology and Therapeutics, 13,* 221–231.

King, D. A., Bouton, M. E., & Musty, R. E. (1987). Associative control of tolerance to the sedative effects of a short-acting benzodiazepine. *Behavioral Neuroscience, 101,* 104–114.

Linnoila, M. (1978). Psychomotor effects of drugs and alcohol on healthy volunteers and psychiatric patients. *Advances in Pharmacology and Therapeutics, 8,* 235–249.

Melchior, C. L., & Tabakoff, B. (1985). Features of environment-dependent tolerance to ethanol. *Psychopharmacology, 87,* 94–100.

Mendelson, W. B. (1987). *Human sleep: Research and clinical care.* New York: Plenum Press.

Mendelson, W. B. (in press). Do studies of sedative/hypnotics suggest the nature of chronic insomnia? In R. Godbout & J. Montplaisir (Eds.), *Sleep and biological rhythms: Application to psychiatry.* New York: Oxford University Press.

Mendelson, W. B., Garnett, D., Gillin, J. C., & Weingartner, H. (1984). The experience of insomnia and daytime and nighttime functioning. *Psychiatry Research, 12,* 235–250.

Mendelson, W. B., James, S. P., Garnett, D., Sack, D. A., & Rosenthal, N. E. (1986). A psychophysiological study of insomnia. *Psychiatry Research, 19,* 267–284.

Mendelson, W. B., Sicuro, F., Starz, K. E., Gupwartz, K., Dorothea, M., and Weingartner, H. (1989). Effects of two preparations of triazolam on cognition and performance in normal volunteers. *Sleep Research, 18,* 63.

Mendelson, W. B., Stephens, H., Giesen, H., & James, S. P. (1987). Effects of flurazepam on sleep, arousal threshold, and the perception of being asleep. *Psychopharmacology, 95,* 258.

Mendelson, W. B., Weingartner, H., Greenblatt, D. J., Garnett, D., & Gillin, J. C. (1982). A clinical study of flurazepman. *Sleep, 5,* 350–360.

Mitler, M. M., Seidel, W. F., Van Den Hoed, J., Greenblatt, D. J., & Dement, W. C. (1984). Comparative hypnotic effects of flurazepman, triazolam and placebo: A long-term simultaneous nighttime and daytime study. *Journal of Clinical Psychopharmacology, 4,* 2–13.

Monroe, L. J. (1967). Psychological and physiological differences between good and poor sleepers. *Journal of Abnormal Psychology, 72,* 255–264.

Montlaisir, J., & Godbout, R. (Eds.). (in press). *Sleep and biological rhythms: Application to psychiatry.* New York: Oxford University Press.

Muzet, A., Libert, J.-P., & Candas, V. (1984). Ambient temperature and human sleep. *Experientia, 40,* 425–429.

Pleuvry, B. J., Maddison, S. E., Odeh, R. B., & Dodson, M. E. (1980). Respiratory and psychological effects of oral temazepam in volunteers. *British Journal of Anaesthesiology, 52,* 901.

Rechtschaffen, A. (1968). Polygraphic aspects of insomnia. In Gastaut, H., Lugaresi, L., Berti, G., and Coccagno (Eds.), *The abnormalities of sleep in man* (pp. 109–125). Bologna, Italy: Gaggi.

Reynolds, C. F., Taska, L. S., Sewitch, D. E., Restifo, K., Coble, P. A., & Kupfer, D. J. (1984). Persistent psychophysiologic insomnia: Preliminary research diagnostic criteria and EEG sleep data. *American Journal of Psychiatry, 141,* 804–805.

Rickels, K. (1983). Clinical trials of hypnotics. *Journal of Clinical Psychopharmacology, 3,* 133–142.

Roehrs, T., Kribbs, N., Zorick, F., & Roth, T. (1986). Hypnotic residual effects of benzodiazepines with repeated administration. *Sleep, 9,* 194–199.

Roehrs, T., Zorick, F., Kaffeman, M., Sicklesteel, B. A., & Roth, T. (1982). Flurazepam for short-term treatment of complaints of insomnia. *Journal of Clinical Pharmacology, 22,* 290–296.

Saletu, B. (1975). Is the subjectively experienced quality of sleep related to objective sleep parameters? *Behavioral Biology, 13,* 433.

Sewitch, D. E. (1984). NREM sleep continuity and the sense of having slept in normal sleepers. *Sleep, 7,* 147.

Sewitch, D. E. (1987). Slow wave sleep deficiency insomnia: A problem in thermo-downregulation at sleep onset. *Psychophysiology, 24,* 200–215.

Siegel, S. (1975). Evidence from rats that morphine tolerance is a learned response. *Journal of Comparative Physiology and Psychology, 89,* 498–506.

Spielman, A. J., Caruso, L. S., & Glovinsky, P. B. (1987). A behavioral perspective on insomnia treatment. *Sleep Disorders, 10,* 541–553.

Stepanski, E., Lamphere, J., Badia, P., Zorick, F., & Roth, T. (1984). Sleep fragmentation and daytime sleepiness. *Sleep, 7,* 18–26.

Stepanski, E., Zorick, F., Roehrs, T., Young, D., & Roth, T. (1988). Daytime alertness in patients with chronic insomnia compared with asymptomatic control subjects. *Sleep, 11,* 54–60.

CHAPTER 11

THE PERCEPTION OF SLEEP ONSET IN INSOMNIACS AND NORMAL SLEEPERS

MICHAEL H. BONNET

The ability to measure the onset of sleep reliably is clearly a central component of modern sleep research. Because behavioral quiescence, muscular relaxation, alpha drop, respiratory decrease, and auditory threshold increase generally show strong agreement, sleep onset may be considered to be well-defined. Unfortunately, subjective reports of sleep onset frequently do not agree well with physiological measures. It is not unusual for people to report having been awake when they are awakened from sleep (Anch, McCoy, & Somerest, 1980; Campbell & Webb, 1981; Rechtschaffen, 1968). Some patients, usually those who are depressed, claim to have had no sleep during nights in which physiological indicators suggest that they had several hours of sleep. One of the most persistent areas of disagreement exists between objective and subjective reports (from patients with reported difficulty falling asleep) of the length of time it initially takes to fall asleep at night. At least nine studies have documented median electroencephalograph (EEG) sleep onset latencies of 51 min compared with subjective median estimates of 82 min in such patients (Carskadon et al., 1976; Frankel, Coursey, Buchbinder, & Snyder, 1976; Hauri & Cohen, 1977; Mendelson, Garnett, Gillin, & Weingartner, 1984; Monroe, 1967; Nease, Monroe, Bonnet, & Kramer, 1981; Olmstead, Hauri, Percy, & Hellekson, 1980; Spielman et al., 1980; Tietz, Zorick, Roth, & Kaffeman, 1980).

SLEEP ONSET ESTIMATES IN NORMALS

We initially began our examination of sleep onset by observing carefully delineated periods of sleep in normal young adults. In all studies reported here, we

148

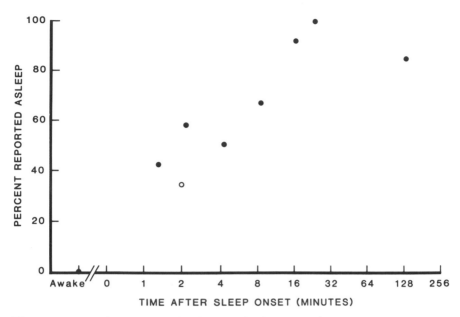

Figure 1 Plot of percentage of subjects subjectively reporting themselves to be asleep at awakening as a function of time after electroencephalograph (EEG) sleep onset. (The open circle corresponds to the initial spindle awakening. Used with permission from Bonnet & Moore, 1982.)

timed EEG intervals from the appearance of the first sleep spindle rather than from the point of alpha drop because alpha may decrease for reasons other than sleep onset (like opening the eyes) and because a substantial proportion of normal young adults do not produce significant alpha at any time. In the initial study (Bonnet & Moore, 1982), 12 subjects spent 5 nights each in the laboratory. The subjects were awakened at specified intervals ranging from the first sleep spindle and 1 min after the first spindle to 140 min after the first spindle. When the subjects were awakened, they were asked if they had been asleep at that point. If they answered no, they were asked how long it had been since the technician had told them good night. If they answered yes, they were asked how long it had taken to fall asleep and how long they had been asleep. Figure 1 plots the percentage of subjects who reported themselves to be asleep as a function of how long they had been asleep when awakened. It can be seen from the figure that, whereas only 40% of the subjects reported being asleep 1 min after the first sleep spindle, 100% of the subjects reported being asleep 25 min after the first sleep spindle. By classical perceptual criteria, the threshold of sleep onset (i.e., the point at which 50% of the subjects reported being

This work was supported by the Veterans Administration and by the Sleep-Wake Disorders Research Institute. The author would like to acknowledge the many sleepless nights of Sarah E. Moore and Ralph Downey III, whose respective master's thesis and doctoral dissertation are described at length in this chapter.

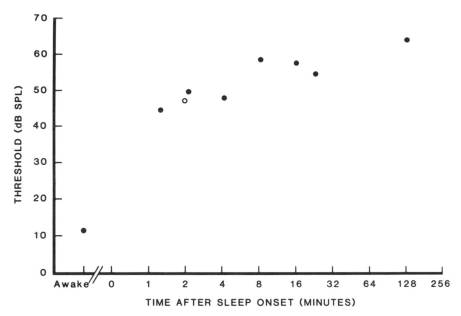

Figure 2   Plot of auditory arousal threshold level in the awake state and after various intervals of sleep. (The open circle corresponds to the initial spindle awakening. Used with permission from Bonnet & Moore, 1982.)

asleep) would fall between 4 min and 8 min. Subjects were always awakened by an audiometer using an ascending method of limits procedure. Figure 2 plots auditory arousal thresholds for the same awakenings displayed in Figure 1. It can be seen that auditory thresholds reached 70% of their stable Stage 2 sleep value after 1 min of sleep. The data reinforce the notion that physiological changes such as muscle relaxation and auditory threshold increase occur rapidly at sleep onset but that cognitive–perceptual changes occur more slowly and that little subjective certainty of sleep occurs for at least the first 8 min of sleep, even in normal young adults. These young adults could clearly differentiate longer periods of sleep, and many studies have shown that normal young adults can estimate their nocturnal sleep latencies with relative accuracy (Baekeland & Hoy, 1971; Frankel et al., 1976; Monroe, 1967).

SLEEP ONSET ESTIMATES IN INSOMNIACS
In our next studies, we sought to compare the abilities of control subjects and sleep-onset insomniacs to estimate their sleep latencies (Moore, 1981; Moore, Bonnet, Warm, & Kramer, 1980). One problem of estimating sleep latency in most studies is that estimates are generally collected in the morning about 8 hr after the actual event. Many things can happen during those 8 hr, including multiple awakenings, movements, and various forms of disturbance. In addition, it can be very difficult for some people to report accurately an event that happened that long ago. Therefore, the first study examined the abilities of an

age-matched (18–35 years) group of 12 normal and 12 insomniac subjects to estimate their latency to sleep onset both at the normal early morning time and when they were awakened at their first sleep spindle on counterbalanced nights. All the subjects had previously had a screening night in the laboratory to rule out other sleep disorders as a cause of the insomnia. Several other variables, such as oral temperature and anxiety level, that are potentially related to sleep-related estimates, were measured or controlled. The subjects were drug free for 2 weeks prior to the study and were allowed no naps, alcohol, or caffeine during the study. Watches and clocks were not allowed in the sleeping rooms. All estimates were made from the time when the technician told the subject good night over the intercom system. This time was also marked by the technician as the beginning of the sleep recording. Oral temperature was measured immediately prior to the beginning of the recording each night and immediately after each estimate of sleep latency. Anxiety levels were measured each evening and each morning. For all sleep latency measures, the values to be presented are geometric means (inverse of the mean of the log transform) because sleep latency estimates are not normally distributed.

Interestingly, it was found that overall EEG-determined sleep latencies did not differ significantly in the two groups of subjects (18 min vs. 26 min). However, as expected, normal subjects' subjective estimates of their sleep latency were significantly shorter than those of insomniac subjects (14 min vs. 38 min), $F(1,22) = 17.64$, $p < .01$. Of primary interest was the lack of a significant interaction between time of estimate (sleep spindle and morning) and experimental group; that is, the insomniacs overestimated their sleep onset latency both in the morning and at the first sleep spindle at night. It was found, however, that both groups estimated that their sleep onset latencies were longer when they made the estimates in the morning. This probably resulted because few of the subjects thought they had actually been asleep yet when they were awakened for their nocturnal sleep spindle estimate. However, it is also possible that there is a circadian rhythm to time perception in general and that insomniacs differ from normal subjects in either the amplitude or phase of that rhythm.

If the circadian rhythm explanation were valid, then one might expect to find body temperature differences in the two groups. Significant differences between insomniac and normal subjects in oral temperature were not found at any test point. In fact, body temperature at lights out was 98.4°F in both groups and was actually 0.2°F lower in insomniacs at the first sleep spindle. Two previous studies have found a significantly higher oral temperature in insomniac than in normal subjects at sleep onset (Monroe, 1967) and two studies have not (Johns, Masterton, & Bruce, 1971; Mendelson et al., 1984). The oral temperature findings are relevant because Monroe and others have hypothesized that insomniacs have increased physiological activation at sleep onset and that it is the activation (most easily indexed by temperature) that is related to the overestimation of sleep latency. Although the time perception literature also suggests that there is a positive correlation between body temperature and magnitude of temporal estimate (Pfaff, 1968), those findings cannot explain the data in the current study.

Significant differences in anxiety were found. A main effect was found showing insomniacs to be more anxious than normal sleepers, $F(1,22) = 10.11$, $p < .01$. Therefore, anxiety may have played a significant role in the estimates of sleep onset, as suggested by other temporal perception studies involving anxiety (Falk & Bindra, 1954; Langer, Wapner, & Werner, 1961).

A second experiment was performed to determine whether insomniacs are simply poor estimators of time. If general anxiety level were the major factor in determining overestimation, then one might suppose that insomniacs would overestimate all intervals of time. However, it is also possible that insomniacs might simply become more anxious when they are left alone for relatively long periods of time (i.e., the 20 min before falling asleep) and might therefore overestimate only longer intervals. Several investigators have shown circadian rhythms in time perception (Aschoff, Geidke, Poppel, & Wever, 1972; Masao, 1978). Because the circadian curve of time perception may be different for insomniac than normal sleepers and because these rhythm differences may have accounted for the results of the initial experiment, we found it important to examine the time estimation of insomniacs at several different times during the day. Alternatively, insomniacs may simply become more anxious in bedroom settings and therefore may overestimate intervals only when they occur in a bedroom setting. Finally, insomniacs may react only to the sleep-specific demand situation and may therefore overestimate only when they are under the pressure to attempt to fall asleep. These possibilities became the experimental conditions for the second study (Moore, 1981; Moore, Bonnet, & Warm, 1982).

The screening, age range, and subject requirements that were specified in the previous experiment were carried over to the second experiment, and 12 new insomniac and 12 new normal sleepers were recruited. The subjects participated for 1 day. During that day, subjects estimated short intervals (5–35 s) and a long interval (19 min) five times (at 7:00 a.m., 11:00 a.m., 3:00 p.m., 7:00 p.m., and 11:00 p.m.). The subjects also took a nap at noon and were given 19 min to fall asleep. Half of the subjects did all of their time estimating in a neutral laboratory setting, whereas the remaining subjects did all of their time estimating in a bedroom setting. All intervals that were estimated were unfilled (i.e., the beginning and end of each interval were marked by a burst of white noise, but there were no intervening events). All estimates were made individually on log sheets that were analogous to those used in the first study. Estimating procedures were practiced by all subjects within 48 hr of participation in the study. To replicate and extend other findings in the first study, anxiety and oral temperature were measured at the beginning and end of each testing session and nap across the day.

The results of this study with comparison data from the first experiment for nocturnal sleep onset estimates are displayed in Figure 3. For all estimates, the ratio of subjective estimate to objective interval length was calculated. The

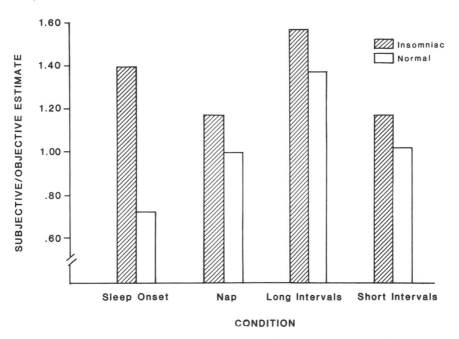

Figure 3   Subjective to objective sleep onset latency ratios in groups of insomniac and normal sleepers at sleep onset, at daytime nap onset, for long intervals during the day, and for short intervals during the day. (Data from Moore, 1981; Moore, Bonnet, & Warm, 1982; Moore, Bonnet, Warm, & Kramer, 1981.)

resulting values were used in an analysis of variance (ANOVA) with terms for group (normal vs. insomniac), place of estimate (bedroom vs. nonbedroom), and time of test. For the short intervals and long intervals, no significant effects were found for group, place, or time of day. For oral temperature, there was no significant effect for group ($F < 1.00$), but there was the expected effect for time of day, $F(4,80) = 15.18$, $p < .01$. As in the first study, it was found that the insomniacs scored significantly higher on the State Anxiety scale of the Spielberger State-Trait Anxiety Inventory (Spielberger, Gorusch, and Lushene, 1968). The significant effect was the main effect, $F(1,20) = 8.22$, $p < .01$. The anxiety ANOVA effects for place of estimate, for time of day, and for interactions were not significant. In the afternoon nap attempt, both insomniac and normal sleepers estimated relatively well. The insomniacs slightly overestimated the interval, and the normal sleepers estimated the interval almost correctly. No significant difference was shown in the subjective to objective sleep latency ratio for normal and insomniac sleepers, $t(22) = 0.72$. As expected from the other data, no nap-associated temperature differences were found, but anxiety again differentiated the groups, $t(22) = 2.54$, $p < .01$.

Sufficient observations of time estimates, oral temperature measures, and anxiety scores were available so that Spearman rank-order correlations could be calculated for each subject across the day. The correlations were then tested for direction (to determine if a positive or negative relation between pairs of variables existed for either insomniac or normal sleepers). No indication of a significant association between subjective time estimates and either state anxiety or body temperature were found in either group.

The two studies together suggest that insomniacs do overestimate their sleep onset latency but that this overestimation is directly linked to events that take place specifically during the first 20–30 min in bed at night as the insomniac attempts to fall asleep. No evidence was found to suggest that insomniacs, as compared with normal sleepers, misperceive any time interval during the day. This implies (a) that insomniacs do not simply misperceive time, (b) that insomniacs do not misperceive long intervals of time, (c) that insomniacs do not become more anxious or misperceive time in the presence of sleep-associated stimuli (i.e., in a bedroom), and (d) that insomniacs do not perceive a nap sleep onset as similar to a nocturnal sleep onset even though the setting contains both the bedroom stimulus and the demand to sleep. This also implies that the nap is viewed as a unique sleep situation without the usual demands (e.g., "If I do not fall asleep quickly, I will feel terrible in the morning"), and this view is supported by the fact that the participating subjects reported that they normally did not take naps.

The data also seem to imply that neither oral temperature nor anxiety is directly related to the misperception of nocturnal sleep onset in insomniacs. Although the insomniacs were significantly more anxious than the normal sleepers, they were more anxious than the normal sleepers at all measuring points. This means that the insomniacs were more anxious than normal sleepers at many points at which their perception of time was just as accurate as that of the normal subjects. These data leave open the possibility of a complex interaction in which insomniacs are stably more anxious than normal sleepers but react differently only when the lights go out and they are faced with the nocturnal sleep period. Conversely, insomniacs may simply ruminate more at their nocturnal sleep onset in a way that is not directly measured by a state anxiety scale. Finally, it is possible that insomniacs have a poor wake/sleep perceptual interface and simply do not know when they actually enter the sleep state. At the subjective level, at least, insomniacs may slide slowly into sleep rather than fall asleep.

SLEEP ONSET INSOMNIA AS A PERCEPTUAL PROBLEM

Recently, we have begun to consider sleep onset problems in insomniacs without other sleep disorders or significant psychopathology as more of a cognitive–perceptual difficulty. Depending on the extent of this cognitive–perceptual problem, we may be able to teach these insomniacs to identify more accurately the time of their own sleep onset and thereby to estimate more accurately their sleep latency. Furthermore, if this perceptual ability can be taught, it may by definition eliminate the insomnia complaint because the long subjective sleep latencies will no longer exist. A current study (Downey & Bonnet, 1989) is directed toward improving perception of the sleep/wake interface.

As in the previous studies, participants were carefully screened to eliminate other sleep disorders such as periodic leg movements or sleep apnea. Patients with significant psychopathology, as measured by the Minnesota Multiphasic Personality Inventory (MMPI) were also eliminated. In the current study, insomniacs were between 18 and 40 years of age and had reported insomnia for more than a year. On a sleep laboratory screening night, subjects were required to overestimate their objective sleep latency by at least 50% but to have relatively normal sleep efficiency (>85%) once they had fallen asleep. The final criterion was used in an attempt to define the insomnia clearly as sleep onset rather than sleep maintenance.

After an adaptation night, subjects were randomly assigned to either a control or a treatment condition. The next laboratory night was an undisturbed baseline night. On the following laboratory night, subjects in both control and treatment conditions were awakened 27 times during the night according to criteria to be described. The control and treatment conditions differed in two respects. First, in the treatment condition, subjects were shown their sleep recording from the adaptation night, and various sleep events were defined for them. At the same time, typical mental content at the various sleep times was described. For example, at a representative period of alpha, the subjects were told that alpha represented relaxed wakefulness and that when people are "awakened" at that point, they usually report thinking about things and being in general control of their thoughts. The initial sleep spindle was differentiated as a state in which thoughts may be drifting, without direct control, or no longer completely linked together with earlier thoughts or concerns. Thoughts 5 min after the initial sleep spindle were characterized as showing more loss of control or contact. Subjects were told that occasionally these latter awakenings may not be accompanied by a clear thought or may seem cognitively unusual. Second, subjects in the treatment condition were given appropriate feedback concerning their sleep/wake state from the experimenter after each awakening, whereas subjects in the control condition were not.

The awakenings were designed to occur at three times around sleep onset to give the subjects three consistent cognitive surrounds as described previously and to help them clarify their own sleep onset process. The three awakening possibilities were labeled *A, B,* and *C.* Point A was preceded by a minute of clear alpha; Point B was the first well-defined sleep spindle; and Point C was 5 min after the first well-defined sleep spindle. Trials A, B, and C were block randomized. Nine trials were given early in the night, nine trials were given in the middle of the night, and the remaining nine trials were given early in the morning.

After all laboratory nights, subjects completed standard morning questionnaires about their night of sleep and provided estimates of their sleep onset latency. Following the treatment/control night, subjects were allowed a normal night at home to recover from any sleep disturbance effects from the awakening procedure. After the home night, subjects returned to the sleep laboratory for an undisturbed night of sleep followed by normal morning estimates. Sleep latency estimates from this last night were used to determine changes in perceived sleep latency. Subjects who received the control condition first received the training condition at least 1 week later. Subjects who received the treatment condition first could not be scheduled for a control condition (because they had already been trained to identify the cognitive surround of sleep onset).

To date, 4 subjects have completed both the control and the treatment conditions, and 1 subject has completed the treatment condition only. The data indicate that insomniacs can learn to differentiate the three sleep conditions. Subjects improved their correct sleep state differentiation from 46% on the control week to 93% on treatment weeks. The 93% correct on treatment weeks implies that a very good discrimination can be made. Of course, the more important issue is the subjective to objective sleep latency ratio. This ratio was also decreased. The mean ratio was 4.0 after the final laboratory night in the control condition and 1.8 after the final laboratory night in the treatment condition, $F(1,4) = 13.26$, $p < .05$. Although this seems to imply that patients had greatly improved estimates, the subjective to objective ratio on the baseline night directly preceding treatment was 2.1, and that was not significantly different from the 1.8 value following treatment. The numbers should stabilize with a greater number of subjects.

Of additional interest, subjects were asked to estimate the probability with which they thought they would be able to fall asleep in less than 30 min on a given night across the course of the study. Those estimates ranged from 18–28% prior to the treatment night. On the final laboratory night, the estimate was 59%, $F(1,4) = 22.62$, $p < .01$. This finding corresponds to reports from subjects that they learned to feel more in control of their sleep behavior. One subject had a long-term (5 month) follow-up. That subject reported that sleep remained improved and that, despite some bad nights, nights were not all bad as they previously had been. When the subject slept in the sleep laboratory once again, she could still identify the three conditions with 85% accuracy. In addition, at 5-month follow-up, that subject had a subjective to objective latency ratio of 1.5 compared with a ratio of 3.3 at the end of the experiment proper.

SUMMARY

If you ask yourself how long it took to fall asleep last night, you will probably be faced with a definition based primarily on absence (i.e., "I do not remember much happening after I went to bed, so I probably fell asleep quickly"). It is difficult to make accurate retrospective judgments of periods without clear markers, and it is surprising how well most people can make such judgments. Our studies have shown that when normal subjects are given clear markers and immediate judgments, there is still a 4–8 min period around sleep onset when cognition is changing and determination of sleep state is uncertain. In most people, this error has little impact. In patients with insomnia, errors in defining sleep state are much greater, and such errors in perception may form the basis for the long-term use of hypnotics or other medication. Thus, the problem of sleep onset in patients with insomnia is real.

The current work was based on a small and select group of insomniacs who appeared to suffer primarily from a problem of misperception of sleep onset. These patients almost certainly had a problem linked to events that occurred during their sleep onset, and the present data suggest that those events were probably cognitive. It is likely that a cognitively based treatment, perhaps the one described here, can be of benefit. However, some cautions are in order. There is no evidence that the results described herein will apply to patients with major depression or with a long history of medication use. It is also unlikely that a cognitive treatment program will be helpful for patients with disorders that significantly fragment sleep, because each brief arousal may bring a return of conscious events that may become mixed with the sleep onset definition. Rather, it is hoped that individuals can begin to apply objective behavioral methods to diagnose and treat some forms of insomnia and that these methods will serve as a starting point for the development of behavioral treatments for more difficult insomnias.

References

Anch, A. M., McCoy, J. S., & Somerest, J. S. (1980). The relationship between EEG alpha activity and perceived awakening. *Sleep Research, 9,* 22.

Aschoff, J., Geidke, H., Poppel, E., & Wever, R. (1972). The influence of sleep interruption and sleep deprivation on circadian rhythms in human performance. In W. P. Colquhoun (Ed.), *Aspects of human efficiency* (pp. 135–150). London: English University Press.

Baekland, F., & Hoy, P. (1971). Reported vs. recorded sleep characteristics. *Archives of General Psychiatry, 24,* 548–551.

Bonnet, M. H., & Moore, S. E. (1982). The threshold of sleep: Perception of sleep as a function of time asleep and auditory threshold. *Sleep, 5,* 267–276.

Campbell, S. S., & Webb, W. B. (1981). The perception of wakefulness within sleep. *Sleep, 4,* 177–183.

Carskadon, M. A., Dement, W. C., Mitler, M. M., Guilleminault, C., Zarcone, V. P., & Spiegel, R. (1976). Self-reports vs. sleep laboratory findings in 122 drug-free subjects with complaints of chronic insomnia. *American Journal of Psychiatry, 133,* 1382–1388.

Downey, R. D., & Bonnet, M. H. (1989, June). *Sleep-wake discrimination in subjective insomnia improves as a function of sleep onset feedback.* Paper presented at the meeting of the Association of Professional Sleep Societies, Washington, DC.

Falk, J. L., & Bindra, D. (1954). Judgments of time as a function of serial position and stress. *Journal of Experimental Psychology, 47,* 279–284.

Frankel, B., Coursey, R., Buchbinder, R., & Snyder, F. (1976). Recorded and reported sleep in chronic primary insomnia. *Archives of General Psychiatry, 33,* 615–623.

Hauri, P., & Cohen, S. (1977). The treatment of insomnia with biofeedback: Final report of Study 1. *Sleep Research, 6,* 136.

Johns, M. W., Masterton, J. P., & Bruce, D. W. (1971). Relationship between sleep habits, adrenocortical activity and personality. *Psychosomatic Medicine, 33,* 499–508.

Langer, J., Wapner, S., & Werner, H. (1961). The effect of danger upon the experience of time. *American Journal of Psychology, 74,* 94–97.

Masao, K. (1978). Performance and time of day: Diurnal variations in physiological and psychological tests. *Journal of Child Development, 14,* 16–24.

Mendelson, W. B., Garnett, D., Gillin, J. C., & Weingartner, H. (1984). The experience of insomnia and daytime and nighttime functioning. *Psychiatry Research, 12,* 235–250.

Monroe, L. J. (1967). Psychological and physiological differences between good and poor sleepers. *Journal of Abnormal Psychology, 72,* 255–264.

Moore, S. E. (1981). *Estimates of sleep latency and of other temporal intervals in insomniac and normal sleepers.* Unpublished master's thesis, University of Cincinnati.

Moore, S. E., Bonnet, M. H., & Warm, J. S. (1982). Time estimation in normal and insomniac subjects. *Sleep Research, 11,* 161.

Moore, S. E., Bonnet, M. H., Warm, J. S., & Kramer, M. (1980). Estimates of sleep latency in the morning and at sleep onset in insomniac and normal subjects. *Sleep Research, 10,* 219.

Nease, N. F., Monroe, S. E., Bonnet, M. H., & Kramer, M. (1981). Perception of sleep latency across nights and conditions in insomniacs. *Sleep Research, 10,* 220.

Olmstead, E., Hauri, P., Percy, L., & Hellekson, C. (1980). Subjective vs. objective estimation of sleep onset in normal sleepers and in insomniacs. *Sleep Research, 9,* 216.

Pfaff, D. (1968). Effects of temperature and time of day on time judgments. *Journal of Experimental Psychology, 76,* 419–422.

Rechtschaffen, A. (1968). Polygraphic aspects of insomnia. In H. Gastaut, E. Lugaresi, G. Berti, G. Ceroni, & G. Coccagna (Eds.), *The abnormalities of sleep in man.* Bologna, Italy: Gaggi.

Spielberger, C. D., Gorusch, R. L., & Lushene (1968). *The state–trait anxiety inventory. Preliminary test manual for form X.* Tallahassee, FL: Florida State University.

Spielman, A. J., Tannenbaum, R., Adler, J., Saskin, P., Pollak, C. P., Roffwarg, H. P., & Weitzman, E. D. (1980). A comparison between objective and subjective sleep latency in patients with chronic insomnia. *Sleep Research, 9,* 225.

Tietz, E. I., Zorick, F. J., Roth, T., & Kaffeman, M. E. (1980). Objective and subjective sleep parameters in documented and undocumented insomniacs. *Sleep Research, 9,* 222.

CHAPTER 12

ARE YOU AWAKE? COGNITIVE PERFORMANCE AND REVERIE DURING THE HYPNOPOMPIC STATE

DAVID F. DINGES

Kleitman (1963) observed that "immediately after getting up, irrespective of the hour, one is not at one's best" (p. 124). It is a paradoxical phenomenon—being more impaired upon awakening from sleep than upon going to sleep—that has been documented for a wide array of behavioral tasks. Typically, such impairment is modest and short-lived due to gradual awakening or to a slow transition out of the hypnopompic state. It can be dramatic, however, if the arousal from sleep is abrupt, regardless of whether the sleep occurs at night or during a daytime nap (Dinges, Orne, Evans, & Orne, 1981). Further, the intensity of the hypnopompic state as evidenced by the severity of cognitive impairment can be most profound if the awakening occurs during the first half of the night or if the person has been awake for a protracted period of time and is aroused after only an hour or two of recovery sleep. In such situations, the sleepiness evident in the hypnopompic state results in vastly impaired performance compared with that seen in a sleep-deprived subject (Dinges, Orne, & Orne, 1985b).

The dramatic nature of hypnopompic disorientation, confusion, and performance impairment has been described by a variety of names, including "sleep drunkenness" (Broughton, 1968, 1973), "postdormital sleepiness" (Association of Sleep Disorders Centers, 1979), and "sleep inertia" (Lubin, Hord, Tracy, & Johnson, 1976). The former terms are now used primarily for sleep pathology, whereas the latter is widely applied to describe transient awakening (i.e., hypnopompic) impairment in healthy persons. This chapter is concerned with hypnopompic cognition during intense sleep inertia and the processes that might account for it.

SLEEP INERTIA AND PERFORMANCE DURING
THE HYPNOPOMPIC PERIOD

The studies cited in Table 1 represent much of what is known about hypno-pompic cognition and the awakening process as it pertains to performance capability. Table 1 does not include a separate body of literature on dream reports at awakening. Virtually all the work conducted on performance during the hypnopompic state has derived from two theoretical perspectives, with slightly different emphases. The first reflects an interest in the functional differences between REM and non-REM (NREM) sleep stages in information processing potential; this is the performance analogue of the studies of sleep stage-dependent dream mentation. The approach typically taken is to awaken subjects from different stages of sleep and evaluate performance on a parame-ter of theoretical import, such as perception (e.g., Lavie & Sutter, 1975) or memory (e.g., Bonnet, 1983; Stones, 1977). The second approach derives from studies of human performance during periods of prolonged quasi-continuous wakefulness, when the adverse effects of sleep loss must be weighed against the adverse effects of sleep inertia upon abrupt arousal from sleep due to an emergency (e.g., Hartman & Langdon, 1965; Haslam, 1982). In these studies, emphasis is placed not on the preawakening stage of sleep but rather on the magnitude of sleep inertia, its duration, and the range of performances affected by it.

At the heart of sleep inertia is the nature of hypnopompic cognition and biobehavioral functioning on arousal from sleep. Although much more has been written about the hypnagogic state (Mavromatis, 1987; Schacter, 1976) than the hypnopompic state, the phenomenon of sleep inertia and its accom-panying cognitive processes are ubiquitous. Because of this ubiquity and be-cause it is typically a transient phenomenon (lasting between 1–20 min) dur-ing which cognition and performance can be grossly altered relative to other times, the hypnopompic period is often ignored in many studies on the effects of sleep on human functioning.

It is, however, precisely because of the dramatically altered cognitive per-formance, reverie, and subsequent amnesia of the hypnopompic period that sleep inertia is worthy of increased attention. At the very least, the phenome-non offers a window to the changes in cognition from sleep to waking. In its extreme form in an otherwise healthy individual, sleep inertia affords a model for cognitive impairment of a kind rarely seen in either experimental (e.g., sleep deprivation) or clinical (e.g., insomnia) studies. What follows is an espe-cially dramatic example of sleep inertia that illustrates how profound the phe-nomenon can become if the appropriate paradigm is used. Following the ex-

The research and substantive evaluation upon which this manuscript is based were sup-ported in part by Office of Naval Research Contract N00014-80-C-0380, in part by National Institute of Mental Health Grants MH-19156 and MH-44193, and in part by a grant from the Institute for Experimental Psychiatry Research Foundation. I am grateful to Kelly A. Gillen for help in preparing the manuscript.

ample is a discussion of factors that contribute to it, including a review of evidence that sleep depth more than the preawakening stage of sleep is the crucial variable that influences hypnopompic cognition. We conclude with a theoretical framework that posits a common process (sleep pressure) underlying hypnopompic, hypnagogic, and sleep-related waking reverie.

A PARADIGM TO STUDY SLEEP INERTIA

To study the role of sleep pressure and various aspects of sleep infrastructure on hypnopompic performance, we conducted two studies of human cognitive functioning upon abrupt awakening from naps (Dinges et al., 1981; Dinges, Orne, & Orne, 1985a, 1985b). Like the studies cited in Table 1, the goal was to use a cognitive task as a probe to investigate the processes underlying hypnopompic cognition. Relatively short periods of sleep (1–120 min) provide a theoretically important way of studying cognitive performance during the hypnopompic state without confounding circadian variation and sleep infrastructure changes, which result when awakening occurs from longer periods of sleep (4–8 hr). Thus, studies of naps under 2 hr, at different phases of the circadian cycle and following varying amounts of prior sleep loss, permit assessment of specific aspects of sleep infrastructure and depth in relation to performance upon awakening.

In both studies, performance on a 3-min descending subtraction task (DST) was used as a cognitive probe on abrupt awakening. Details of the task have been published elsewhere (Dinges et al., 1985a). Briefly, it was developed to permit the subject to perform it while lying on a bed in the dark, thereby allowing assessment within a few seconds of sleep offset. The task requires an oral rather than a nonverbal response from the subject, which permits reverie intrusions to be observed. The subtractions are done silently, and the answers are said aloud. Both speed and accuracy are emphasized, and because the subtrahend and minuend change after each response, a considerable load is placed on memory. If a subject does not give a response on the DST for 20 s, the experimenter then says, "Please continue, guess if you have to," and thereafter pushes the subject every few seconds to respond. (This was necessary often during the hypnopompic period but was necessary only infrequently during baseline, presleep, or sleep deprivation phases of the studies.) Thus, no subject could score poorly on the task merely by not responding for the bulk of the allotted 3 min.

In our studies, DST performance was assessed repeatedly before each nap (to ensure that performance was asymptotic) and immediately following a motor response (answering a telephone) and an affirmative oral response (to the question "Are you awake?"), as well as repeatedly thereafter. In all 198 awakening nap protocols we have run to date, sleep was polysomnographically recorded, and the EEG was monitored during hypnopompic performance. Naps were either 1 hr (Dinges et al., 1981) or 2 hr (Dinges et al., 1985a) in duration, although subjects were not told how long they would be permitted to nap. They were aware, however, that they would be expected to perform

Table 1

STUDIES OF PERFORMANCE UPON AWAKENING

Study	Task
Dinges, Orne, Evans, and Orne (1981)	Simple reaction time
Dinges, Orne, and Orne (1985a)	
Okuma, Nakamura, Hayashi, and Fujimori (1966)	
Rosa, Bonnet, and Warm (1983)	
Webb and Agnew (1964)	
Wilkinson and Stretton (1971)	
Williams, Morlock, and Morlock (1966)	
Feltin and Broughton (1968)	Complex reaction time
Goodenough, Lewis, Shapiro, Jaret, and Sleser (1965)	
Scott (1969)	
Seminara and Shavelson (1969)	
Jeanneret and Webb (1963)	Grip strength
Tebbs and Foulkes (1966)	
Wilkinson and Stretton (1971)	Steadiness/coordination
Hartman and Langdon (1965)	Complex simulation
Hartman, Langdon, and McKenzie (1965)	
Langdon and Hartman (1961)	
Seminara and Shavelson (1969)	
Fort and Mills (1972)	Letter cancellation
Haslam (1982)	Logical reasoning
Akerstedt and Gillberg (1979)	Memory tasks
Bonnet (1983)	
Gastaut and Broughton (1965)	
Grosvenor and Lack (1984)	
Stones (1977)	
Dinges et al. (1981)	Mental arithmetic
Dinges et al. (1985a)	
Pritchett (1969)	
Wilkinson and Stretton (1971)	
Scott (1969)	Clock reversal

Table 1 (continued)

Study	Task
Carlson, Feinberg, and Goodenough (1978)	Time estimates
Koulack and Schultz (1974)	Vigilance, trailmaking
Lavie and Giora (1973)	Visual-perceptual
Lavie and Sutter (1975)	
Scott (1969)	
Scott and Snyder (1968)	

the DST immediately upon awakening from sleep. Awakening was done auditorily by a telephone, which rang continuously for 1 min and, if not answered, rang on and off every 2 s for another minute. If the subject still did not respond, his or her name was spoken over the intercom until a verbal response was elicited. After answering the phone, the subject was asked how much time had elapsed since he or she had last spoken with the experimenter (immediately prenap) and was asked to estimate his or her sleepiness on a 10-point analogue scale. Following this, the subject was instructed to hang up the phone, lie back down (in the dark), and perform the DST. The polygraph was kept running throughout awakening performance, which was audio tape-recorded. After electrode removal, DST performance was again assessed repeatedly.

In one major study (Dinges, 1986; Dinges, Orne, Whitehouse, & Orne, 1987; Dinges, Whitehouse, Orne, & Orne, 1988), the amount of continuous wakefulness (sleep loss) prior to a 2-hr nap opportunity was varied from 6 hr to 52 hr. This had the effect of producing marked differences in nap sleep-stage infrastructure and amount, which permitted an assessment of hypnopompic cognition as a function of varying sleep depths or intensities. At the most extreme intensity, sleep inertia was profound, and intrusions of hypnopompic reverie occurred during the DST at awakening. The following example illustrates the power of our experimental protocol to produce a dramatic hypnopompic condition that is characterized by social interaction with simultaneous performance impairment, hypnopompic reverie, misjudgment of sleepiness, and a dissociation between the electroencephalogram (EEG) and behavior.

SOCIALLY AWAKE YET FUNCTIONALLY ASLEEP
The nature of the cognitive impairment in DST performance that was evident at awakening, especially after subjects had been sleep-deprived and therefore had slept very deeply, was such that it was often accompanied by dramatic intrusions of reverie as subjects attempted to say the answers aloud. Table 2 provides a transcript of the interaction between one of our sleep-deprived subjects (18-year old healthy man) and the experimenter after the subject had been awake for 52 consecutive hours in the sleep-deprivation protocol, during

Table 2

DIALOGUE BETWEEN SUBJECT AND EXPERIMENTER DURING
PRESLEEP PERFORMANCE OF DESCENDING SUBTRACTION TASK
AND UPON AWAKENING FROM SLEEP

Minute	Speaker	Content
		Presleep Performance
0	Experimenter:	I would like you to do the subtraction task again. Remember to work as fast and accurately as you can. Your starting number is 931.
1–3	Subject:	931 922 914 907 901 *895* 891 888 886 869 862 . . . . 509 503. [75 correct, 2 errors]
4–5	Experimenter:	That's good. On a scale from 1 to 10, where 1 is very wide awake and 10 is very sleepy, how do you feel now?
	Subject:	8
	Experimenter:	Please lie quietly with your eyes closed, but stay awake, until I tell you that you can go to sleep.
	Subject:	Okay.
	Experimenter:	Remember that the end of the nap will be signalled by the telephone ringing, which you should answer as quickly as possible. You will then be asked to do the subtraction task. Okay, you can go to sleep now.
		Postsleep Performance
128–129	Experimenter:	Are you awake?
	Subject:	Yes!
	Experimenter:	Can you hear me okay?
	Subject:	Yeah.
	Experimenter:	How long since I spoke to you last?
	Subject:	Um . . . um . . . 90 minutes.
	Experimenter:	On a scale from 1 to 10, where 1 is very wide awake and 10 is very sleepy, how do you feel now?
	Subject:	Um . . . about um . . . 6.
	Experimenter:	Hang the phone up and lie back. I would like you to do the subtraction task. [S having difficulty hanging up telephone.]
	Experimenter:	Can you see to hang it up?
	Subject:	There, got it.
	Experimenter:	Remember to work as fast and accurately as you can. Your starting number is 648.

Table 2 (continued)

Minute	Speaker	Content
130	Subject:	648 64 . . ah 63 . . ummm 500 and ah . . (sigh)
	Experimenter:	Continue!
	Subject:	500 and um . . let's see . . um . . 696 685 640, ah, um . . . *632* *631* *631*
	Experimenter:	Continue!
132	Subject:	What if people ran faster than normal people run home—than the normal person runs faster than the square root of two times . . . (mumbles incoherently) . . . and normal quote-unquote people take up two derivatives of normal people in skin brackets . . .
		[1 correct, 4 errors]
133	Experimenter:	That's good.

Note: After the presleep test, the subject, who had been awake for 52 hr, took a 2-hr nap. After the nap, the subject did not respond to the telephone bell but picked up the phone when his name was called.

which the DST was repeatedly performed. The script in Table 2 begins as the subject is lying on a bed, in a dark quiet room, just before being allowed to sleep. His presleep (postsleep-loss) DST performance for 3 min of 75 correct answers and 2 errors was below his presleep-loss levels of 82–99 correct answers and 0–2 errors; this net loss in number completed is characteristic of the cognitive slowing on subject-paced tasks that typically occurs with sleep loss (Dinges, 1989b).

Following this performance, as is typical for intensely sleepy persons, the subject fell asleep (Stage 1) within 30 s of being permitted to do so and had his first epoch of slow wave sleep (SWS) 4 min later (Dinges, 1986). He remained asleep for the entire 2-hr period. He had no REM sleep but accumulated 82.5 min (69% of total sleep time) of SWS (70 min of Stage 4 sleep), which is nearly as much SWS as healthy young adults of his age acquire in an average 8-hr nocturnal sleep (cf. R. L. Williams, Karacan, & Hursch, 1974)! He was in Stage 3 sleep at the time of the awakening bell. Although he did not answer the awakening telephone call until his name was spoken, which indicates an intense sleep depth, he interacted immediately thereafter, affirming that he was awake, estimating the time since he had last spoken to the experimenter, and providing a rating of his sleepiness.

Curiously, he estimated his sleepiness at a score of 6 at awakening, indicating that he was less sleepy than he had been before the nap (rating of 8). This was a clear dissociation between his self-report and his DST performance, which was far worse at awakening than it was after 52 hr of wakefulness, just prior to the nap. We have analyzed enough data to show that this hypnopompic misjudgment of sleepiness is common in subjects whose sleep has followed a sustained period of wakefulness beyond 18 hr, but that it does not occur if the nap is taken before sleep deprivation (Dinges, 1988). The intensity of the sleep inertia seems to make it difficult to estimate how sleepy one feels. This finding is consistent with Sewitch's (1984) report that the length of continuous NREM sleep affects the normal sleeper's perception of having been awake or asleep, such that awakenings from SWS or after prolonged periods of NREM sleep most often result in subjects being least able to identify accurately whether they had been awake or asleep.

Following his time and sleepiness estimates and his interaction with the experimenter over the phone, the subject was asked to perform the DST. He was totally unable to execute subtractions correctly (only his repeat of the starting number was correct; his four subtraction errors are in italics in Table 2), and he could not remember where he was in the sequence, despite two prods to continue from the experimenter.

He also had considerable difficulty preventing hypnopompic reverie from intruding into his oral output. The spoken reverie that occurred 2 min into the awakening DST performance (132 min in Table 2) began after the experimenter prompted him a second time to continue. It is noteworthy that the apparent evocation of this spoken reverie by the experimenter is consistent with the observations of Broughton (1968, 1982) that parasomnic episodes such as sleep walking and enuresis can be triggered by external stimuli and, therefore, can be considered disorders of arousal or of partial arousal. In fact, the awakening performance behavior of this subject is reminiscent of the confusional arousals from SWS described by Broughton (1968), which he suggested were due to "impaired cerebral responsiveness or of functional deafferentation" (p. 1074). The actual reverie of our subject at 2-min postawakening is illustrative of the semicoherent material we have observed in the awakening reverie of other subjects. Neologistic phrases such as "normal people in skin brackets" are referred to, along with phenomenological material appropriate to the individual such as "the square root of two times" (this subject was a math major and, indeed, the reverie has the quality of a statement of a mathematical problem).

Interestingly, the subject indicated that he had dreamed during the nap; this response was made in a questionnaire booklet he completed while electrodes were being removed, 15 min after awakening. No dream content was asked for and, consequently, it is unknown whether the dream related to his hypnopompic reverie. This was not the only reverie he experienced, however. Despite coherent social interaction and the completion of performance tasks, he experienced other reverie intrusions into his cognitive performance oral output at 6 min and 35 min postawakening. Although reverie was less dramatic in many other subjects to the extent that it lasted only a few seconds rather than a full minute, it was apparent in most who had undergone intensive sleep loss in the form of one- to five-word intrusions into oral performance output. Such intrusions were most common in the hypnopompic period.

Record

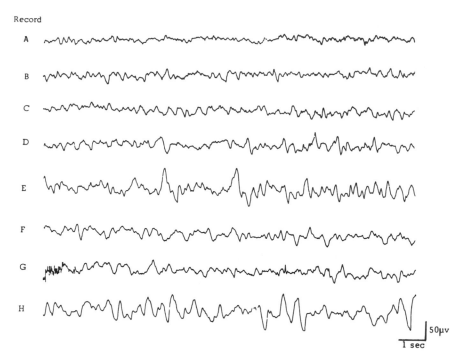

Figure 1   Vertex (C_z-A_1A_2) EEG recordings from a healthy young adult with eyes closed lying on a bed in a dark quiet bedroom, taken at eight different times. Record (A) after 6 hr of wakefulness—instructed to lie awake quietly. (B) after 52 hr of wakefulness—minute 1 after being instructed to lie awake quietly. (C) 2 min after B—still attempting to stay awake. (D) 1 min after C and after being instructed to go to sleep. (E) 2 min after D (asleep by polysomnographic criteria). (F) after 2-hr nap—minute 1 of DST performance at awakening (see text). (G) 2 min after F—during reverie of final minute on DST (see Table 2). (H) 2 min after completion of DST at awakening— instructed to remain awake, but S fell asleep.

FUNCTIONALLY ASLEEP YET ELECTROENCEPHALOGRAPHICALLY AWAKE

The EEG recording obtained during the awakening reverie of our subject was compared with recordings made under comparable conditions (e.g., eyes closed, prone in bed) prior to and following sleep deprivation, during wakefulness and sleep onset, in an effort to determine whether the reverie was accompanied by a clear change in EEG. Increased theta and delta activity in particular is characteristic of a period of reverie, and one would expect the EEG to be visibly different during reverie than during the prenap DST performance, when the subject was intensely sleepy but able to perform 75 correct subtractions in 3 min.

Figure 1 displays vertex EEG recordings made at eight times for this subject. The presleep-deprivation record (Record A) taken after only 6 hr awake is notably different from all others because it contains less slow wave activity (delta and theta) and more beta activity. All records (Records B–H) from the sleep-deprivation period show increased slow wave activity. Of particular interest is the comparison between Records C and G. Although no EEG recording was made during the presleep DST performance, Record C (at 52 hr and 2 min of sleep loss) was obtained 2 min into the 3-min presleep wake, eyes-closed baseline (i.e., 1 min before the subject was allowed to sleep). Record G was obtained 2 min into the postsleep awakening DST performance, when the reverie at the bottom of Table 2 was elicited. There is no obvious difference between these records, and they are clearly different from the high-amplitude, slow-frequency waveforms apparent in the sleep records at 1 min and 2 min of nap onset (Records D–E) and when the subject fell asleep after completing the awakening DST (Record H). Despite the lack of EEG differences between Records C and G, differences at these times in DST performance and cognitive coherency are profound (Table 2).

SLEEP DEPTH AND SLEEP INERTIA

The depth of sleep achieved by our subject during the 2-hr (recovery) nap following over 2 days without sleep was intense, as it has been in every subject we have examined who was sleep deprived. Recovery sleep following sleep loss has long been known to involve a greater depth of sleep. Consistent with other studies, the greater depth of sleep was evidenced by a decreased latency to SWS (Dinges, 1986), an exceptionally high amount of SWS, especially during the first NREM cycle of sleep (Borbely, Baumann, Brandeis, Strauch, & Lehmann, 1981; Dinges, 1986; Feinberg, Floyd, & March, 1987; Hume & Mills, 1977; Webb & Agnew, 1967, 1971), decreased body movement during sleep (Naitoh, Muzet, Johnson, & Moses, 1973), a failure to respond to the awakening bell (Rechtschaffen, Hauri, & Zeitlin, 1966; Rosa & Bonnet, 1985; Williams, Hammack, Daly, Dement, & Lubin, 1964), and a rapid return to sleep following awakening (Bonnet, 1978). All of these parameters provide an index of sleep depth. Ironically, sleep depth often has not been considered in studies of performance upon awakening.

There has been considerable interest in determining which aspects of sleep account for sleep inertia or the performance impairment evident in the hypnopompic period. The typical experimental paradigm used to study it has consisted of abrupt, forced awakening from REM or NREM sleep stages. Thus, when performance during the hypnopompic period has been investigated (Table 1), the paradigm for studies of sleep-stage-related mentation has been most commonly used. In these studies, it is often assumed that the severity of performance sleep inertia is directly related to the preawakening stage of sleep, such that awakenings from SWS yield the most dramatic hypnopompic phenomena, whereas those from REM sleep yield more wakelike performances. Although the results of most studies that have investigated arousal from different sleep stages support this view, the bias of evaluating only the preawakening stage of sleep is so pervasive that other aspects of the sleep infrastructure are rarely examined to determine whether they are more consistently associated with the magnitude and nature of hypnopompic phenomena.

There is reason to hypothesize, however, that the intensity of hypno-pompic reverie and the extent to which cognitive performance is impaired during awakening are most accurately characterized as being a function of the depth of sleep, of which the preawakening stage of sleep is but one facet (Dinges et al., 1985a, 1985b). This is evidenced in three ways: (a) awakenings exclusively from Stage 2 NREM sleep yield performance decrements that vary as a function of time of night (circadian phase) (Rosa, Bonnet, & Warm, 1983); (b) awakenings from recovery sleep following prolonged wakefulness yield decrements greater than those found for awakenings from the same stage of sleep prior to deprivation (Akerstedt & Gillberg, 1979; Fort & Mills, 1972; Rosa et al., 1983); and (c) abrupt awakenings from naps yield increasingly more severe cognitive performance decrements as the amount of NREM (Stages 2 + 3 + 4) sleep increases (Dinges et al., 1981) and as the amount of wakefulness prior to sleep increases, regardless of the stage of sleep from which subjects are awakened (Dinges et al., 1985a).

How can we account for the fact that most of the studies in Table 1 have observed greater hypnopompic impairment on awakenings from SWS relative to Stage 2 or REM sleep? This may have resulted because SWS is consistently associated with greater sleep depth, especially in the first NREM cycle (Dinges 1986; Feinberg et al., 1987). Generally, the preawakening depth of sleep may be more important than the depth of sleep at other times in the sleep period (Bonnet, 1983), making the preawakening stage of sleep a salient variable for hypnopompic cognition. On the other hand, at least one study has reported that the behavioral performance variables at repeated awakenings from recovery sleep following (40 hr and 64 hr of) sleep loss are generally more sensitive than sleep stages to different amounts of prior wakefulness (Rosa & Bonnet, 1985).

In fact, it is not clear that SWS is essential for severe hypnopompic performance impairment to occur in response to sleep depth. Bonnet (1985) observed that hypnopompic disorientation could be profound in subjects who were permitted to sleep but who were denied most of their SWS and REM sleep during repeated nights of experimentally induced sleep disruption every minute. In his study, auditory arousal thresholds increased dramatically by the second night of sleep disruption, indicating increased sleep depth, while subjects began to become confused on awakening:

> They often could not give ratings. One subject later recounted that at awakening she could hear the technician talking but his words did not seem to make sense. Other subjects could not perform simple tasks such as being able to respond with "a" when prompted for the letter that precedes "b". One explanation for this behavior is sleep drunkenness (i.e., arousal from very deep sleep resulting in confusion). (p. 18)

SLEEP PRESSURE AND THERMOREGULATION

It is my contention that sleep pressure, or the probability of transition from wakefulness to sleep, ($Pr[W \to S]$) underlies sleep depth, SWS, and the magnitude of sleep inertia effects during the hypnopompic period. The simplest way to manipulate sleep pressure is through prior wakefulness. But which physiological process underlies sleep pressure and correlates with manifestations of sleep depth, especially pressure for SWS? Although biochemical changes must underlie any such process, and candidates have been proposed (e.g., see Chapter 2 by Hobson in this volume), there is reason to suggest that body core temperature and, presumably, brain metabolic activity may be an essential link in the hypnopompic process. Body core temperature shows a circadian rhythm, but sleep (especially the first SWS period of the night) also has the (evoked) effect of thermal down-regulation (Gillberg & Akerstedt, 1982). There is evidence that this effect may be enhanced whenever the pressure for sleep is increased. Aschoff, Giedke, Poppel, and Wever (1972) observed that "after two days without sleep, one night of uninterrupted sleep results in an exaggerated drop in rectal temperature" (p. 144). A significant covariation between oral temperature and performance upon awakening has been reported (Rosa & Bonnet, 1985). But the relation between SWS and temperature may go both ways (Sewitch, 1987). Experimentally induced lowering of rectal temperature at sleep onset has been associated with an increase in Stage 4 sleep and a lengthening of the first NREM/REM cycle (Sewitch, Kittrell, Kupfer, & Reynolds, 1986). Passive afternoon body heating has been observed to result in an enhanced drop in rectal temperature during the first 2–4 hr of subsequent nocturnal sleep (Horne & Staff, 1983).

One possible mechanism underlying the increasingly impaired performance at awakening of subjects who have experienced intense pressure for sleep is a decline in cerebral metabolism resulting from thermal down-regulation exacerbated by sleep pressure. The purpose of such down-regulation is unclear, although speculation is easy (e.g., the increased need for protein synthesis, which is favored during sleep, especially during periods of lowest basal metabolic level). Whatever its purpose, such basal drops may have a longer time course than the EEG manifestation of specific sleep stages and may make coherent cortical function impossible until metabolic or specific biochemical activity has been increased through the passage of time (e.g., circadian variation), a change in sleep stage (e.g., accumulation of REM sleep), or increased physical activity at awakening (e.g., getting out of bed)—all of which are intercorrelated such that REM sleep is more likely to occur as body core temperature is rising, and awakenings are more likely to occur from REM sleep (Dinges, 1989a). Unfortunately, despite many studies of hypnopompic performance, none have assessed body core temperature as a covariant of sleep inertia beyond looking at circadian variability.

The hypothesized widespread metabolic decline in cortical activity that would covary with pressure (and therefore with depth) of sleep would probably make it exceedingly difficult for a person to perform well if aroused abruptly from sleep when basal metabolic levels are low. Virtually every type of performance, especially all cognitive performances involving memory and attention, would be adversely affected. There is no reason to believe, however, that the subject could not interact socially at some simple level such as name acknowledgment; indeed, this is what appeared to be the case with our subject. On the other hand, when performance is demanded, reverie can intrude, especially in response to a stimulus (e.g., the experimenter says "continue"). The nature of such semicoherent reverie may be determined by the extent to which the "functional deafferentation" suggested by Broughton (1968) has taken place. The reverie would, therefore, be the result of insufficient neural metabolism for coherent mentation. The inhibition needed for directed cognition would be lacking.

THEORETICAL MODEL OF REVERIE
BASED ON SLEEPINESS

The concept of pressure for sleep, which is expressed as the probability of transition from wakefulness to sleep, $(Pr[W \rightarrow S])$, is in effect a definition of sleep tendency or of sleepiness. To the extent that sleep-related reverie occurs without exception during sleep stages, especially during Stage 1 sleep, then a sleepiness model can account for it. That is, as the probability of a transition to sleep increases, the probability of reverie will increase: Increased pressure for a thermoregulatory down-regulation may underlie this phenomenon. Whatever its physiologic basis, it can account for the "semi-dreaming" (Kleitman, 1963, p. 221) of sleep-deprived subjects, which was observed in the earliest human sleep loss study (Patrick & Gilbert, 1896) as well as for both hypnagogic and hypnopompic reverie.

Figure 2 displays the manner in which sleep pressure manifests itself in behavior and physiology, depending on the context. If the context is one in which the subject is attempting to remain awake, as in sleep-deprivation studies, then increased microsleeps (Stage 1 intrusions), cognitive slowing, response blocks or lapses, and response habituation will be increased. Semi-dreaming or dreaming while awake during tasks that require oral output will be more likely. If the subject is attempting to go to sleep, then increased sleep pressure will be evident in decreased sleep latencies (e.g., as seen on the multiple sleep latency test) and hypnagogic reverie will be more likely to occur sooner. If the context is one of attempting to awaken from sleep, then increased sleep pressure will result in increased sleep depth, and the probability of hypnopompic reverie will be increased. There is, therefore, no reason to posit that the reverie resulting from these three instances is qualitatively different. The various effects of sleep pressure in Figure 2 are intercorrelated. The word used to describe the resulting reverie is more aptly thought of as a descriptor of the context in which each occurs, not of any unique characteristic of the mentation.

Differences can occur, of course, in the severity of reverie intrusions (i.e., pressure for sleep). Hypnopompic mentation may be the most dramatic form of reverie because it involves transition from sleep to wake (sleep inertia), whereas waking and hypnagogic mentation involve transition from wake to sleep ("wake inertia"). In all three cases, the process underlying the emanation

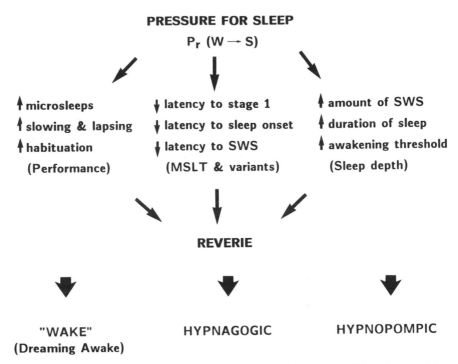

Figure 2   Theoretical model of how sleep pressure (i.e., probability of a transition from wake to sleep) can manifest in sleep-related behavior and physiology, depending on the context, and result in reverie. To the left is the sleep-deprivation context, in which the subject is attempting to remain awake but microsleep intrusions result in "semi-dreaming" reverie. Center is the sleep onset context, in which the subject is attempting to go to sleep and intense sleepiness leads to rapid sleep onset and hypnogogic reverie. To the right is the awakening context, in which the subject is attempting to transition out of sleep but sleep inertia resulting from increased sleep depth leads to hypnopompic reverie. In all three cases, the resulting reverie is the product of increased physiological sleepiness.

of reverie and the nature of cognition in general may well be the same. What happens to this process as REM sleep (and circadian time) accumulate remains to be determined.

References

Akerstedt, T., & Gillberg, M. (1979). Effects of sleep deprivation on memory and sleep latencies in connection with repeated awakenings from sleep. *Psychophysiology, 16*, 49–52.

Aschoff, J., Giedke, H., Poppel, E., & Wever, R. (1972). The influence of sleep interruption and sleep deprivation on circadian rhythms in human performance. In W. P. Colquhoun (Ed.), *Aspects of human efficiency* (pp. 135–150). London: English Universities Press.

Association of Sleep Disorders Centers. (1979). Diagnostic classification of sleep and arousal disorders, first edition, prepared by the Sleep Disorders Classification Committee, H. P. Roffwarg, Chairman. *Sleep, 2,* 1–137.

Bonnet, M. H. (1978). The reliability of depth of sleep and the effects of flurazepam, pentobarbital and caffeine on depth of sleep. *Dissertation Abstracts International, 38,* 5632.

Bonnet, M. H. (1983). Memory for events occurring during arousal from sleep. *Psychophysiology, 20,* 81–87.

Bonnet, M. H. (1985). Effect of sleep disruption on sleep, performance, and mood. *Sleep, 8,* 11–19.

Borbely, A. A., Baumann, F., Brandeis, D., Strauch, I., & Lehmann, D. (1981). Sleep deprivation: Effect on sleep stages and EEG power density in man. *Electroencephalography and Clinical Neurophysiology, 51,* 483–493.

Broughton, R. J. (1968). Sleep disorders: Disorders of arousal? *Science, 159,* 1070–1078.

Broughton, R. J. (1973). Confusional sleep disorders: Interrelationship with memory consolidation and retrieval in sleep. In T. J. Boag & D. Campbell (Eds.), *A triune concept of the brain and behavior* (pp. 115–127). Toronto: University of Toronto Press.

Broughton, R. J. (1982). Human consciousness and sleep/wake rhythms: A review and some neuropsychological considerations. *Journal of Clinical Neuropsychology, 4,* 193–218.

Carlson, V. R., Feinberg, I., & Goodenough, D. R. (1978). Perception of the duration of sleep intervals as a function of EEG sleep stage. *Physiological Psychology, 6,* 497–500.

Dinges, D. F. (1986). Differential effects of prior wakefulness and circadian phase on nap sleep. *Electroencephalography and Clinical Neurophysiology, 64,* 224–227.

Dinges, D. F. (1988). When we can and cannot judge our sleepiness upon awakening. *Sleep Research, 17,* 83.

Dinges, D. F. (1989a). The influence of the human circadian timekeeping system on sleep. In M. Kryger, W. Dement, & T. Roth (Eds.), *Principles and practice of sleep medicine* (pp. 153–162). Philadelphia, PA: Saunders.

Dinges, D. F. (1989b). The nature of sleepiness: Causes, contexts and consequences. In A. Stunkard & A. Baum (Eds.), *Perspectives in behavioral medicine: Eating, sleeping, and sex* (pp. 147–179). Hillsdale, NJ: Erlbaum.

Dinges, D. F., Orne, E. C., Evans, F. J., & Orne, M. T. (1981). Performance after naps in sleep-conducive and alerting environments. In L. C. Johnson, D. I. Tepas, W. P. Colquhoun, & M. J. Colligan (Eds.), *Biological rhythms, sleep and shift work: Advances in sleep research* (Vol. 7, pp. 539–552). New York: Spectrum.

Dinges, D. F., Orne, M. T., & Orne, E. C. (1985a). Assessing performance upon abrupt awakening from naps during quasi-continuous operations. *Behavior Research Methods, Instruments, and Computers, 17,* 37–45.

Dinges, D. F., Orne, M. T., & Orne, E. C. (1985b). Sleep depth and other factors associated with performance upon abrupt awakening. *Sleep Research, 14,* 92.

Dinges, D. F., Orne, M. T., Whitehouse, W. G., & Orne, E. C. (1987). Temporal placement of a nap for alertness: Contributions of circadian phase and prior wakefulness. *Sleep, 10,* 313–329.

Dinges, D. F., Whitehouse, W. G., Orne, E. C., & Orne, M. T. (1988). The benefits of a nap during prolonged work and wakefulness. *Work and Stress, 2,* 139–153.

Feinberg, I., Floyd, T. C., & March, J. D. (1987). Effects of sleep loss on delta (0.3–3 Hz) EEG and eye movement density: New observations and hypotheses. *Electroencephalography and Clinical Neurophysiology, 67,* 217–221.

Feltin, M., & Broughton, R. (1968). Differential effects of arousal from slow wave versus REM sleep [Abstract]. *Psychophysiology, 5,* 231.

Fort, A., & Mills, J. N. (1972). Influence of sleep, lack of sleep and circadian rhythm on short psychometric tests. In W. P. Colquhoun (Ed.), *Aspects of human efficiency* (pp. 115–127). London: English University Press.

Gastaut, H., & Broughton, R. J. (1965). A clinical and polygraphic study of episodic phenomena during sleep. In J. Wortis (Ed.), *Recent advances in biological psychiatry* (Vol 7, pp. 197–221). New York: Plenum Press.

Gillberg, M., & Akerstedt, T. (1982). Body temperature and sleep at different times of day. *Sleep, 5,* 378–388.

Goodenough, D. R., Lewis, H. B., Shapiro, A., Jaret, L., & Sleser, I. (1965). Dream report following abrupt awakening from different kinds of sleep. *Journal of Personality and Social Psychology, 2,* 170–179.

Grosvenor, A., & Lack, L. C. (1984). The effect of sleep before or after learning on memory. *Sleep, 7,* 155–167.

Hartman, B. O., & Langdon, D. E. (1965). *A second study on performance upon sudden awakening* (School of Aerospace Medicine Report No. TR-65-61). Brooks AFB, TX: USAF.

Hartman, B. O., Langdon, D. E., & McKenzie, R. E. (1965). *A third study on performance upon sudden awakening* (School of Aerospace Medicine Report No. TR-65-63). Brooks, TX: U.S. Air Force.

Haslam, D. R. (1982). Sleep loss, recovery sleep, and military performance. *Ergonomics, 25,* 163–178.

Horne, J. A., & Staff, L. H. E. (1983). Exercise and sleep: Body-heating effects. *Sleep, 6,* 36–46.

Hume, K. I., & Mills, J. N. (1977). Rhythms of REM and slow wave sleep in subjects living on abnormal time schedules. *Waking and Sleeping, 3,* 291–296.

Jeanneret, P. R., & Webb, W. B. (1963). Strength of grip on arousal from full night's sleep. *Perceptual and Motor Skills, 17,* 759–761.

Kleitman, N. (1963). *Sleep and wakefulness.* Chicago: University of Chicago Press.

Koulack, D., & Schultz, K. J. (1974). Task performance after awakenings from different sleep stages. *Perceptual and Motor Skills, 39,* 792–794.

Langdon, D. E., & Hartman, B. O. (1961). *Performance upon sudden awakening* (School of Aerospace Medicine Report No. 62-17). Brooks, TX: U.S. Air Force.

Lavie, P., & Giora, Z. (1973). Spiral aftereffect durations following awakening from REM and non-REM sleep. *Perception and Psychophysics, 14,* 19–20.

Lavie, P., & Sutter, D. (1975). Differential responding to the beta movement following awakening from REM and NONREM sleep. *American Journal of Psychology, 88,* 595–603.

Lubin, A., Hord, D., Tracy, M. L., & Johnson, L. C. (1976). Effects of exercise, bedrest and napping on performance decrement during 40 hours. *Psychophysiology, 13,* 334–339.

Mavromatis, A. (1987). *Hypnagogia.* London: Routledge & Kegan Paul.

Naitoh, P., Muzet, A., Johnson, L. C., & Moses, L. (1973). Body movements during sleep after sleep loss. *Psychophysiology, 10,* 363–368.

Okuma, T., Nakamura, K., Hayashi, A., & Fujimori, M. (1966). Psychophysiological study on the depth of sleep in normal human subjects. *Electroencephalography and Clinical Neurophysiology, 21,* 140–147.

Patrick, G. T. W., & Gilbert, J. A. (1896). On the effects of loss of sleep. *Psychology Review, 3,* 469–483.

Pritchett, T. P. (1969). An investigation of sudden arousal from rest: A study of impaired performance on an addition task (Doctoral dissertation, University of Kentucky, 1964). *Dissertation Abstracts International, 30,* 2934B. (University Microfilms No. 69-20, 443)

Rechtschaffen, A., Hauri, P., & Zeitlin, M. (1966). Auditory awakening thresholds in REM and NREM sleep stages. *Perceptual and Motor Skills, 22,* 927–942.

Rosa, R. R., & Bonnet, M. H. (1985). Sleep stages, auditory arousal threshold, and body temperature as predictors of behavior upon awakening. *International Journal of Neuroscience, 27,* 73–83.

Rosa, R. R., Bonnet, M. H., & Warm, J. S. (1983). Recovery of performance during sleep following sleep deprivation. *Psychophysiology, 20,* 152–159.

Schacter, D. L. (1976). The hypnagogic state. A critical review of the literature. *Psychological Bulletin, 83,* 452–481.

Scott, J. (1969). Performance after abrupt arousal from sleep: Comparison of a simple motor, a visual-perceptual, and a cognitive task. *Proceedings of the 77th Annual Convention of the American Psychological Association, 4,* 225–226.

Scott, J., & Snyder, F. (1968). "Critical Reactivity" (Pieron) after abrupt awakenings in relation to EEG stages of sleep. *Psychophysiology, 4,* 370.

Seminara, J. L., & Shavelson, R. J. (1969). Effectiveness of space crew performance subsequent to sudden sleep arousal. *Aerospace Medicine, 40,* 723–727.

Sewitch, D. E. (1984). NREM sleep continuity and the sense of having slept in normal sleepers. *Sleep, 7,* 147–154.

Sewitch, D. E. (1987). Slow wave sleep deficiency insomnia: A problem of thermo-downregulation at sleep onset. *Psychophysiology, 24,* 200–216.

Sewitch, D. E., Kittrell, E. M. W., Kupfer, D. J., & Reynolds, C. F. (1986). Body temperature and sleep architecture in response to a mild cold stress in women. *Physiology and Behavior, 36,* 951–957.

Stones, M. J. (1977). Memory performance after arousal from different sleep stages. *British Journal of Psychology, 68,* 177–181.

Tebbs, R. B., & Foulkes, D. (1966). Strength of grip following different stages of sleep. *Perceptual and Motor Skills, 23,* 827–834.

Webb, W. B., & Agnew, Jr., H. (1964). Reaction time and serial response efficiency on arousal from sleep. *Perceptual and Motor Skills, 18,* 783–784.

Webb, W. B., & Agnew, Jr., H. (1967). Sleep cycling within 24-hr periods. *Journal of Experimental Psychology, 74,* 158–160.

Webb, W. B., & Agnew, Jr., H. (1971). Stage 4 sleep: Influence of time course variables. *Science, 174,* 1354–1357.

Wilkinson, R. T., & Stretton, M. (1971). Performance after awakening at different times of night. *Psychonomic Science, 23,* 283–285.

Williams, H. L., Hammack, J. T., Daly, R. L., Dement, W. C., & Lubin, A. (1964). Responses to auditory stimulation, sleep loss, and the EEG stages of sleep. *Electroencephalography and Clinical Neurophysiology, 16,* 269–278.

Williams, H. L., Morlock, Jr., H. C., & Morlock, J. V. (1966). Instrumental behavior during sleep. *Psychophysiology, 2,* 208–216.

Williams, R. L., Karacan, I., & Hursch, C. J. (1974). *EEG of human sleep: Clinical applications.* New York: Wiley.

PART FOUR

CLINICAL TOPICS

CHAPTER 13

A NETWORK MODEL OF DREAMS

ROSALIND CARTWRIGHT

BACKGROUND AND HISTORY

Given that we first learned the technology almost 40 years ago that permitted us to tune in on the dream channel to identify when dreams occur, how long they last, and (roughly) how exciting they are, and given the enormous public interest in dreams, the progress we have made on understanding this part of our regular mental life has been very slow. There are several obvious reasons for this. The working conditions are terrible. Dreams must be collected from the sleeping human, who typically sleeps long hours at an inconvenient time, at night. Sleepers are affected by laboratory sleep circumstances and, thus, must be accommodated over a period of nights before typical dream data can be collected. Dreams have not yielded easily to manipulative studies in which, prior to sleep, subjects were deprived of or satiated with water, social stimulation, and so forth. Nor have clear incorporations come from exposing subjects to specific stimuli before or during sleep (Webb & Cartwright, 1978). All in all, the area has been a tough one for the experimentalist. Subjects tend to ignore our best efforts and to go along dreaming their own dreams, providing very little evidence of incorporation (Berger, 1963).

We do not start from zero, however. A good deal of descriptive work has been conducted and replicated to broadly outline the landscape of the night mind. Clear differences exist between REM and non-REM (NREM) reports, and blind judges can make these discriminations with 90% accuracy (Monroe, Rechtschaffen, Foulkes, & Jensen, 1965). However, an examination of auditory awakening thresholds has shown that light sleepers have more NREM fantasy reports than do deep sleepers (Zimmerman, 1970). Within REM periods, reports from the beginning are less dreamlike than reports from the end (Foulkes, 1966). The dreamlike character of the reports is also related to the eye movement density of the epoch preceding the awakening. Low eye movement density leads to no recall or to recall that is "thoughtlike." High density is related to more storylike content (Cartwright, Stephenson, Kravitz, & Eastman, 1987). The REM reports also become more dreamlike as the night progresses, and because eye movement density also increases with time of night, these two measures can be somewhat confounded.

Generally, the progression across the night shows movement from short, reality-oriented thought in the first half of the night, when more NREM sleep is present, to longer, perceptually vivid, nonreality tested experiences in the second half of the night, when REM sleep is proportionately higher.

The field has been troubled not only by how to grasp dream content experimentally but also by how to define dreaming itself: Should the definition focus on its psychological properties whenever and wherever it occurs (e.g., at sleep onset and in NREM sleep) or on only the mental content that accompanies REM periods? This question remains debatable. In my own work, I prefer to sample REM periods and to define dreaming as the content of these periods, which may be scaled as more or less dreamlike psychologically. This decision was made because so much theorizing about dreaming starts from the properties of REM sleep, which is highly activated and closely associated with the PGO spiking that, in man, appears to be related to the REMs that, in turn, are associated with the dreamlike quality of mentation. Not that dreaming only takes place in REM periods: Several good studies have shown that dreaming occurs in NREM periods (Brown & Cartwright, 1978). However, I chose to examine the REM stage because dreaming is most often associated with REM. In fact, dreaming probably occurs cyclically throughout the 24-hr cycle, but it is only sustained long enough to produce the narrative continuity necessary for these experiences to be recalled when a highly aroused brain state persists in the absence of demands for attention from external sources (Koulack & Goodenough, 1976).

QUESTIONS ABOUT DREAMING

Given that we can collect distinctive psychological material by sampling REM, and given that this material is rather resistant to manipulation, how can we best proceed with our study? We must answer four questions:

1. Do dreams have intrinsic meaning, or is this added from waking associations?
2. Does dreaming serve a psychological function or functions, or are these epiphenomena to the physiological functions of activated sleep?
3. How do dreams relate to the prior waking state and to personality traits? Are these relations consistently or alternately, compensatory or continuous?
4. Do dreams have an impact on the subsequent waking state or on the more enduring personality traits?

Table 1

CURRENT MODELS OF DREAM MEANING AND FUNCTION

Variable	Crick-Mitchison (1983)	Hobson-McCarley (1977)	Breger (1969)	Freud (1955)
Meaning	None	Degraded	Emotional	Hidden
Function	Purging	Synthetic	Assimilation	Safety valve

The theories of dream meaning and function are many, but they can be grouped into four rough categories (see Table 1).

The Crick and Mitchison (1983) theory relates dreaming to previous waking but views content as accidental and useless material to be purged to make room in memory for better data. The Hobson and McCarley (1977) theory, at least as originally published, postulates that the images originate randomly from the pons but grants that associated meaning is then synthesized by the cortex to express the current concerns carried over from waking into sleep. Breger is one of many modern theorists who believe dream meaning depends on the structure of the individual's memory networks, particularly those related to affect, and believe the function of dreaming is assimilative, "integrating contemporary material into the adaptive solutions worked out in the past" (Breger, Hunter, & Lane, 1971, p. 188). This position relates dreams both to the immediate and recent presleep experience and to related memory networks from the past. It implies no immediate impact on subsequent waking behavior unless the material becomes conscious and is worked on to accommodate a change in outlook or behavior on the basis of an insight from a dream. In this view, dreams have meaning and function but exert no effect on postsleep states or traits without further integrative work. These theorists are thus closer to the Freudians, who see the work of dreams as the gratification of hidden impulses. Dream work is regularly done at night; only with a lot of additional work during waking, to make the unconscious conscious, will this effect any change in the waking personality.

Breger's information-processing hypothesis has been taken one step further by Greenberg, Pillard, and Pearlman (1972), who see the assimilation work of dreams as adaptive for waking functioning in the original stress-producing situation. According to these authors, behavior after a night of dreaming should be more productive (or at least less distressed) and should contribute to better coping in the situation that originally provoked anxiety. Jones (1962), also associated with this position, took one more theoretical step to relate dreams to postsleep waking by suggesting that dreams preserve and protect the waking self-image. In other words, Jones believed that dreams serve not just a stress-related adaptive function but a full-time job.

To go beyond the descriptive level and test some of these theories has been enormously difficult. The controlled studies have largely been failures. Even the dream deprivation studies have run afoul because of the amount of individual variability that occurs in studies with small sample sizes. The meaning of the situation to the subject, including both the experiment itself and the target stimulus; the subjects' long-term traits and coping styles; and the subjects' own transformation language as it relates to what is in the memory network of like experiences must be taken into account before much headway can be made in understanding dream meaning and function.

How then can we best proceed? One good method is to take advantage of anything promising from past work and to build better designs to clarify helpful insights. I focused on work that has tested the assimilative function as that starting point, particularly on the two studies reported by Breger, Hunter, and Lane in "The effect of stress on dreams" (1971), which represents a landmark in this area. Breger et al. took advantage of the laboratory to collect dreams through sleep monitoring and, thus, avoided all the problems associated with home-recalled dreams. However, they used not experimenter-designed manipulations to produce affect but genuine experiments in nature. One consisted of presleep group therapy sessions and the other consisted of dream collections prior to and following elective surgery. The studies were not tightly controlled, but they are important because they took real-life events that have tremendous personal meaning and traced their impact on dream content. The studies were conducted in 1964–1966, more than 20 years ago, and they stand today as the best in the field.

The thinking is clear: External input is replaced in REM sleep by internally generated images, bits of memories generated by systems activated from the presleep period, which becomes increasingly distant in the course of the night. By looking at these images, we can make inferences about the memory systems. To do this, we put the system under stress, generate good strong affect, and watch the work of assimilation take place through dreams. This can best be done by finding a distressing event that will threaten the currently organized self-structure in some basic way so that the work of dreams and their relevance to the specific emotional turmoil can be highlighted and examined. For this reason, I undertook the study of the dreams of people undergoing divorce. Divorce is a stressful event. No matter how strongly one wishes to end a bad relationship, no one gets out scot-free. One partner may retaliate and cause so much trouble that both partners become stressed beyond measure for a considerable time before they reach a new reorganization as self-respecting singles. Divorce involves a lot of loss, not only the loss of love but also the loss of physical security (a home), of economic security (a standard of living), of a social network of friends and shared relatives, and (most of all) of self-esteem.

Although bereavement is credited with creating more stress on most recent events scales, many divorcing people have told me that life would be so much easier if only their spouse would "drop dead." Divorce provides a good natural stressor to work with. There is also a large pool of subjects to draw from (there were 1.5 million divorces last year). The distress lasts a long time—most divorces take 1 to 2 years because the courts are crowded—and people vary in how well they cope. Some people are initially upset but then take back their investment in the shared life and reach a new internal reorganization. Others proceed from the state of stress to focus on the loss, shame, and guilt of failure and become clinically depressed. This gives us some ability to stratify a sample into those who are coping well with the stress of a major life change and those who are not. Depression rates are high among those who are divorcing (approximately 37% according to recent work).

What does it take to get through this life event successfully? Time, good friends, good genes, good luck, and a good dream system was my hypothesis.

We know that stress disrupts sleep and that stress that culminates in the hopelessness of depression can create a type of sleep disruption that affects REM sleep. The work by Kupfer (1976) and Reynolds, Shaw, Newton, Coble, and Kupfer (1983), which has been replicated by Rush, Giles, Roffwarg, and Parker (1982); by Gillin and Borbely (1985); and by Cartwright (1983), shows major affective disorder to have some usual (although not universal) effects on the first REM period of the night and some additional effects on the distribution of REM across the night (see Table 2).

If REM sleep is disrupted, what happens to dreams? Do they malfunction in some way and fail to assimilate affective experience into memory networks? Is that why depressed patients feel at their worst first thing in the morning? If dreaming has an assimilative function, can we see this at work in subjects who are going through divorce without becoming depressed? If good copers under stress show productive dreaming, is there a threshold of affect above which dreaming is overloaded and breaks down? Since we have methods of indexing depression in both the waking and sleep states (high eye movement density and reduced REM latency), we have measures to help identify those with good and poor dream functioning.

THE DIVORCE STUDY

This study builds on a previous study conducted with a small sample of 29 divorcees, all women, diagnosed only on the Beck Depression Inventory (Beck, 1967). (No psychiatric diagnoses were obtained). Nonetheless, there were clear sleep differences in REM latency and eye movement density (Cartwright, 1983; see Figures 1 and 2). There were also some clear dream differences between the depressed and nondepressed women (Cartwright, 1986; see Table 3). Traditional women who had more invested in the homemaker/wife/mother role were more often depressed; showed reduced REM latency; and had dreams that were short, past-oriented, negative in motivation, and featured a self-character who was inadequate to cope in the dream. The nondepressed women, who often chose alternate roles, had longer and more complicated dreams with wider time frames and positive motives. In addition, not the self but some other character was inadequate in the dream (Trenholme, Cartwright, & Greenberg, 1984).

The present study was designed to look at a larger sample of people (including both sexes) undergoing divorce who had been better diagnosed for

Table 2

DIFFERENCE BETWEEN REM SLEEP IN DEPRESSED
AND NORMAL PERSONS

Variable	Normal Group	Depressed Group
First REM		
Latency	80–120 min	<65 min
Eye movement density	<1.5	>1.5 per min
Duration	8–12 min	20 min
All night		
REM distribution in first half of night	1/3	1/2
Eye movement distribution	Successively higher with each REM stage	Sequence irregular

depression. The study is still in progress. The target sample contains 300 people (150 men and 150 women) who are examined at the time of marital separation when the decision to divorce from a first marriage has been made. All are unmedicated volunteers who have agreed to return in 1 year for a follow-up. So far, 170 subjects have been seen (85 men, 85 women). Of these, 87 (40 men, 47 women) have returned for follow-up. Of the original sample, 42 subjects (19 men and 23 women) were currently depressed according to the conjoint criterion of meeting a Schedule of Affective Disorders and Schizophrenia (SADS) (Endicott & Spitzer, 1978) Research Diagnostic Criteria (RDC) (Spitzer, Endicott, & Robbins, 1978) diagnosis and yielding a Beck score above 15. On SADS RDC criteria alone, the figures were much higher, with 47% of the men and 51% of the women classed as currently in an episode of major affective disorder. Most people get over this. At follow-up, only 7.5% of the men and 6.3% of the women remained depressed.

The original evaluation was used to select 90 subjects (45 men and 45 women) for the sleep laboratory study to examine the effects of divorce on the sleep and dreams of 30 depressed and 15 nondepressed subjects of each sex at the initiation of the break-up and a year later. To date, 54 subjects have been studied for 3 nights, and 36 subjects have been restudied at a 1-year follow-up.

The study of sleep showed that 18 subjects had short REM latencies (less than 65 min when averaging Nights 2 and 3), and 13 subjects had high eye movement density at the first REM stage (greater than 1.5 on the Kupfer scale), but only 3 subjects had both markers. Both markers were relatively stable over a 1-year period. The product-moment correlation for REM latency was .53 and for eye movement density was .55. The factor most heavily contributing to this stability was family history of depression. For those with family history positive ($n = 21$), the correlation between the two REM latency measures (at the breakup point and 1 year later) was .73. For those without a

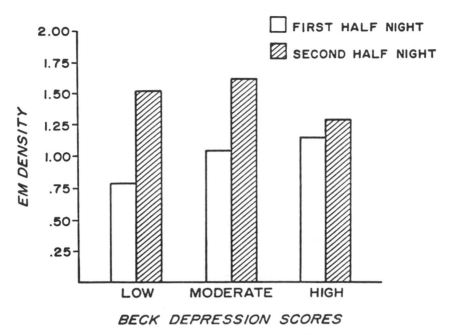

Figure 1   Eye movement density in first and second half of night in relation to Beck depression scores.

family history for affective disorder (n = 13), the correlation was .06. Not all subjects who showed the markers of depression, however, were currently depressed on their own self-reports. Twelve of 18 subjects with short REM latencies had Beck scores above 14.5, and 8 of 13 subjects with high eye movement density had Beck scores above 15. For those with a SADS diagnosis and self-reported current depression, short REM latency was associated with higher dreamlike fantasy ratings (on a 1–5 scale) and higher affect scores (1 = *no affect,* 2 = *mild,* and 3 = *strong*) for the dream collected from the first REM than those with normal REM latencies. In contrast, high eye movement density was associated with lower than normal dreamlike fantasy scores and neutral affect in the first REM period (see Table 4).

Both sleep markers of depression were stable over 1 year, but they seemed to represent two different subgroups. Short REM latency subjects had earlier, more affective and storylike dreams, whereas high eye movement density subjects showed poor dream formation and reduced dream affect. The numbers are too small for formal testing of an interaction effect at this time, but the presence of an affective disorder seems to heighten the differences in dreaming that are represented in these sleep groups.

Things are never as straightforward as one would wish. The so-called depression markers are not statelike but rather are more traitlike. None of the 3 subjects who showed both markers were currently depressed, but all 3 had past divorce-related depression episodes by RDC. The two markers seem to represent two different sleep sub-groups: Those with early REM are affect re-

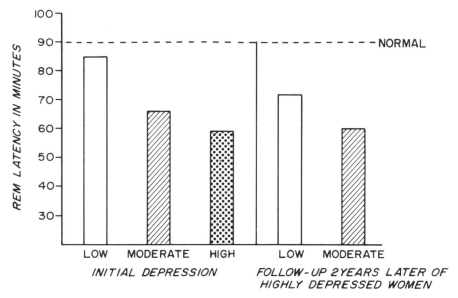

Figure 2   REM latency at time of divorce and 2 years later in relation to Beck depression scores.

sponsive in terms of generating more and better fantasies, and those with higher than normal phasic events at the beginning of the night have disrupted dreaming. This means we need a large sample size to examine how stable these findings are over time and what happens to these groups psychologically.

What does the sequential dream content look like in the laboratory for those subjects who are coping well and those who are not? What theory do they match, if any? Are Hobson and McCarley (1977) right in stating that, because REM is turned on by the unthinking pons, the images are not selected to tell a story but rather give the cortex the work of trying to interpret them as best it can in the light of its own agenda of emotional concerns? Or are images selected from a memory network that has been stimulated in response to some particular type and level of affect aroused in connection with a recent experience, and do they relate the issues to specific memory components?

My best guess leads me to accept the latter premise. Because dreams from the beginning to the end of the night often have repeated images, memory networks seem to be activated not randomly but in response to some persistent issues. Dreams look like creative constructions, drawing on memory systems that are activated by persistent emotional concerns. Memories are encoded as unique bits but are organized into networks of related materials and are decoded according to our needs, without our conscious attention or direction. Emotional connections are made via earlier memories. These are then lit up selectively when the brain is activated in REM sleep. Dream meaning relates to the status of our ongoing needs, and dreams function to assimi-

Table 3

DIFFERENCES IN DREAM CHARACTERISTICS BETWEEN
DEPRESSED AND NONDEPRESSED WOMEN (N = 29)

Dream Characteristic	Depressed Group	Nondepressed Group
Length	Short	Long
Time reference	Past	Wider range of time
Anxiety	Low	Higher
Self	Inadequate	Other inadequate
Motivation	Abasement, avoidance (negative)	Affiliation, achievement (positive)

late new data and reorganize related memories. Once the network is stimulated in the first REM period, it is held in a state of readiness, and other parts of it are more likely to be stimulated the next time REM occurs when older elements of the same network are stimulated (see Figure 3).

Which network comes into play is governed by the type and level of affect carried over from the day. When all is well with our world, the level is low, and different networks may be stimulated in the same night. When we are in an unstable state and affect runs high, the system may jam or fail to work at its best. This appears to happen with higher then normal eye movement density. Then dreams do not seem to progress across the night.

Dreaming appears to be a part of our normal information processing, which relates waking experiences to past emotional experiences to past emo-

Table 4

DREAM CONTENT SCORES FOR DEPRESSED AND NONDEPRESSED
SUBJECTS

Group	Dreamlike Fantasy[a]			Affect[b]		
	Short REM Latency	High EMD	Normal REM	Short REM Latency	High EMD	Normal REM
Depressed						
M	3.40	2.38	3.00	1.90	1.00	1.60
SD	1.07	0.92	0.71	0.88	0.76	0.55
Nondepressed						
M	2.67	2.20	2.70	1.00	1.40	1.60
SD	0.82	1.10	0.82	0.63	0.89	0.84

Note: EMD = eye movement density. For short REM latency, $n = 18$; for high EMD, $n = 13$; for normal REM, $n = 19$.
[a] Measured on a 1–5 scale, where 1 = *no recall* and 5 = *well-developed dream*. [b] Measured on a 1–3 scale, where 1 = *neutral* and 3 = *strong*.

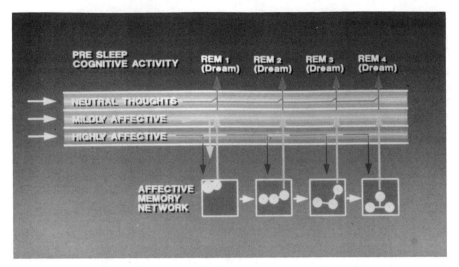

Figure 3   A network model of dream construction.

tional paradigms expressed as story images. Dreaming is involved in reviewing, reorganizing, and rehearsing conceptions of who we are and how we are doing in our own eyes. The system shows up best when we are under stress and threatened with a major life change that requires new responses. The system can be overloaded, which seems to happen in those with a biological vulnerability for REM sleep disruption. This may be adaptive, with reduced REM latency, or it may be maladaptive, with eye movement storms that create chaos.

References

Beck, A. (1967). *Depression.* New York: Harper & Row.

Berger, R. (1963). Experimental modification of dream content by meaningful verbal stimuli. *British Journal of Psychiatry, 109,* 722–740.

Breger, L. (1969). Dream function: An information processing model. In L. Breger (Ed.), *Clinical–cognitive psychology* (pp. 182–227). New Jersey: Prentice-Hall.

Breger, L., Hunter, I., & Lane, R. (1971). The effect of stress on dreams. *Psychological Issues Monograph, 27*(7, Suppl. 3).

Brown, J., & Cartwright, R. (1978). Locating NREM dreaming through instrumental responses. *Psychophysiology, 15,* 35–39.

Cartwright, R. (1983). Rapid eye movement sleep characteristics during and after mood-disturbing events. *Archives of General Psychiatry, 40,* 197–201.

Cartwright, R. (1986). Affect and dream work from an information processing point of view. *Journal of Mind and Behavior, 7,* 411–427.

Cartwright, R., Stephenson, K., Kravitz, H., & Eastman, C. (1987). Life events effects on REM sleep. *Sleep Research, 16,* 267.

Crick, F., & Mitchison, G. (1983). The function of dreaming sleep. *Nature, 304,* 111–114.

Endicott, J., & Spitzer, R. (1978). A diagnostic interview: The schedule for affective disorders and schizophrenia. *Archives of General Psychiatry, 35,* 837–844.

Foulkes, D. (1966). *The psychology of sleep.* New York: Scribners.

Freud, S. (1955). *The Interpretation of Dreams.* New York: Basic Books. (Original work published 1900.)

Gillin, J., & Borbely, A. (1985) Sleep: A neurobiological window in affective disorders. *Trends in Neuroscience, 8,* 537–542.

Greenberg, R., Pillard, R., & Pearlman, C. (1972). The effect of dream (stage REM) deprivation on adaption of stress. *Psychosomatic Medicine, 34,* 257–262.

Hobson, A., & McCarley, R. (1977). The brain as a dream state generator: An activation-synthesis hypothesis of the dream process. *American Journal of Psychiatry, 134,* 1335–1348.

Jones, R. (1962). *Ego synthesis in dreams.* Cambridge, MA: Schenkman.

Koulack, D., & Goodenough, D. (1976). Dream recall and dream recall failure: An arousal-retrieval model. *Psychological Bulletin, 83,* 975–984.

Kupfer, D. (1976). REM latency: A psychobiologic marker for primary depressive illness. *Biological Psychiatry, 11,* 159–174.

Monroe, L., Rechtschaffen, A., Foulkes, D., & Jensen, J. (1965). Discriminability of REM and NREM reports. *Journal of Personality and Social Psychology, 2,* 456–460.

Reynolds, C., Shaw, D., Newton, T., Coble, P., & Kupfer, D. (1983). EEG sleep in outpatients with generalized anxiety: A preliminary comparison with depressed outpatients. *Psychiatric Research, 8,* 81–89.

Rush, A., Giles, D., Roffwarg, H., & Parker, R. (1982). Sleep EEG and dexamethasone suppression test findings in outpatients with unipolar and major depressive disorders. *Biological Psychiatry, 17,* 327–341.

Spitzer, R., Endicott, J., & Robbins, E. (1978). Research diagnostic criteria: Rationale and reliability. *Archives General Psychiatry, 35,* 773–782.

Trenholme, I., Cartwright, R., & Greenberg, G. (1984). Dream dimension differences during a life change. *Psychiatric Research, 12,* 35–45.

Webb, W., & Cartwright, R. (1978). Sleep and dreams. *Annual Review of Psychology, 29,* 223–252.

Zimmerman, W. (1970). Sleep mentation and auditory awakening thresholds. *Psychophysiology, 6,* 540–549.

CHAPTER 14

NIGHTMARES (DREAM DISTURBANCES) IN POSTTRAUMATIC STRESS DISORDER:
IMPLICATIONS FOR A THEORY OF DREAMING

MILTON KRAMER

Sleep that comes on quickly at an appropriate time and place, proceeds without incident to terminate in a smooth awakening at a desirable time, and leaves us feeling refreshed is what most of us seek from Somnos, the god of sleep. Dreaming, Freud (1900) suggested, maintains the sleeping process by binding the affective stimuli that might otherwise disrupt the continuity of the process. How then are we to understand the disturbing dream that seems to disrupt the process it was designed to protect? Is the disturbing dream, as Freud (1920) suggested, a failure in an otherwise effective mechanism? Does the dream lead to disruption because it cannot bind the emotion that surges up periodically during the night?

Certainly this view of the sleep-protective function of dreaming is consonant with two observations about REM sleep that are generally well-established (Anch, Bowman, Mitler, & Walsh, 1988). First, if dreams maintain sleep, and if the longer one sleeps the more likely one is to wake up after the initial settling down process, then the distribution of REM sleep across the usual sleep period is appropriate: It is positively accelerated, with more REM occurring later in the night. This progression contrasts with that of deep sleep (Stages 3–4), which decelerates (i.e., less occurs) as the night goes on. Second, a period of dreaming sleep (REM sleep) often ends in a brief arousal. However, sleepers generally do not remember this brief arousal. The importance of the arousal for understanding the disturbing dream, which leads the sleeper to awaken and recall a troublesome event, is that the nucleus for an awakening exists in the nature of the dreaming process itself: A brief, unrecalled arousal is available to be converted into a troublesome awakening.

An example of a disturbing dream will concretize some of the problems the experience presents and will call attention to some of the factors that predispose one to disturbed dreaming and that stimulate its appearance. The following dream was reported by a 26-year-old man who was a patient in a Veterans Administration Hospital.

> I dreamed I was back in Vietnam and I had thrown a grenade into one of the Vietnamese huts. I went inside and there was one of the babies blown up all over the inside of the hut. I woke up and was terrified, nauseated and crying.

This dream meets our criteria for a disturbing dream: Troubling contents lead to an awakening associated with negative affect and the recall of a prior troubling dream.

Most dreams have no accompanying feeling. However, when a feeling tone is recalled, a negative feeling is more common than a positive one (Hall & Van de Castle, 1966). The romantic notion of the "land of dreamy dreams" is not borne out by the experience of dreaming.

In fact, in a study (Taub, Kramer, Arand, & Jacobs, 1978) that compared recalled dreams, recalled nightmares, and the concept of nightmares, the concept of nightmares was reported to be more intense than the experience of the nightmare. In addition, the nightmare and the recalled dream were reported to have different contents. The disturbing dream is troublesome, does not live up to its advance billing, and is clearly distinguishable from the ordinary dream.

Although dream meaning is not the topic of this chapter, I will offer an interpretation of this dream of infanticide that I arrived at without any knowledge of the dreamer. The interpretation conforms with an analysis subsequently provided by the dreamer's therapist. (A more detailed examination of this dream appears in Kramer & Roth, 1977.)

It was my impression that the dreamer felt he had committed a sanctioned, aggressive (destructive) act, at a distance, against a fragile, possibly pregnant woman and had caused her (or perhaps her unborn child) to die. The dreamer did not want to be held responsible for the act (which he felt was disgusting).

What do we know about the dreamer from the report given by his therapist? He had been in Vietnam. He felt very guilty about some of his behavior there. In his personal life, he had assaulted his second wife and had been accused of causing his first wife to abort by having intercourse late in the pregnancy and rupturing her membranes. He was the oldest of nine children in a rural family. His father was a vagrant, violent alcoholic with whom he often fought in defense of his mother. He had to assist on one occasion in delivering one of his siblings because the doctor could not come and they could not get his mother to the hospital. During his treatment, he reported a dream similar to the one already described in which the baby was his daughter. The first dream was described in the second session, and the dream about his daughter was described in the sixth session.

Although one could discuss at length the meaning of this disturbing dream and could raise a number of questions about predisposing factors, proximal stimuli, the selection of content, internal organization, and so forth, these speculations are not our current focus. We must focus instead on the awakening with negative affect that the dreamer reports.

The REM dream is often terminated by a brief arousal. The intensity of the dream experience shows a systematic development across the REM period (Kramer, Roth, & Czaya, 1975). The periodicity of the development of dream content intensity is similar to the periodicity of the density of eye movements seen during REM sleep. The intensity of the dream increases rapidly, peaking at 10–20 min, then declines and starts up again. This rise and fall of emotion across the dream period is consonant with the notion that there is a surge of emotion during REM sleep, which the dream contains or attempts to contain. The rise and fall of emotion, anxiety, fright, and so forth parallels physiological activity, as reflected in eye movement density, which suggests a possible psychophysiological parallel. Does the terminal arousal become an awakening because the intensity surge exceeds the integrative capacity of the dream experience? This question must be explored further.

If an emotional surge exceeds the integrative capacity of the dream experience and results in a dream disturbance, is the surge related to the content of the dream, to the preoccupation with and recall of dreams by the dreamer, to the emotional condition (psychopathology) of the dreamer (i.e., predispositional issues), or to the responsivity of the dreamer to the experience (i.e., failure to bind or integrate an experience). Kramer, Schoen, and Kinney (1984a) examined these issues and found that subjects who reported two or more disturbed dream experiences per week had the same content categories and dream frequencies as vivid dreamers. The vivid dreamers also reported much higher dream recall in general than did the disturbed dreamers (89% vs. 54%).

The disturbed dreamers, however, were more troubled people both from a trait and a state point of view. Their scores were higher on all Minnesota Multiphasic Personality Inventory (MMPI) scales and on the emotionally based scales of the Cornell Medical Index, and they reported a greater number of psychiatric hospitalizations. Their daily frequency of disturbed dreams appeared to be related to current feelings (e.g., anger, sensitivity, and general emotion). Of greatest interest was the fact that the disturbed dreamers showed a greater degree of emotional responsivity to the dream experience than did the vivid dreamers, and more of them had been described by others as acting frightened in their sleep.

Dream disturbance sufferers, selected for having bad dreams, are more psychologically troubled, recall fewer normal dreams, and are more responsive to their dreams than are vivid dreamers. The increased responsivity suggests an integrative failure that may be affected by the altered emotional state (increased psychopathology) of disturbed dreamers.

The work of Kramer, Schoen, and Kinney (1984a) would lead to the prediction that disturbed dreamers would be more responsive to stimuli (e.g., the dream experience) than normal subjects. Indeed, that was the case. Above-threshold tones were presented during sleep to a group of disturbed dreamers and a group of control subjects (Kinney & Kramer, 1985). Control subjects responded in 52% of the trials, but disturbed dreamers responded in 93% of the trials. Related to this was a stimulus identification in 40% of the control subjects but in only 8% of the disturbed dreamers.

The dreaming process is linked to a process of repeated arousal. Arousal followed by awakening in disturbed dreamers appears to result from increased responsivity to the dream experience, which is related to the psychophysiological alterations associated with being emotionally troubled. In chronic sufferers from dream disturbance (e.g., patients with chronic delayed posttraumatic stress disorder), the arousal threshold is increased (Schoen, Kramer, & Kinney, 1984), which suggests that their emotional focus may be internal (i.e., on the dream experience) and supports the theory that patients are more responsive to the negative dream experience.

There is reason to believe that the sleep process is related to alterations in subjective state, particularly affect, mood, or feelings. If the sleep process has been successful, it is generally agreed that one feels down, tired, and sleepy before sleep and feels refreshed after sleep. This view of sleep relates, in a general way, to the theory that dreaming is related to emotional alterations during sleep and that bad dreams are related to (and often the consequence of) altered feeling states during the day (Kramer, Schoen, & Kinney, 1984a).

To examine the relation between sleep and subjective states, we assessed mood, as indexed by an adjective check list, before and after sleep (Kramer & Roth, 1972; Roth, Kramer, & Roehrs, 1976). Mood at night, before sleep, is generally experienced more intensely; that is, one is more unhappy, aggressive, friendly, clear thinking, or anxious prior to going to sleep at night than in the morning. Further, moods experienced at night are more variable than those experienced in the morning. Mood, therefore, generally decreases from night to morning and becomes less variable.

As mood changed systematically from night to morning, the relation of sleep physiology (Kramer, Roehrs, & Roth, 1976) and dream content (Kramer & Roth, 1980) to mood change across the night was studied. The decrease in unhappiness from night to morning was found to be related to whom and (to a lesser extent) to what one dreams about, and changes in sleepiness and clear thinking across the night were related to the amount of non-REM (NREM) sleep the dreamer had experienced. These observations were utilized in formulating the mood regulatory theory of sleep (Kramer, in press). From the perspective of the dream, the theory suggests that the dream subserves a selective, affective regulatory function (Kramer & Roth, 1978). The dream may be thought of as an "emotional thermostat" that corrects the level and range of the person's mood.

If dreaming functions to protect sleep by absorbing the emotional surge that appears to occur during REM sleep, then dreaming ought to be related to the emotional state of the dreamer. That is indeed the case: Changes in emotional state across the night are related to the content of the dream.

Multiple dream periods across the night are part of the periodicity of REM sleep. These multiple dreams are also related to the emotional preoccupations or current concerns of the dreamer. Just as pre- and postsleep mood is related to the intervening dreams and sleep physiology of the night, so is the dream content of the multiple REM periods of the night related to what is on the dreamer's mind before and after sleeping (Kramer, Roth, Arand, & Bonnet, 1981; Kramer, Moshiri, & Scharf, 1982; Kramer, Roth, & Palmer, 1976).

Two principal patterns of thematic dream development across the night are discernable (Kramer, Whitman, Baldridge, & Lansky, 1964): A *progressive-sequential* pattern in which problems are stated, worked on, and resolved and a *repetitive-traumatic* pattern in which the problem is simply restated and no progress occurs.

The effectiveness of the night's dreaming varies from night to night within the same subject. This may result from the differential pattern of dreaming across the night. If one has experienced a progressive-sequential dream pattern, one may also experience a positive alteration in emotional state. The problem solving that takes place is emotional in nature. If the problem that one goes to sleep with is simply restated and is not solved, then a less successful night's dreaming has occurred. It could be through this mechanism of success or failure in problem solving (French & Fromm, 1964) that the affective alteration takes place. The problem-solving function may also parallel the change in the degree of unhappiness and may be related to the appearance of appropriate character types.

It may be useful to illustrate the patterns of dream development by reviewing the experiences of a subject who slept in the experimental laboratory who showed both patterns of dreaming. Subjects do show both patterns, which suggests that there is not universal success in altering the emotional preoccupations of the previous day. This may account for some of the variability in how one feels on awakening from a night's sleep.

SEQUENTIAL DREAM PATTERN

The sequential pattern shows an alternating ascendancy of disturbing and reactive motives and a concomitant tension accumulation, discharge, and regression pattern. Each dream report obtained was from an REM-period awakening (Kramer et al., 1964). This illustration is from a female subject on the sixth dream night.

Sequential Dreams

1. This little girl was asleep. She was being real cute, prolonging things for money or to stay in the hospital longer.

2. I passed Frank's wife in a car. She saw me come . . . she pulled away. I got kind of mad. I decided that it didn't make any difference.
3. I was playing tennis. I hit it back real hard. We won the game.
4. A patient didn't need the doctor after all. She started out thinking she needed a doctor but she didn't. She had a big bandage on her stomach.
5. Doctor was not able to treat patient because he was not properly licensed. The patient is planning to use surgery against the doctor.

Sequential Interpretations

1. The thematic pattern focuses on the subject's wish to depend on or cling to the doctor and hospital even if she has to claim illness, but the cuteness reveals a seductive motive as well.
2. The subject expresses, vis-á-vis the wife of a friend, the feared and expected rejection, which she tries to minimize.
3. This dream can be seen as a turning point because the victory in the tennis game appears to discharge effectively the tension generated by the conflict between the wish to be close to the doctor/experimenter for care and love (the disturbing motive) and the feared rebuff of abandonment (reactive motive). The subject switches to a successful competition that she wins with a partner and thus finds a successful solution. The inference is that whatever she was struggling with has been conquered.
4. The successful victory with a partner in the previous dream permits the subject to deny her need for the doctor, which she admits she once had. The bandage provides evidence that the need continues.
5. Recognition of her continuing repressed need for the doctor for care and love causes the patient to intensify her rejection of him by being critical of the doctor's qualifications and by expressing her wish to get even or to hurt him. It is the familiar double assertion: "Not only do I not need you, but you're no good anyway."

The sequential pattern in this series expresses a dependent/sexual longing toward the experimenter/doctor, which leads to a feared (expected) rejection by the wife/mother in the second dream. The subject masters the conflict in the third dream by an aggressive victory with her own partner. The fourth dream reveals a rejection of the previous need, although a recognition is present that the need still exists. In the last dream of the night, a more intense rejection in the form of an attack on a doctor serves to deny the need further.

REPETITIVE DREAM PATTERN

The repetitive pattern provides a restatement of the conflict, often in different settings and at different degrees of concreteness or abstraction. Although some interrelation of events is suggested, the dreams predominantly restate the situation within a narrow range without sequential progression. Each dream was obtained from a female subject (on the third dream night) after an REM-period awakening (Kramer et al., 1964).

Repetitive Dreams

1. Somebody was lost. It was a dog and they were trying to find out where it lived. It wasn't my dog, though. I wasn't lost. This person who was lost was always fumbling around leading everybody else around because he didn't know what he was doing. Some boy, I think. Somehow we had telephone numbers trying to find the right one. It was supposed to be that little boy that was lost.
2. They filled up the car. There wasn't enough room, unless I went back with the people we went back with before. I could go back with someone else. The place we were going was an orphanage someplace, some house, a place like that.
3. I was dreaming about visiting, I think it was some EEG laboratory, or something like that where the mothers could leave their children, and they could go shopping. I doubt whether they could, there wouldn't be enough room for all of these people.

Repetitive Interpretations

1. The boy (association = experimenter) is seen as lost and misleading others. Not the subject but the boy is lost. There is concern in the dream that she will be misled by the experimenter because of his inexperience, so she tries to call home.
2. In a setting of abandonment (orphanage), the subject hopes anxiously that there will be room for her to return home. She has a ride home, but the car is crowded.
3. The subject is in the laboratory temporarily and her mother is going to return for her (implied). There isn't enough room. In all the dreams of the night, the subject deals with her fear of being abandoned and her method of recontacting her family: calling on the phone, riding in a car, or being picked up.

These patterns are elaborations of the general thesis that dreams may subserve a problem-solving function (French & Fromm, 1964). Through this effort at emotional problem solving, the dream may succeed or fail to contain the emotional surge that leads to the arousal/awakening that is the hallmark of disturbed dreaming. Difficulty in emotional problem solving in waking life is certainly more characteristic of the psychopathologically disturbed subjects who have been found to be more responsive to arousal/awakening after a REM period and who report more bad dreams.

Sleep is generally a successful process, although there is much concern expressed about a disturbed night's sleep. Given that the process is generally successful, one would expect to see the progressive-sequential pattern occur more often than the repetitive-traumatic pattern: In the two laboratory subjects, that was the case (50% vs. 32%; Kramer et al., 1964).

If the progressive-sequential pattern is more common, one ought to see dream content change across the REM periods of the night. This change indeed was found when the dreams were analyzed of 22 subjects who slept for 20 consecutive nights in the laboratory and described dream content from each REM period of the night (Kramer, McQuarrie, & Bonnet, 1981). Word count and dream content showed systematic and statistically significant change across the night. Three character variables in particular showed an increase and decrease across the night, in keeping with the inverted U-shaped curve that the progressive-sequential pattern describes. And the character variable was best correlated with change on the dimension of unhappy mood across the night (Kramer & Roth, 1980).

A number of studies have shown evidence that dreams are a regular and orderly process (Kramer, 1982). The dreams of the same person on one night are distinguishable from those on another night. This supports the notion that the dreams of the night are indeed focused on a single topic, whether they are handled in a progressive-sequential or a repetitive traumatic manner. Dreams in individuals are differentiable, but the dreams of one night are highly correlated with the dreams of the next night. Dreams, therefore, are unique to the individual dreamer.

The emotional preoccupations or current concerns of the dreamer, assessed from Thematic Apperception Test (TAT) stories (Kramer, Roth, & Palmer, 1976) and presleep and postsleep verbal samples (Kramer, Roth, Arand, & Bonnet, 1981), have been shown to be significantly correlated with the content of a night's dreams. The dream content is linked thematically (Kramer, Moshiri, & Scharf, 1982) both to the current concerns of the subject before sleep and to the emotional preoccupation of the dreamer the subsequent morning. The notion of emotionally relevant material being processed by the dreamer during his or her dreams is supported by these observations. Thus, dream content is related across the waking-sleeping-waking continuum.

What occurs at times of emotional upheaval, when disturbing dreams occur with increased frequency, such as those that occur in chronic delayed posttraumatic stress disorder (CDPTSD)? There may be a process of reactivation of previously troubling life experiences. This reactivation may be a response to a breakdown in a current emotionally significant relationship (e.g., marriage), and the previously troubling experiences may become a metaphor to express feelings such as hostility and rage stirred by the breakdown. This previous experience is then linked to earlier childhood experiences.

This rather traditional psychodynamic view is supported by a study of the sleep (Kramer & Kinney, 1988), dreams (Kramer, Schoen, & Kinney, 1984b), and psychological states (Kinney & Kramer, 1985) of CDPTSD patients. The sleep and dreams of Vietnam combat veterans with disturbed dreaming were explored. They were then compared with combat-matched control subjects without CDPTSD and with normal nonveterans.

Dream-disturbed Vietnam combat veterans with CDPTSD have clear disturbances in their sleep, both spontaneously and in response to nonspecific stimuli (Schoen et al., 1984). These sleep difficulties may help sustain their disturbance. These subjects sleep more poorly and awaken and arouse spontaneously in NREM sleep (across the night) more often than control subjects. In response to auditory stimuli above waking thresholds (Kinney & Kramer, 1984), dream disturbed subjects have more physiological systems activated in NREM sleep during the first half of the night (especially respiratory and motor) than control subjects but report less awareness of the source of the arousals.

This pattern of disturbance in dream-disturbed Vietnam combat veterans suggests that their sleep is potentially more disruptable by random (meaningless) noise that can lead to an arousal/awakening without subjects knowing what the source of the arousal/awakening is. Subjects are then in the position of being awakened without cause, which is often experienced as frightening.

Were these dream-disturbed subjects hypervigilant? In Vietnam, combat veterans had felt it wasn't safe to sleep in the field. Therefore, one might predict that they would have lower arousal thresholds to auditory stimuli. On the contrary, they had higher arousal thresholds (Schoen, Kramer, & Kinney, 1984) and appeared to be more inwardly vigilant than externally vigilant. The source of their disturbance seemed to exist on the inside rather than on the outside.

An investigation of CDPTSD subjects' internal experience (i.e., dream content) showed that they recalled dreams more often than did control subjects (55% vs. 45%) but were alone in reporting military references in their dreams (Kramer, Schoen, & Kinney, 1984b). The threat, if the military experience indexes a threat, is now within the individual, and he is focused on it.

Interestingly, only half of the dreams of the CDPTSD subjects were manifestly about the Vietnam experience. The other half were about other aspects of their lives. Therefore, these subjects were not exclusively focused on Vietnam, although in the waking state they certainly felt this to be the case.

It might be helpful to illustrate the dream findings from these CDPTSD patients with a case example. A Vietnam veteran volunteered to sleep in the laboratory at the Veterans Administration Hospital. He was stymied in his therapeutic work on his problems. Two years earlier, his wife had left him. Following that, he became more and more troubled and preoccupied with his Vietnam experiences. Approximately 4 months earlier, he had quit his job and had given his gun to his boss for fear of getting into difficulty with it. A brief synopsis of his dreams from five consecutive dream periods of one night follows (Kramer, Schoen, & Kinney, 1987).

1. He tries to cross a river, and a big guy is trying to help him. It seems that they are in the Mekong Delta. Every time they try to get to the other side, they are back at the beginning.
2. He is a young boy at home and is fighting with one of the neighborhood kids. His brother is around. The kid they are fighting with is later killed in Vietnam.

3. He goes with others to a construction site. He is a sapper, like in Vietnam. He blows the site up. The consequence of blowing up the construction site is that his brother's house is flooded.
4. He remembers being a young boy at his parents' house. There is some argument and he leaves. He writes them post cards without a forwarding address. When they try to contact him, he has moved elsewhere.
5. He is driving very fast, and his wife is worried that he will have an accident.

The patient has clearly interdigitated his current life stresses, his Vietnam experiences, and his childhood. A brief review of the dynamic implication of the material may be useful.

In the first dream, the subject might well be referring to his therapeutic efforts with the doctor (the big guy). He is making efforts to go across a dangerous area, the Mekong Delta, to get to the other side. This could be a metaphorical statement about going from one state to another, from one position to another, or from one place in life to another. The more he tries, the more he ends up in the same place. His dream may reflect the stalemated condition he alluded to in coming to seek help.

In response to the subject's frustration with change, he recalls an earlier difficulty in succeeding. Themes related to moving ahead, and problems associated with moving ahead, are clearly repeated in his dreams. He is struggling with a neighborhood youngster in his dreams, and his brother is in the background. The young man with whom he is struggling is one who later dies in Vietnam. Peer competition (fighting, hostility) in his dreams is linked to death in Vietnam. Sibling competitive issues are further suggested by the brother's presence.

In the third dream, the competitive situation becomes a bit clearer, as does the link to Vietnam. In performing his job in Vietnam, which is destructive but legitimate, he damages things, which leads to the damage of his brother's home. One recalls that in the second dream he was fighting with a peer, with his brother in the background. In the third dream, the direct consequence of his action is to bring damage to his brother's possession. The potential for a sibling problem is clearly underlined.

A tension with his parents is reflected in the fourth dream. The point of sibling rivalry is to gain the approbation of his parents. He flees from tension with the parents (i.e., the argument) but longs to remain in contact with them. He writes them and invites a response, but directs them to where he has been, not to where he is going. He cannot form an effective relationship with his parents, although he would like to. The dream has a Tom Sawyer quality: "They'll miss me when I'm gone."

The last dream reflects a current peer (but possibly a parental) relationship as well. His wife (i.e., a peer/parent) is concerned about him. She's afraid that his being out of control will lead to an accident. She cares about him as he wants his parents to care.

The subject was surprised that a significant portion of his dreams focused on his family. We learned later that, following the experience in the laboratory, he went back and sought out his wife to see if there could be a reconciliation. His therapeutic work was rejuvenated by work on both past and current problems.

The dreams of this subject reflect his use of the Vietnam situation in a metaphorical sense to reflect his difficulties (i.e., his difficulties in changing). His hostility, which goes back to childhood and is directed toward his brother, is manifested again in Vietnam, but it affects both a brother in arms and his own brother from the past. His act of sibling rivalry results in a disruption of his relationship with his parents. He is ambivalent about this disruption and flees from them but also wishes to remain in contact with them. He cannot resolve this tension. His plight leads him to be potentially out of control, perhaps because of the intensity of his emotion. This potential loss of control is reflected in his current situation with his wife. It is the breakdown with his wife that stimulated his current difficulty, which is focused on Vietnam.

It is apparent from this case that the Vietnam experience can become a metaphor for chronic interpersonal difficulty with peers and parental figures, both current and past. The wish to dominate the peer leads to competition with destructive consequences. It serves to alienate the subject from the parents (and parental support figures) and potentially leads to a loss of control.

This example illustrates three levels of problems in the Vietnam veteran. A breakdown in current life situations echoes and stirs up similar problems from the past. Vietnam then serves as a metaphor to express the difficulties. Those aspects of Vietnam that are in focus currently are those that have some meaning as determined by events in the subject's past, prior to Vietnam. The Vietnam experience is a factor, but not the only factor, that dominates the life of the Vietnam veteran.

The current precipitant is the new trauma in CDPTSD. In the illustrative case, the current "universal stressor" is marital disruption. These stressful events may occur in predisposed individuals. The Vietnam combat control group may be a high-risk group for developing CDPTSD. The sleep of the control group (Kramer & Kinney, 1988) was disturbed when compared with that of the normal group: 87% sleep efficiency, eight awakenings per night, more light sleep, less REM sleep, and decreased deep sleep. Furthermore, their dream recall was strangely low both overall (45%) and in REM sleep (50%) (Kramer, Schoen, & Kinney, 1984b).

It may be that these combat veterans without dream disturbances are vulnerable to developing CDPTSD in response to a current stress. This development would facilitate the return of dreams about Vietnam, and those dreams would also be expressive of the subject's current problems. Disturbing dreams and troubled awakenings are reinforced (perpetuated) by nonspecific, intermittent stimuli (apparently meaningless noise) at night.

The experience of the Vietnam veteran with CDPTSD may be placed in a more traditional psychodynamic perspective. The Vietnam experience reflected but did not completely determine their later lives. The patients with CDPTSD had a reactivation of memories of Vietnam brought about by some breakdown in their current life equilibrium. The case illustration involved a disruption in a marital relationship. The current preoccupations of the patient echoed both his Vietnam experience and his childhood experience. This form of illness is not particularly unusual. Once the dynamic is started, psychophysiological factors (i.e., alterations in sleeping and dreaming) may serve to keep it alive.

Theories of dreaming need to address dreams that go on automatically, outside of awareness, and those that enter awareness and have the potential for a more direct effect on the dreamer's consciousness (Kramer, 1981). One needs both an assimilative and an accommodative theory of dreaming, with the former being reductive and the later being potentially transforming. The selective-affective mood regulatory theory of dreaming (Kramer & Roth, 1978; Kramer, in press) is an example of an assimilative theory. The experience of the disturbing dream opens the possibility for an extension of this assimilative view to encompass some degree of transformation and accommodation.

References

Anch, A. M., Bowman, C. P., Mitler, M. M., & Walsh, J. K. (1988). *Sleep: A scientific perspective.* Englewood Cliffs, NJ: Prentice-Hall.

French, T., & Fromm, E. (1964). *Dream interpretation.* New York: Basic Books.

Freud, S. (1900). The interpretation of dreams. In J. Strachey (Ed. and Trans.), *The standard edition of the complete psychological works of Sigmund Freud* (Vols. 4–5). London: Hogarth Press.

Freud, S. (1920). Beyond the pleasure principle. In J. Strachey (Ed. and Trans.), *The standard edition of the complete psychological works of Sigmund Freud* (Vol. 18). London: Hogarth Press.

Hall, C., & Van de Castle, R. (1966). *The content analysis of dreams.* New York: Appleton.

Kinney, L., & Kramer, M. (1984). Sleep and sleep responsivity in disturbed dreamers. *Sleep Research, 13,* 102.

Kinney, L., & Kramer, M. (1985). Personality differences among disturbed dreamers, "sick" controls and normal veterans. *Sleep Research, 14,* 130.

Kramer, M. (1981). The function of psychological dreaming: A preliminary analysis. In W. P. Koella (Ed.), *Sleep 1980* (pp. 182–185). Basel, Switzerland: Karger.

Kramer, M. (1982). The Psychology of the dream: Art or science. *Psychiatric Journal of the University of Ottawa, 7,* 87–100.

Kramer, M. (in press). The mood regulatory function of sleep. In A. Moffit & M. Kramer (Eds.), *The function of dreaming.* Albany, NY: SUNY Press.

Kramer, M., & Kinney, L. (1988). Sleep patterns in trauma victims with disturbed dreaming. *Psychiatric Journal of the University of Ottawa. 13,* 12–16.

Kramer, M., McQuarrie, E., & Bonnet, M. (1981). Problem solving in dreaming: An empirical test. In W. P. Koella (Ed.), *Sleep 1980* (pp. 174–178). Basel, Switzerland: Karger.

Kramer, M., Moshiri, A., & Scharf, M. (1982). The organization of mental content in and between the waking and dream state. *Sleep Research, 11,* 106.

Kramer, M., Roehrs, T., & Roth, T. (1976). Mood change and the physiology of sleep. *Comprehensive Psychiatry, 17,* 161–165.

Kramer, M., & Roth, T. (1972). The mood-regulatory function of sleep. In W. P. Koella & P. Levin (Eds.), *Sleep 1972* (pp. 563–57). Basel, Switzerland: Karger.

Kramer, M., & Roth, T. (1977). Dream translation, *Israel Annual of Psychiatry, 15,* 336–3561.

Kramer, M., & Roth, T. (1978). The dream as selective affective modulator. Acad. Form, *22,* 13.

Kramer, M., & Roth, T. (1980). The relationship of dream content to night-morning mood change. In L. Popoviciv, B. Asgian, & G. Badiv (Eds.), *Sleep 1978* (pp. 621–624). Basel, Switzerland: Karger.

Kramer, M., Roth, T., Arand, D., & Bonnet, M. (1981). Waking and dreaming mentation: A test of their interrelationship, *Neuroscience Letters, 22,* 83–86.

Kramer, M., Roth, T., & Czaya, J. (1975). Dream development within a REM period. In *Sleep 1974* (pp. 406–408). Basel, Switzerland: Karger.

Kramer, M., Roth, T., & Palmer, T. (1976). The psychological nature of the REM dream report and T.A.T. stories. *Psychiatric Journal of the University of Ottawa, 1,* 128–135.

Kramer, M., Schoen, L. S., & Kinney, L. (1984a). Psychological and behavioral features of disturbed dreamers. *Psychiatric Journal of the University of Ottawa, 9,* 102–106.

Kramer, M., Schoen, L. S., & Kinney, L. (1984b). The dream experience in dream-disturbed Vietnam veterans. In B. A. Van der Kolk (Ed.). Washington, DC: American Psychiatric Press.

Kramer, M., Schoen, L. S., & Kinney, L. (1987). Nightmares in Vietnam veterans. *Journal of the American Academy of Psychoanalysis, 15,* 67–81.

Kramer, M., Whitman, R., Baldridge, B., & Lansky, L. (1964). Patterns of dreaming: The interrelationship of the dreams of a night. *Journal of Nervous and Mental Disorders, 139,* 426–439.

Roth, R., Kramer, M., & Roehrs, T. (1976). Mood before and after sleep. *Psychiatric Journal of the University of Ottawa, 1,* 123–127.

Shoen, L. S., Kramer, M., & Kinney, L. (1984). Auditory thresholds in the dream disturbed. *Sleep Research, 13,* 102.

Taub, J., Kramer, M., Arand, D., & Jacobs, G. (1978) Nightmare dreams and nightmare confabulations, *Comprehensive Psychiatry, 19,* 285–291.

INDEX

Across States Connectionist Model of Imagery and Thought (ASCIT), 5, 7, 9
Activation, Input Source, Modulation (AIM), 25–40
Alzheimer's disease, 100–101
Amnesia, 80, 83, 85, 98, 134, 160
  anterograde, 69, 72–74, 144
  waking, 85, 92, 97
Anesthesia, 127–135
  awareness under, 128
  cognitive processing under, 128–133
Animal models, 27
Anxiety, 152–154
Artificial intelligence, 73
Auditory item presentation
  air conduction, 94
  bone conduction, 94
Atonia, 33
Awakenings, 62, 155, 168–169

Beck Depression Inventory, 183–186
Behavioral response
  after anesthesia, 130
  in sleep, 77–87
    response latency, 64–65, 80
Blind sight, 134
Brain metabolism, 170–171

Cerebellum, 14, 16–17, 20, 73
Circadian rhythm, 151–152, 161, 170, 172
Classical conditioning , 70–75, 128
  conditioned stimulus, 71
  in sleep, 70–72, 78, 89
  of tolerance to hypnotics, 145
  unconditioned stimulus, 71
Cognitive performance tasks
  clock reversal, 163
  letter cancellation, 163
  logical reasoning, 162
  memory tasks, 162
  mental arithmetic, 161–168

reaction time. *See* Reaction time
time estimation. *See* Time perception
vigilance, 163
Cornell Medical Index, 192

Demand characteristics, 111, 152
Depression, 184–188
Dichotic listening, 134
Disorders of Initiating and Maintaining Sleep (DIMS). *See* Insomnia
Dream deprivation, 181–182
Dreams, 179–189
  Activation–Synthesis model, 7–10, 17
  and affect, 191–197
  bizarreness, 8–10, 17–20
  Crick and Mitchison theory, 17–18, 181
  and depression, 183–188
  Freud's theory of, 181, 190
  function of, 181–183, 186–188
  lucid dreams, 36–38, 109–126
  network model, 179–189
  NREM dreams, 180
  recall of, 90, 96, 166
  repetitive dreams, 194–197
  reports, 160, 179–180, 198–200
  and stress, 182–202
    combat, 198–201
    divorce, 182–188

Electroencephalogram (EEG)
  alpha, 60, 62, 69–72, 78–79, 83–85, 88–92, 120, 149
  K-complexes, 49, 71, 95
  NREM sleep. *See* NREM sleep
  REM latency, 183–188
  REM sleep. *See* REM sleep
  sleep efficiency, 140
  sleep onset latency. *See* Sleep onset latency
  sleep spindles, 63, 149, 151
  slow wave sleep, 140, 142, 144, 165–172

spectral analysis, 64, 141
speeding, 62
stage shifts, 62
EMG, 62, 141
submental, 4
Event-related potentials. *See* evoked
potentials
Evoked potentials, 12–13, 43–57
auditory, 45–46, 128
brainstem evoked response, 45–46
contingent negative variation, 44, 47–50,
52
middle latency responses, 46
mismatch negativity, 44, 50–51
readiness potential, 44, 52
selective attention, 44
semantic processing, 44, 52–53
in sleep, 44–53
in NREM sleep, 45–46, 49–51
in REM sleep, 48–52
Eye movements, 3–21, 29–31, 33, 37, 95, 110,
112–117, 119, 180, 183–188
and visual imagery. *See* Visual imagery

Galvanic skin response, 89, 130

H-reflex, 112
Habituation, 70–72, 74, 89
Heart-rate, 71, 89, 112
Hippocampus, 69, 72–75
Homophones, 98–99
Hypnogogic state, 160, 171–172
Hypnopompic state, 159–175
Hypnosis, 69, 77–86, 129, 133–134
posthypnotic amnesia, 85–86
Hypnotics, 139–147
barbiturates, 142
benzodiazepines, 140–145
Hypnotic susceptibility, 81–82, 85, 101–105
Harvard Group Scale of Hypnotic
Susceptibility, 81–82, 85
Stanford Hypnotic Susceptibility Scale,
81–82, 85, 104

Information processing, 67–69, 128–129, 181,
187
Insomnia, 139–147, 150–157
psychophysiological, 140, 145
subjective, 139–140, 145

Korsakoff patients, 98, 133

Language processing, 52–53
Learning
acquisition, 67

classical conditioning. *See* Classical
conditioning
escape/avoidance, 58–59
extinction, 67
habituation. *See* Habituation
reinforcement, 58–60
in sleep. *See* Sleep learning

Memory
declarative, 72–75
and dreams, 186–187
echoic, 50
episodic, 144
explicit, 97–99
implicit, 52, 97–99
long-term, 68–75, 89–90
procedural, 52, 72–75
recall, 96–97, 128–129, 131–133
recognition, 96–99, 128–131
retrieval, 91, 93–94, 128–129
short-term, 68–75, 89–90
and sleep, 67–76
state-specific, 70, 91–94
alcohol, 93
drugs, 93
mood, 93
Mental states
subjectivity, 26–27
isomorphism, 27
Middle ear muscle activity (MEMA), 4, 9
Minnesota Multiphasic Personality Inventory
(MMPI), 155, 192
Multiple Sleep Latency Test (MSLT), 141

Naps, 152–153, 161, 163–167
Neural nets, 17–18
Neurotransmitters
aminergic, 32–35, 38–39
cholinergic, 32–35, 38–39, 48
Nightmares, 122, 190–202
Night terrors, 38
Nocturnal myoclonus, 139, 141, 143, 155
NREM sleep
evoked potentials in. *See* Evoked
potentials
neurophysiology, 4, 9, 11, 14–15, 18–19,
26–30, 34–38
sleep learning. *See* Sleep learning
visual imagery in. *See* Visual imagery

Orienting response, 128–130

Parallel processing, 7–8,
Periodic leg movements. *See* Nocturnal
myoclonus

Periorbital Integrated Potential (PIP), 4, 9
Placebo, 145
Pontine-geniculate-occipital (PGO) activity,
    3–21, 28–31, 33, 38, 180
Posttraumatic stress disorder, 190–202

Reaction time, 47–48, 162
REM sleep
    dreams. *See* dreams
    evoked potentials. *See* Evoked potentials
    neurophysiology, 3–21, 26–36
    phasic events. *See* Eye movements,
        Middle ear muscle activity, or
        Periorbital integrated potential
    sleep learning. *See* Sleep learning
    visual imagery. *See* Visual imagery
Research diagnostic criteria, 184
Respiration, 112
Reticular formation, 6, 11–13, 15, 17, 47–48
Retina, 10, 26
Reverie, 38–39, 81, 159–175
    EEG during, 167–168

Saccade. *See* Eye movements
Schedule of Affective Disorders and
    Schizophrenia, 184
Sleep
    auditory thresholds, 35, 45, 142, 145, 150
    awareness during, 60, 109–126
    perception of, 142
Sleep apnea, 139, 141, 143, 155
Sleep deprivation, 38, 141, 159–169
Sleep drunkenness, 159
Sleep inertia, 159–163
    and sleep depth, 168–169
Sleep learning, 58–76, 78, 88–108
    classical conditioning. *See* Classical
        conditioning

dishabituation, 71
habituation. *See* Habituation
and hypnosis, 83–85, 101–105
learning set, 101–105
in NREM sleep, 59, 61, 64, 84–85, 90–91,
    96, 103–104
in REM sleep, 59, 64–65, 69, 78–85, 96,
    103–104
Soviet Union studies, 83–85, 89, 91, 95,
    101–103
stimulus control, 58–66
subject factors, 99–105
Sleep onset latency, 91, 143, 148
    perception of, 148–158,
Sleepiness, 159–175
    daytime, 63, 141
    postdormital, 159
Somnambulism, 90
Subliminal perception, 134
Suggestibility. *See* Hypnotic susceptibility

Temperature
    ambient, 144
    body, 45, 64, 143–144, 151–154, 169–
        171
Thematic Apperception Test (TAT), 197
Time percpetion, 151–154, 163, 166

Vestibular activity. *See* Cerebellum
Visual imagery
    brightness, 19
    clarity, 19–20
    color saturation, 19
    dreams, 10–14, 18–20
    and eye movements, 18–20, 119
    measurement of, 19–20
    NREM sleep, 18–20
    REM sleep, 18–20